OUT ON THE DEEP BLUE

Also by Leslie Leyland Fields

The Entangling Net

The Water Under Fish (poetry)

OUT ON THE
DEEP
BLUE

WOMEN, MEN, AND THE
OCEANS THEY FISH

Edited by Leslie Leyland Fields

THOMAS DUNNE BOOKS

ST. MARTIN'S PRESS NEW YORK

THOMAS DUNNE BOOKS.
An imprint of St. Martin's Press.

Grateful acknowledgment is made for permission to print the following: "Staying Afloat" by Marie Beaver. Copyright © 2001 by Marie Beaver. "Striper" by John Cole. Copyright © 2001 by John Cole. "Greenhorn" by Michael Crowley. Copyright © 2001 by Michael Crowley. "Pieces of the Wind" by Wendy Erd. Copyright © 2001 by Wendy Erd. "Climbing the Ladder" by Robert Fritchey. Copyright © 2001 by Robert Fritchey. "Payin' Your Dues in Togiak" by Joel Gay. Copyright © 2001 by Joel Gay. "Mug-up" by Linda Greenlaw. From *The Hungry Ocean: A Swordboat Captain's Journey* by Linda Greenlaw. Copyright © 1999 Linda Greenlaw. Reprinted by permission of Hyperion. "Working Below the Waterline" by Seth Harkness. Copyright © 2001 by Seth Harkness. "A Day in the Life" by Nancy Lord. Copyright © 1997 by Nancy Lord. Printed by permission of Nancy Lord and Island Press. "Under Montauk Light" by Peter Matthiessen. Excerpt taken from *Men's Life* (Vintage, 1988). Reproduced with permission from Peter Matthiessen. "The First Kill" by Gavin Maxwell. Copyright © 2001 by Gavin Maxwell. "Asking for It" by William McCloskey. Excerpt taken from *Their Father's Work: Casting Nets with the World's Fishermen* (McGraw-Hill, 1998). Reproduced with permission from The McGraw-Hill Companies. "Swordfish" by Paul Molyneaux. Copyright © 2001 by Paul Molyneaux. "Catch and Release" by Debra Nielsen. Copyright © 2001 by Debra Nielsen. "Out West: Notes from the Bering Sea" by Toby Sullivan. Copyright © 2001 by Toby Sullivan. "Cashing Out on the Bering Sea" by Martha Sutro. Copyright © 2001 by Martha Sutro. "The Long Road Home" by Joe Upton. Copyright © 2001 by Joe Upton. "Nights of Ice" by Spike Walker. Excerpt taken from *Nights of Ice* (St. Martin's Press, 1999). Reproduced with permission from St. Martin's Press.

www.stmartins.com

Library of Congress Cataloging-in-Publication Data

Out on the deep blue : women, men, and the oceans they fish / edited by Leslie Leyland Fields.—1st U.S. ed.
p.   cm.
ISBN 0-312-27726-1
1. Fisheries.   I. Fields, Leslie Leyland, 1957-

SH331.2 .O88 2001
639.2'2—dc21

2001041983

First Edition: October 2001

10   9   8   7   6   5   4   3   2   2   1

CONTENTS

INTRODUCTION

It started in 1977 when I put on my first pair of hip boots on a tiny island in the Gulf of Alaska and vaulted into a small wooden skiff full of salmon. In my previous life in New Hampshire I had written about everything, surreptitiously scribbling stanzas on restaurant napkins, fussing over line endings on index cards while in line at the store. My step into the skiff, though, was a step into silence. I was sucked under with such force, working twelve to eighteen hours a day, seven days a week, for four months on a remote island incommunicado with the rest of the world, that all literary thoughts fled. And though this world was astonishing—volcanoes spouting over the roofs of the cabins, whales, seals, sea otters, sea lions daily sights, winds that blew eighty knots, living on a scrap of land flung onto the Shelikof Strait, sometimes hanging on for life itself—for all of this my journal, which I had kept faithfully for ten years, became the equivalent of a series of grunts: *picked two skiffs of pinks this morning, worked past dark on 7-mile in a NE blow, kicker broke down around the island, arms going numb at night, can't sleep.* Language was a luxury. There was no place in my fishing life for literary allusion; I was body and muscle only. This was the active life, the life of doing, where salmon were salmon, the ocean was itself and nothing more, and the day's object was to pick and deliver as many hundreds and thousands of fish as possible. I wrote no poems or essays about fishing for nearly ten years.

I shouldn't have expected otherwise. Commercial fishing has rarely been viewed as the realm of the contemplative. This belongs to fly-fishing, sportfishing—men and women at rest in the wilderness, senses awakening, losing and so finding themselves, restored for return to that other world. Fishing here is not doing but being, or some magical alchemy of their perfect merging. Books and anthologies abound connecting the spiritual and the natural with sportfishing.

Commercial fishing, though, is a business and so the second cousin from the other side of the tracks, the world of doing and action, where the bottom line governs all activities. Tasks are done in fast forward, so repetitive and at such speeds and for such a length of time that they are best done unthinkingly, instinctively, automatically. Your worth, both economic and personal, is often measured in terms of how fast you can bait the halibut hooks, how quickly you can pick fish, how long you can work without sleep. The all-absorbing intensity of the work coupled with many fishermen's schedules and lives on the water do not allow for languid introspection.

And should a fisherman have the time for such, revelatory communication about his life's work cuts against every tradition and fiber of this occupation. In fishing, sport and commercial alike, secrecy is required and assumed. As many resources decline, and even among those still vigorous, competition for the halibut, cod, pollock, and salmon is intense, even cutthroat. When any kind of fisherman, sport or commercial, speaks, gross understatement or gross overstatement rule the day. No one expects otherwise: There is so much that cannot be said.

The traditional seal has been recently broken though. Sebastian Junger's *The Perfect Storm,* on the bestseller list for fifty-three weeks, and then Patrick Dillon's *Lost at Sea* opened this hermetic world to millions of readers. Commercial fishing became, almost overnight, literary territory. *Outside* magazine, noting the growing appetite for such stories, writes wryly, "If you're a commercial fisherman, you've probably been contacted by an agent."

Why, at the turn of the millennium, in the post-information age, when 85 percent of Americans live in urban or suburban areas, are we turning to books about men and women who break their backs, and sometimes lose their lives, pulling fish from the sea?

It is not hard to hazard a few theories. Commercial fishing, as many know, is ranked as the most dangerous job in the nation, with a death rate from seven to one hundred times the national average. Indeed, as I write this, yesterday two people who work a few miles from our fishcamp off Kodiak Island in Alaska died when their skiff was swamped in a fifty-knot gale. We were out in that storm as well. It does not require flights of imagination or verbal high jinks to create from such a setting and occupation the necessary elements of story: plot, conflict, tension, drama, and tragedy—all of this is built into the business of commercial fishing. But even story is sometimes not a large enough container. This is epic, even, the primeval, universal struggle of man against nature: men and women alone in a fifty-seven-foot boat against a twenty-foot raging sea, or wrestling a leviathan in steep waters, adrift in a suffocating fog. Yet these stories are not *Odysseys* or *Iliads*, where the Greek heroes, godlike figures, ultimately and inevitably triumph against all the malevolent forces that would keep them from reaching home and hearth. For all their courage and daring, in these recent writings we see fishermen as thoroughly human, as beset by flaws, pride, and mortality as the rest of us. Their obituaries appear in our local papers; we leave their funerals weeping. Their stories read like sagas, feeding our deep human hunger to understand the ultimate battle against nature and death; but the lives are real, the losses are personal.

Yet, even for those of us who commercial fish, reading about the losses of our own, thrilling to adrenaline-laced accounts of fishermen's rescues and near rescues at sea is not macabre; it is human and it is necessary. Scott Russell Sanders wrote in "The Most Human Art: Ten Reasons Why We'll Always Need a Good Story" (*Utne Reader*, Sept/Oct 1997) that story, whether fiction or nonfiction, "is to teach us how to be human," and to "help us deal with suffering, loss, and death." Those who have suffered tell and write their stories "as a way of fending off despair," and as a way of teaching us to live consciously and wisely.

There is something here, too, about our national passion for frontier and wilderness. We are losing both the imaginative, mythical frontier, and the actual wilderness lands themselves, we feel. Where do we go now to explore, to test our American mettle? Where else but out past the continents' boundaries to the oceanic plains beyond. This is our Wild West. It is not by chance that the commercial fishermen who work this expanse are often called "the last of the cowboys." At our fishcamp, we speak a piece of this analogy daily. Our own boat, a modest sixty-five-foot scow we bought at an auction for a song, and used mostly to tender our supplies to fishcamp, was bought with the name crudely and audaciously stenciled on the stern: *Cowboy.* The twelve hundred miles of the Aleutian chain are called "Out West" by those who live and fish there. In Alaska's most audacious fisheries, where fleets of wheeling boats stir a single bay to dust, reeling lines on lines, nets over nets, every boat unbridled, every set a maniacal, defiant few minutes' ride—these are rodeos, we say: one of the last Wild West shows still playing.

The mythos of the cowboy carries with it a rugged individualism we still prize, but even more we are drawn by the physicality of the fisherman-cowboy's life. As our physical interactions with the natural world atrophy, we hunger for sensual, whole-body experience with the forces of nature—earth, air, fire, and water. Even the agrarian culture that remains, accounting for less than 4 percent of the population, is increasingly distanced from feet-in-the-soil, hard-muscle extraction of the harvest, often laboring in air-conditioned computerized cabs and rounding up herds of cattle from helicopters.

It is nothing but romanticism to insist that someone somewhere still tills the earth, herds the cattle, and fishes the sea as his forefathers did. No one can compete and survive as a business in this global economy with such ideals; a population of 275 million couldn't be fed. And yet, the fishermen remain, some fishing just as their fathers and grandfathers have fished: in fleets of small boats clustering the nation's coast, working in home-made vessels with crews of two or three, salmon seining in forty-two-foot Deltas, setnetting in open skiffs, hand-hauling the beach seine, pulling a living from the depths with backs, arms, ungloved hands. We are anomalies, indeed.

Many of us in this book are still fishing close to the ancient ways. But nostalgia and literary trends may not save us nor others here from the same fate as the small family farm and ranch. A short time ago, there were many threats on the horizon. Today they are here among us: at-sea catcher-processors and factory ships that catch and produce mass volumes of fish product, threatening the resource; fish farms that raise penned fish, routinely feeding antibiotics against the diseases that proliferate, risking infection and destruction of the wild stocks; increasing pressure from sportfishermen to augment their own share of the resource by reducing the commercial fisherman's catch. This is just the beginning.

Much has been lost already. It is no longer enough to weigh anchor and risk life and health on the North Pacific or the Bering Sea or the mid-Atlantic for a hold of fish. Many fishermen have become activists, lobbyists, consultants, working off-season with the same determination as in-season to preserve the resource, or their own right to a share of it.

While fishermen are becoming increasingly vocal and public in their fight to preserve their livelihood and the natural resources, they are just now beginning to write their own stories. Until very recently, most books about fishing were written by outsiders, writers and journalists afforded a peek or gaze into this other world. This is the first collection of essays written by fishermen themselves, not written about them. There is no filtering journalist; the writing and the events here are intense, direct, first person. The lives and waters represented here range from Alaska's far west Aleutian chain to the Gulf of Mexico to the northern waters of New England, out to the Grand Banks, north and east to the coast of Scotland. Collectively, the fishermen-writers have fished cod, halibut, salmon, sea urchins, crab, herring, shark, and swordfish. Some writing here have fished commercially for several seasons; others have spent much of their lives on the water. The rousing sea stories are here: the dramas of near-death battles, the sickening tragedy of lovers and friends lost to the waters, but this is not the whole story. This collection represents the most holistic view of fishing to date: not just the dying, but the living; not just the obsessive doing of fishing, but the passionate being as well. Together, they'll take you out on the deep blue. Hold on.

Leslie Leyland Fields

STAYING
AFLOAT

MARIE BEAVER, *a wilderness guide in
the Brooks Range, takes her first
commercial fishing trip with her
fisherman boyfriend while in decisional
angst about marrying him and
becoming a full-time fisher herself.*

THE THREE MEN sat at the galley table, slumped over steaming coffee mugs, unusually quiet. Their hair stuck out in wild tufts, and bed-creases were etched into their faces. Tony eventually rose, toasted some muffins, and offered them around. Dale shook his head no.

"Can't eat before an opening," Lars said as he poured himself another cup of coffee. "Too nervous."

He downed the mug, climbed the ladder to the wheelhouse, and started the engine. It gave a raspy shriek, causing my shoulders to seize, before it subsided to a bulldozer-decibel purr. Tony and Dale quickly dumped their coffee in the sink and hurried outside. I ascended to the wheelhouse to view the two men, who were already on the bow helping to draw up the anchor. The chain made a terrible clatter as it spooled, like a jackhammer striking the hull. When the anchor landed on deck, they latched it and retreated to the wheelhouse.

It was 7:00 A.M. In two hours, Kodiak's herring fishery would begin, marking the start of herring season for the *Raven* crew. There would be a three-hour opening this morning and probably one this afternoon, after Alaska Fish and Game officials counted the morning's catch to make sure the quota had not been exceeded. Later in the month, the Cook Inlet and Togiak fisheries, each, like Kodiak, comprising a few short openings, would take place. And that—amounting to roughly twenty-four hours of fishing—would be it until next year.

I was on the boat at the behest of Tony, my boyfriend of two years, who was trying to convince me to become a fishing team with him. I enjoyed guiding wilderness trips in Alaska's Brooks Range, my job for the past eight

3

years, but I was growing tired of cooking for the clients, adjusting their packs, reassuring them when it rained, and the low wages. Fishing, especially with Tony, whom I someday hoped to marry, struck me as a great possibility. I envisioned a total sensory experience. I wanted to work my muscles to an ache and sweat until I stunk. I wanted to cover myself in fish slime, smell it, taste it, get close to the muck of life. I wanted to be outside all day with the wind and the rain and the snow, laughing with the elements in true King Lear fashion. I was looking for a job that went beyond economic satisfaction, that would include the things I loved to do, my interests and convictions, something that would inspire me and fill me with a sense of belonging. The difference between a purely financial pursuit and the one I sought would be the difference, I thought, between renting a house owned by someone I didn't know and living in a home that I had built with my own hands and creative impulses.

We were on the west side of Kodiak Island, deep inside Uganik Bay where it split into three long triangles. The water was choppy with whitecaps that looked like handkerchiefs strewn about. Nearby were fifty other seine boats. All had massive booms from which hung power blocks as big as car engines, smaller-scale booms, and masts that held various antennae. Piles of black web, each large enough to fill a school bus, lay on the decks. Bulky aluminum skiffs towed at the seiners' sterns.

"Let's take the west arm," Lars said as he shifted into gear. "I have a good feeling about it."

Tony and Dale stood inches from the sonar screen. At intervals, one of them pointed to the screen and exclaimed, "What's that?" Lars then swiveled in his seat to study the picture and usually pronounced, "Rock," with a trace of disappointment. Occasionally, however, he murmured an interested "hmmm," and maneuvered the boat in a circle around the object. But after an hour of this, we had found no herring.

Soon, the spotter pilot, Craig, contacted us on the radio. I was surprised since I hadn't heard his Super Cub. It took a while to locate it, extremely high, a speck lost in the blue.

"There's no fish," Lars told him.

"I see something across the bay from you," Craig said. He had a quiet voice, one you would expect to find on a meditation tape, not from someone whose job involved keeping one eye on the fish, another on the boats, and whatever was left on the forty other planes sharing the same pocket of sky. "It's off the bow of that black seiner—"

Lars increased the throttle, producing a heavy rattle, like a bulldozer straining to get unstuck from the mud. As we crashed through the choppy water, Craig directed us. "A little more to your right. Now a little more."

Twenty feet from the black boat, the *Misty Morning*, we stopped suddenly, sending binoculars and pens on the chart table tumbling.

"Bingo," Lars said. He glanced at the *Misty Morning* and lifted an eyebrow. In his early forties, Lars had fished for twenty years in Alaska in almost every fishery—crab, black cod, shrimp, pollock, herring of course, and salmon. He had a chest the size of a kiddie wading pool and veiny, swollen biceps. His straight hair cut in the shape of a bowl made him look like an overgrown Beaver Cleaver, but Lars was far from goody-goody. One night in a bar in the town of Kodiak where we had spent two weeks preparing for herring season, only casually drunk, he had approached a stranger, stuck both hands inside a hole in the thigh of the man's jeans, and ripped the entire pant leg. If I were the recipient of a lifted eyebrow from Lars, I'd be worried.

Craig flew off to help the *Order of Magnitude* and the *Natalia*, both of which were members of our combine, a quasicommunistic arrangement in which we shared trade secrets and profits. These days, with the voluminous nets and spotter planes and

5

sonar equipment, seiners caught either hundreds of tons in one swoop or nothing. To compensate for those inevitable missed seasons, most boats belonged to combines.

Lars eased up on the throttle and we very slowly circled the herring, which were easily spooked. The *Misty Morning* followed close behind, once attempting to pass us, at which Lars lifted his eyebrow and sent the *Raven* shooting ahead. As the two boats resumed their relentless circling, I felt like we were riding a carousel of hungry piranha.

At ten minutes to nine, Tony and Dale took their positions outside. The crew on the *Misty Morning* did the same. Seining worked like this: The net was shaped like a long rectangle. One of the short ends was attached to the seiner, the other to the skiff towing behind the seiner. When above a school of fish, the two boats separated and drove in opposite directions in a wide circle. One of the long sides of the net was made of lead and sank when it entered the water. The other long side was threaded with floating beads of cork. When the seiner and skiff reunited, the net underwater took the shape of a circular wall. Along the lead line, strung through metal hoops, was a pink line, called the purse line. As soon as possible after reuniting with the skiff, the seiner reeled in this line, in turn cinching up the bottom of the net, producing a giant sack, which, if all went well, contained fish.

Craig showed up right before the opening. With one minute to go, he said in his preternaturally calm voice, "Don't worry about those boats coming at you, Lars. They're too far away."

Boats? I peered out the window. A quarter mile away, looking all too close to me, two seiners were speeding our way, churning up fat wings of water. I closed one eye, unsure if I could watch. Craig started counting down from ten. A boat edged in front of us.

"Two. One."

"Go!" Lars called to the guys on deck.

Tony yanked on the tow hitch, releasing the skiff. The *Raven* surged forward while the net unfolded with astonishing speed, thumping and clacking over the roar of the engine. I went to the deck, careful not to step on the wrong side of the many lines. If I caught a foot, I'd be long gone.

The skiff quickly shrank as the corkline between us grew, an endless string of white beads. Everywhere I looked, seiners were spitting out cork as if they were production factories.

Craig was uncommonly agitated. "Close her up," he said. "No! Wait. Okay, close her up now!"

The net ran out with a heavy clunk. With maddening slowness, the *Raven* and the skiff drew close and finally met. Our corkline now formed a misshapen ring. The entire bay was filled with circles of glinting cork, giant pearl necklaces adrift on the sea.

Dale in the skiff handed the end of the net and purse line to Tony, who leaned over the rail for it. Then, Dale drove to the opposite side of the boat. I threw him a line, which he caught and looped around the bit on the skiff. The *Raven* couldn't run its propeller for fear of shredding the net, so Dale towed us away from obstacles such as rocks and other seiners.

Lars came downstairs, ran the hydraulics, and shouted in monosyllables, "Whoa. Go. Stop. Go," as Tony messed with a tangle of lines.

Finally, Tony cried, "Okay!" One by one, the purse rings rose out of the water and collected on a long rod, each landing with weighty force, like a trap being sprung. When the last ring clanged onboard, everyone went to the gunwale and peered into the net.

Often, the herring stayed deep, below the sunlit stratum of the water. However, nothing came to view.

"Oh well," Lars said with a sigh, walking away. I waited a while, willing the fish to appear. After the enormous stress of playing piranha for the last two hours, it seemed inconceivable and somehow unfair that our net was empty. In other areas in life, if you worked hard, you were often rewarded for it. If I ran six miles a day, say, I could count on being in pretty good shape. But apparently in fishing, no one was guaranteed a fat net.

Craig had departed to help the other combine members, leaving us to sleuth out the herring by ourselves. Back and forth across the bay we drove, passing boats in various stages of making a set. A few cozied up to tenders, large boats that transported the herring to processing plants. You could judge how much fish a boat had caught by how long it stayed by a tender. Dale and Tony took turns peering through binoculars and announcing pumping times.

By the end of the opening, the *Raven* had made four fishless sets. In a small cove, we dropped anchor. The temperature was warm for mid-April, and we ate lunch outside on the web pile. With the pressure off for the moment, the guys were back to their usual buffoonery.

"Do not lose hope, crew," Lars said, faking a deep, authoritative voice. "The fish appeared in my dreams last night and vowed to fill our net."

Dale snorted and said, "Who hired the cheerleader?"

"All they asked for was a small human sacrifice." Lars looked slyly at Dale. "Our oldest and weakest crew member."

"That would be you, I think."

"Perhaps, but I look younger than you."

"I don't think so."

"Marie, who looks the youngest?" Lars pushed his face close to Dale's and fluttered his eyelids.

Dale shoved Lars's shoulder and said with exaggerated exasperation, "You see what I have to put up with?"

Dale and Lars were old friends. In his late thirties, Dale had curly hair cropped close to his head, an extravagant beard, and piercing blue bedroom eyes. He wore Patagonia-everything and smelled like a men's magazine. He had fished for almost as long as Lars in just as many fisheries and loved to talk about the glory days of salmon during the early eighties when men made eighty thousand dollars in a three-month season and where towns like Kodiak and Dutch Harbor teemed with drugs and alcohol and men shnockered on both.

The radio blurted out static, then someone called for the *Raven*. Lars hurried to the wheelhouse. Minutes later, he poked his head out the door to report that the *Order of Magnitude* had caught a hundred tons.

"Not bad," Dale called up. Most years, one hundred tons was like receiving a plump Christmas bonus from the boss—excellent but not extraordinary—while a three-hundred-ton catch approximated finding a soda bottle on the beach with a luminescent pearl inside.

But this year, Japan, the sole buyer of herring caught in the Pacific Northwest, had a surplus from last year's harvest and was currently offering two hundred dollars a ton, way down from last year's eight hundred a ton.

Complicating the problem, all three members of the *Raven* crew were struggling financially. Their main trade was not herring but salmon fishing, lately a failing industry, due in part to declining wild salmon runs, but primarily to the rapidly growing farmed salmon industry, which competed directly with the wild salmon fishery, sending prices for both farmed and wild breeds plummeting. Lars had once estimated that wild salmon would garner four times its current price if the farmed industry did not exist.

As Tony liked to put it, salmon fishing was only good for a summer job. And that was if you were lucky enough to be a deckhand, like him. If you owned your own boat and permit, as did Lars and Dale, bought during salmon's heyday when gillnetters could cost $500,000 and permits went for as much as $400,000, you were in serious trouble. Neither man could generate enough cash from salmon fishing to make payments on their boats and permits. Worse, both owned lavish homes, purchased again when salmon was doing well, and had families to support. Lars's gillnetter and home were tentatively up for sale. Dale had not yet resorted to such drastic measures, although one of his favorite pastimes involved perusing the classified section of *Pacific Fishing* magazine and lamenting how low boat and permit prices had sunk—on average, they were one-third the prices of ten years ago.

The *Raven* crew were counting on herring to make up for those vanished salmon dollars. But with herring at two hundred dollars a ton, their only hope was that they make as many of those pearl-inside-soda-bottle sets as possible.

Later, Fish and Game announced that sixty percent of Kodiak's quota had been caught and a two-hour opening would begin at four. Lars drained his coffee and turned on the engine. Tony and Dale raced to draw up the anchor, then took stations by the sonar screen, their arms crossed and eyes fixed ahead, the easy mood of lunchtime apparently over. As we combed the same waters we had this morning, the fish proved even more elusive than before. The fleet had made an obvious dent in the population.

At fifteen minutes before four, Craig came on the radio, excited. "There's a big streak on the other side of the bay. Maybe one hundred tons."

We hurtled across the water, meeting up with an aluminum seiner called the *Zone* jetting in from the north. Tony and Dale rushed to their positions and the two boats began a brutal game of cat and mouse, neither able to take the lead for long without the other jockeying ahead. The men on the *Zone* kept glancing at us, as if nervous.

At three minutes before four, the skiff on the *Zone* broke loose, trailing a string of corks. Their net flew overboard, flop after flop.

"He skunked you," Craig said in dismay. Lars wordlessly navigated the *Raven* above the school of fish and shoved the throttle to its highest pitch, which, under normal circumstances, was considered poor etiquette. Right now, however, it was entirely appropriate.

In the distance, a small boat skimmed motorcycle-speed toward us.

"Good," Lars said. "That's Fish and Game. They're busted."

When the boat drew near, the skipper of the *Zone* emerged from the wheelhouse and made a big show of looking at his watch.

"Ya right," Lars said and laughed bitterly. The skipper had no excuse. At intervals before an opening, the time was announced on the radio.

"Is there a big fine?" I asked.

"Sometimes."

This was small consolation for the lost opportunity to catch a Christmas bonus of herring. We left with the *Zone* backhauling its net, the skipper staring at his feet while a Fish and Game official scribbled on a pad.

By the end of the opening, we had not even wetted our net, although the other combine boats had done well: one hundred and ten tons between the two.

"Good work," Lars radioed to the skipper of the *Natalia*. But his voice was strained, and after he got off the microphone, he muttered something about "intracombine competition."

For dinner, we broke into a box of red wine, and the guys got rowdy and a bit raunchy. They had a remarkable ability to forget about the stress of their job when off-duty. I on the other hand could not shake my disappointment. Herring seining, I was discovering, was about as sweat-inducing as watching television.

The real work was mental. It was hard work employing the right mix of patience and aggression to duke it out with the other seiners. It was hard work knowing that you had only a few brief chances in which to make a successful season. Already, we were one-third done, and even though I was not officially a crew member, I could feel the pressure hanging over me like a descending ax. Above all, it was hard work, not catching fish.

When Tony and I stepped outside to brush our teeth, he said, as if reading my mind, "Fishing's tough, isn't it?"

"The stress is enough to make me melt. How do you do it?"

Tony didn't hesitate. "It's all I know how to do. I grew up on water. I bought a kayak before a car. I was born with gills. See!" He sucked in his cheeks so that his upper lip became bulbous and wiggled it gymnastically—one of the best fish impersonations I had ever seen.

I laughed, in part at the Prince Valiant haircut he had given himself the other day, when in a fit of frustration at being blinded by his long bangs he had whipped out his Swiss Army knife and hacked them short. Tony was always making me laugh—that was one of the things I loved most about him. But there had been a tremble of emotion in his voice when he said, "I was born with gills," that caused me to abbreviate my laughter. At thirty-one, he had done a lot more fishing than most his age—fourteen years' worth. Now that I had seen him in action on the boat, studying the sonar screen like it held a secret, rushing to tie a line that had gotten loose, sensing immediately when the wind shifted directions, I understood what that tremble of emotion signified, what those fourteen years really meant to him. In fishing, he had found what I was looking for, something that went beyond money, something into which you poured a large part of yourself and which poured itself back to you, something that felt like a place, a home, a foundation, at once a shelter and a support. Lars and Dale, I was sure, shared the same close connection to fishing, perhaps even more so since they had been at it longer than Tony. It made the stakes higher, this understanding. Now, the season struck me as a matter of going broke or staying afloat not only for the men's finances but for their sense of how to live and be in this world, for their capacity to accept and know and believe in and ultimately feel good about themselves.

In the morning, we headed for Cook Inlet. Uganik Bay was wonderfully calm with just a spatter of rain. But only a few miles across Shelikof Strait, famous for its high winds and strong tides that often collided, producing unpredictable, roller-coaster waves, the *Raven* began to heave one way, then the other, throwing me off my feet. Green white-streaked water filled the portholes downstairs. I soon felt queasy. Tony came down from the wheelhouse and offered me sea bands, stretchy bracelets, each with a bead that according to acupressure theory would press into a spot on my wrist that supervised my stomach and so alleviate the nausea.

"Thanks," I said, putting them on. It was hard to talk. He sat with me, at intervals asking, "Feel any better?"

After my third time of answering, "not really," he pulled out a package. "Dramamine then?" Tony had the craziest knack for withdrawing from his pocket whatever you needed at the precise moment: knife, cord, even chocolate.

"Perfect," I said. In my bunk, as I waited for the drug to swirl me away to unconsciousness, the irony of my condition did not escape me. The wind and rain had arrived, but I was not outside, feeling their wildness, as I had imagined myself doing. I was not bidding them to "rage and blow," as King Lear had done in the glory of his madness. I was more like Lear in his weakened state, uttering the infant words of "do, de, de, de."

A storm hit Cook Inlet on the first day of the opening. Along with a few other boats, the *Raven* retreated to the only sheltered place, the mouth of the McNeil River, which went dry during low tide and left the boats leaning in the mud like wind-hammered shacks. Every day, we listened to the weather report and every day we heard the same dismal news: "Fifty knots, northeast." Several times, when the storm temporarily relented, during high tide, the crew took the Zodiac raft to shore and explored the narrow spit protecting our cove. The rest of the time, stuck on board, we tried not to bump into each other and tried not to look at the clock. I went through four or five books. However, if Tony was born with gills, I was born with cayenne in my blood and trampolines under my feet. I had to go, go, go all the time, and if I didn't, I became fretful, anxious, claustrophobic. Currently on day nine of no exercise, I felt like I was wearing a straitjacket.

"Are any of the tenders going to Kodiak before the next opening?" I asked at one point.

"Why?" Tony asked.

"I have to get off this boat."

"Does this mean you don't like fishing?" he joked.

Lars looked up from his magazine. "What's wrong with you, Marie? Isn't this fun?"

"I was under the impression that fishing was a little more active."

"This is herring fishing," Lars said. "Wait, wait, wait, then bust your ass."

"I hate it," I said, in no mood for tact.

"But you won't hate salmon," Tony said, eagerly. Lately, observing my decline, he had taken to listing the virtues of salmon gillnetting, in which you didn't purse up the fish with your net as in seining but you set it adrift in the current and the fish got snagged in its mesh. The gillnet was then hauled on board and you handpicked the salmon out of it—a highly aerobic activity, apparently. Also, the season was open for almost three months straight—there were none of these three-hour openings amid week-long closures.

"Crap, Tony," Lars said. "You're trying to talk her into salmon fishing?" He turned to me. "There's no money in salmon anymore. The last good season I had was ten years ago. Don't listen to your boyfriend—he's in denial!"

"Denial!" Tony sounded shocked. "Salmon's just going through a slump. It's only a matter of time before those fish farms go broke, the way they've over-invested themselves. If that doesn't happen, then all those fake fish are going to get eaten by some parasite."

Lars raised his famous eyebrow. "All I know is, I'd love to sell my boat and permit right now, but with the prices so low these days, I'd lose my shirt."

"You hear that?" Tony said to me. "It's a good time to buy in."

I laughed hesitantly. Tony was joking, as usual, but I didn't think Lars was in the mood for humor.

"Don't be stupid, Tony." Lars wagged a finger at him. "You've got two reasons not to buy in: me and Dale. You want to be like us in ten years? You want to have families to support while trying to figure out what the hell you can be in life besides a fisherman?"

"Salmon's going to get better," Tony said, weakly.

Lars shook his head in disgust and returned to his magazine. I had to agree with him—Tony was in denial. But I saw this as a measure of how deeply fishing penetrated into his life. Tony and fishing were like two ribbons intertwined: inseparable. Most people I knew had jobs in which they sat bug-eyed and humpbacked in front of computers or they waited tables with plastic smiles and plastic voices, all the while counting the hours until they could go home and do the things they really liked to do, like read or garden or bake cookies, if, that is, they had enough energy after work to do these things. It was a privilege, finding the perfect blend that Tony had discovered with his job, and like him, I'd go into enormous denial before I gave it up. How far would Tony take his denial, how much seriousness existed behind his joke of buying a salmon boat and permit, I couldn't say. If he ever decided to buy in, I'd want to support him in his determination to stick to his high standards of living, but in the end, in the name of financial sanity only, I'd probably try to discourage him. However, if the opportunity arose for me to be a deckhand with him on a salmon boat, because he loved it so and because I still hoped that fishing, as long as it wasn't herring seining, would lead to the full and affirming experience I was seeking in a job, I thought I might give it a try.

When the storm finally quit a week later, the fish were getting ready to spawn in Togiak, a five-day boat ride away. No one had seen skin nor fin of the herring in Cook Inlet since before the storm. I would not be able to hitch a ride with a tender going to Kodiak, because the entire fleet was heading directly to Togiak.

We drove day and night. On the third morning, the wind escalated from negligible to forty knots. That evening it snowed, creating such a dizzying whiteness in the glare of the crab lights with the boat rising and slamming and rising and slamming that Dale, at the helm, got sick for the first time in ten years. I spent the next thirty-six hours in my bunk, thoroughly Dramamined, waking only occasionally with one thought on my mind: Fishing was surely demented.

We arrived in Togiak the evening before the fishery was due

to begin. This was the most cutthroat fishery of all. Since no permit was required here, as many as four hundred boats participated. To prevent overharvest, Fish and Game often limited each opening to as few as thirty minutes. With three or four openings, we'd be lucky to get in two hours of fishing, all told. We ate a quick dinner and went straight to bed.

In the middle of the night, I awoke and looked up into the wheelhouse. Lars was sitting on his bunk, staring out the window. I could only imagine the pressure he felt. On tomorrow hinged not just a successful herring season, but possibly his fishing career, all that over the past twenty years had encompassed his thoughts, his feelings, his habits, the movements of his body, the people with whom he spent time, the conversations he had, the places he lived and to which he traveled, even the clothes he wore, the food he ate, and the music he listened to. I wished I could flick a wand and have herring rain down on the *Raven* tomorrow.

In the morning, we began patrolling the bay not two hours in advance as we typically did, but three. In no time, we reached the conclusion that the majority of the fish were crammed inside a small cove, the size of a football stadium. Unfortunately, the rest of the fleet had made this observation as well, and the tiny bay looked like it was harboring a full-scale naval engagement inside it.

We decided to try our luck on the other side of the spit that separated the cove from the rest of the bay. "Miracles can happen," Lars said, sounding more discouraged than I had ever heard him sound. Ten minutes into the opening, he shouted in surprise at the sonar screen and without hesitation cried, "Let's go!" to Tony and Dale, who stood in position. Soon, our net held a small load of herring.

I sat on the gunwale as we waited for the tender to arrive. Dozens of herring scuttled on the water's surface, their charcoal skins shifting silver when struck by the sun. It didn't look like we had caught much, but when I peered into the depths, a shadowy mass differentiated into hundreds of slow-moving fish. Soon, another deeper chamber of drifting fish appeared. All those layers of all those languid fish made me feel very sleepy.

When the tender drove up, it dropped into our net a hose big enough to suck me up. The thing roared and the herring each trembled slightly before disappearing. *Whoosh.* Soon, fish spilled out of the other end of the hose and into the one-ton bin on the tender. Excited, I whooped every time the bin filled up and the tender guy opened its door and an inky stew spilled into the hold.

After a while, I noticed that the tender guy had fish blood and scales all over his raincoat and face. Meanwhile, my hair smelled of shampoo and my clothes of laundry detergent. During the entire season, I hadn't so much as touched a fish, much less gotten parts of it all over me. Looking at the guy on the tender, I realized, was as close to the muck of life as I would get in herring seining. The whole trip had been a procession of disappointments. Earlier, I had discovered that I would not be required to sweat and grunt; then I had found that my tolerance for rough weather on the boat was very low. This was strike three. I no longer felt like whooping.

The catch was forty tons. "Hardly enough to salvage our ego," Dale said.

Toward the end of the second opening, the *Order of Magnitude* scooped sixty tons, astonishingly inside the battle zone. The *Natalia* caught nothing.

It was the third and last opening. Craig directed our entire combine inside the small cove. "The herring are simply nowhere else," he said, and we had to admit that after our lucky break earlier in the day, the outside-cove area had been utterly dead. The naval engagement, it appeared, had switched to fast-forward. Seiners everywhere darted and slalomed and bucked over choppy waves. Boats drove so close to us, I could read the deckhands' sweatshirts. In the sky, a swarm of planes mirrored the activity on the water.

"We might die," I whispered to Tony.

"We might," he said, smiling, as if he enjoyed the adrenaline of it all.

With ten minutes to go, Craig guided us to a school of fish. "It's not much," he said, "but it's as good as it gets."

A black boat with a purple stripe called the *Juniper* cut in front of us.

"Oh, no, you don't," Lars said, his voice threatening as he lurchingly maneuvered the *Raven* slightly ahead and to the inside of the black boat. A small seiner, the *Juniper* deftly shot in front of us. When we tried to regain the lead, the boat skirted around us again.

"She's got us," Lars said.

With two minutes remaining, Craig said, "Let them have this batch. There's another streak building one hundred yards to your left. Go!"

The *Raven* leaned as if sinking. Downstairs, dishes clattered to the floor. On the deck, Tony embraced the capstan, and in the skiff, Dale crouched. The *Juniper* hurtled ahead of us.

"Is he crazy?" Lars cried, incredulous. "I just gave him that last batch."

"Time's up!" yelled Craig.

Tony released the skiff and the *Raven* looped toward the beach. On our inside, the *Juniper* produced a smile of corkline. Just as I was thinking that we seemed rather close to the shoreline, the *Raven* stopped short and made a sock-in-throat sound.

Lars shoved the gear in reverse but the boat wouldn't budge. When he tried forward again, the gravely, strangling sound only grew louder.

"Shit!" Lars pummeled the dashboard with his fist. I thought he might break some knuckles.

Meanwhile, all around us, boats were closing up their sets. Circles of cork littered the bay like garlands of flowers thrown on a stage. While Dale in the skiff towed the *Raven* out of the sand, one hundred yards away the *Natalia* caught sixty tons. The corkline jittered from the weight of the fish, and a deckhand raced around the circumference of the net in a Zodiac, adding buoys. On the far side of the cove, the *Order of Magnitude* hit the jackpot with an eighty-ton catch. Our one consolation was that the *Juniper* didn't catch anything.

After the opening, the combine boats tied together for a brief respite before they headed back to Kodiak. Craig was flying to Anchorage with an empty seat and invited me to join him. I accepted, not wanting to be on the boat another day. Without much ado, I said good-bye to Lars and Dale and thanked them for letting me fish with them.

Tony walked me to the plane, unusually quiet. "Does this mean you've written off salmon fishing?" he asked after a while.

"Ask me again much, much later," I said, sadly. I would have laughed at his perseverance, but I was too disappointed that seining, something I had so wanted to believe in, had failed me. It was like hiking in the desert and coming to a clear pool of water that was undrinkable. Tony, I knew, was also disappointed that I had not fallen in love with fishing. However, we had gained something immeasurable, I believed. We had gained the knowledge that we shared a commitment to a job well lived, to finding the one calling or experience in life that held our passions and interests and beliefs, the one that allowed us to feel the expanse of ourselves. Neither he nor I wanted to settle for anything less. The only difference between us was that Tony was at risk of losing the life he had found most suited for him, while

I was at risk of not finding mine. I felt that the space between us had shrunk just a little.

We hugged and I promised to pick him up at the airport when he arrived in Fairbanks. Craig started the plane and we took off among a scattering of seiners. I sighed. Thank God I was off the boat. Down below, the *Raven* crew were already backhauling the net into the hold. I cringed to think of the five-day drive in store for them, with nothing to do but dwell on their untriumphant season. Though our combine had done slightly better than the fleet average, with this year's feeble price, the men's take-home salary would not amount to much, perhaps $1500 for Tony and Dale and twice as much for Lars. I thought it very possible that I had just accompanied them on one of their very last expeditions.

The plane soared. The cloudless, pale blue sky looked washed out, as if overfull of sun. Craig pointed out some streaks of herring, the ones that had escaped this year's thrashing. There were lots of them in Togiak Bay. Murky brown and huge, they resembled thunderclouds building above a prairie floor. From here, catching them looked like a breeze.

STRIPER

JOHN COLE *lives in Maine and has written about commercial and sport fishing for several decades in such books* as Stripers: An Angler's Anthology, Fishing Came First, *and, most recently,* Tarpon Quest.

L IKE THE GULLS, we follow the fish as they head east along the beach during May and on into the long days of June—that most luminous month. We are up before the sun at three-thirty, ready to set on first light at four, and before another hour has gone, we discuss whether to make a second set. It is not yet five in the morning, but the sun is already bulging orange above the southeast horizon, squat and heavy with its throbbing warmth. Crimson dervishes dart over the slick sea's surface as the sun's velvet reflection stretches, breaks, and moves with the ocean's easy summer undulations.

Sharks follow the warming; we can expect them in the seine in most dawn sets—threshers slapping their scythe tails at the cork line, sand sharks snapping with their ugly, grinning mouths, makos leaping the twine, or crashing through it, and, every so often, hammerheads and blue sharks cruising from wing to wing, their fins slicing the slick surface, slowly at first and then faster as the net tightens and the sharks turn to shred their filmy trap with convulsive bites and the spasmodic turning, twisting, and thrashing of their tails. Inevitably, the larger sharks leave us with much mending. We stand there, sweating in our waders as the sun climbs higher, pulsing faster with the fierceness of its heat, and move the needles back and forth, over and under, closing as best we can the open meshes riven by shark teeth. Some mornings I can look down the beach and see the first of the vacationing city bathers running through the surf, splashing and playful. How many, I wonder, would be as abandoned if they had watched the fins moving back and forth within our seine's small arc?

If we escape severe shark damage to the twine, we can make two sets by seven. After that, it is almost too warm to work, and, Ted tells us, the bass move offshore to deeper, darker, cooler waters. We go back, take care of the catch, wait until two or three in the afternoon and return to the beach—a place that is no longer ours. Wherever we go, we are followed by bathers, beach-goers, men, women, and children on holiday. They gather and watch, and most of them coo with sympathy for the fish that come writhing in the bunt. We stay silent, removed, dutiful, and as we go about the work, our eyes on the gear and the sand, I look for myself among the watchers, skinny in my bathing trunks, horsing around with Chick and my companions, taking the summer for a playroom, wondering what these men in the rubber suits are doing in June, working, sweating, covered with sand, stinking with fish when they should be swimming, riding the waves, bodysurfing like the me I watch for.

By dusk, the audience thins and vanishes with the sunset. We wait through the long twilight, watching for the flickering of bait fish, a stirring of the waters that may mark the turning of a bull bass moving inshore for his feeding. There is ample twilight to set as late as eight-thirty, and it is often ten by the time we head back to Ted's to end a day that has spanned more than eighteen hours.

We are deranged, in a way, by the sweetness of the season. The weather seems perpetual, the slick ocean caresses the sand instead of pounding it; even the rain is soft, we can fish through it. The days are extruded like golden wire, stretched longer and longer, thinner and thinner, vibrating with the sun's vitality, hot with the friction of their stretching. We walk the golden wire, sustained by the spinning equilibrium of our own excitement at the prospect of more of the same tomorrow. We are like drunkards in a wine cellar, intoxicated as much by the vista of a long row of casks as we are by drinking all our bellies can hold.

But there is no glut of fish. The same heat and the same long sun that keep us sleepless send the striped bass to the cool refuges off the rocks at Montauk. As June pulls past us, even our dawn sets produce barren bunts, flapping sleeves of twine that twitch only with whiptail rays, a sand shark, or a handful of sea robins. Ted says we should not be discouraged; he wants to haul right through July and August, pulling his seine across summer until he finds autumn in the net. But Alex must work longer at tending the gardens of his boss's big house, making the roses opulent for the family's July arrival; Peter wants to go purse-seining porgies in the bay on Milt's groaning hulk of a dragger. Our spring season ends at a time so rich in the sensual luxury of summer that the sparse call of the geese that began this episode is a needle-slim memory lost in fields of fat grass rippling in the afternoon breeze.

I go to Montauk to find Jim, still working his gear alone, setting gillnets in the bay now, trying for a catch of bluefish before the market is glutted by the July and August arrival of the Point's vast summer schools. I remember what Jim said about charter boats, I recall his stories of the charter skippers he knows, and I ask if he can steer me to a captain who may need a mate.

"Try Al, on the *Skip Too*, over at the town dock," Jim answers, after pondering for one of his long pauses. He is sitting on the sand on the beach that runs west of the breakwater, mending a gillnet. His shirt is off and his compact shoulders and muscular back are a dark tan. He must already have spent days on this beach, sunning and mending. He will not give up his stubborn search for a system that will make fishing more of a sure thing for him, even if that search forces him to endure days of solitude and discouraging drudgery.

Such a sense of aloneness hovers about him here, working on this sweep of bay beach, bent over his net, fingering every bar in every mesh, compelled by some push within him toward a kind of perfection few, if any, fishermen would consider practical. Jim will mend, and mend again any weakness in his gear because he wants no equipment failures to cloud his testing of the fish. If his nets fail to catch, it will be for other reasons than their readiness and their ability. I feel a kind of guilt that I am not here working with him, staying at the side of the man who let me stay at his when I was useless and knew nothing about fishing, nothing about woodcutting, nothing about working as hard as I have since I learned a fisherman's work.

"Thanks, Cap," I say. "I'll get right over there." Jim nods, the needle moves. "Cap, I'll let you know what he says. How is it going with you? I mean, are you catching enough to pay for your gas? Is it panning out, you fishing alone?"

The needle stops, Jim looks up, smiles. "Finest kind, John, finest kind. Those blues will show here any day, and I'm ready, I'm ready. I'm going to set around on the outside, off Caswell's. I figure those big blues will strike in there first. I'll be shipping them in while the price is still a quarter, instead of a nickel like it's going to be two weeks later."

"Well, Jim . . ." I can't quite say it. "Well, if you need any help, you let me know."

"I'm doing fine. Just like New York." He waves his arm, pointing with the seine needle in his raised hand. "Get on over there and see Al."

The *Skip Too* is a high-sided, V-bottom slab of a charter boat, narrow, roll-y, with an unreliable converted Buick engine yanked from a car that rolled over on the Montauk Highway. Al has to use her because he doesn't have the fifteen thousand dollars it takes to get a charter captain properly started with a new boat, a dependable engine. He's just a year or so older than I, busting his ass, trying to support a growing family, trying to put enough aside to get a better boat. "One more winter in Florida," he tells me, "if the stock market holds up, and I'll log enough charter for a down payment on a new boat. Then watch me go. Right now, we got to make do with what we have. I want you to know that before I take you on." He stops, gestures at the beat-up fishing chairs, the clean but worn decks. "Last mate I had figured he wanted to work on a yacht, I guess. Left me high and dry Sunday for a job with a private boat at the club. I had to give up a charter, too.

"What you get is what you see," he says, turning all the way around as he stands in the cockpit talking to me on the dock. "Take a good look. Then, if you still want to mate for me, be here at four in the morning. I got a party for the early tide."

That's how it begins. From that morning in late June until two weeks after Labor Day, I put in seven days a week aboard the *Skip Too*. We don't miss a day. Even with this slab of a hull, even with Al reluctant to go offshore after tuna, swordfish, and marlin because he doesn't trust the engine, we get charters every day.

Some mornings we watch as the other boats leave. We get depressed as we become one of the two or three charter boats that remain at the dock when the rest of Montauk's hundred-boat fleet has gone. But by noon, something always turns up. A man and his wife walk the docks, looking for a bargain; half-a-dozen Chinese who have driven down late from Chinatown want to go bottom-fishing for sea bass off the Elbow. Or we get striper fishermen who figure the afternoon is just as productive as the morning, so why should they get out of bed in the pre-dawn dark and go roll around off the Point while Al trolls back and forth, back and forth over the rips, or works Shagwong, edging the wire lines and lures closer and closer to the bottom where stipers wait in undersea ravines for the tide to tumble bait fish their way.

We are a seagoing taxi, a fish-catching machine, a plane that flies in circles. Al is the captain-pilot, remote, up on the flying bridge; his dark glasses and his preoccupation with navigation put a barrier between him and the passengers. I'm the passengers' man. I'm their stewardess, telling them the rules, making them coffee, tea, and drinks, letting out their lines, untangling the snarls. I hook the fish, jig the rods, gaff and boat the fish, gut and clean the fish, make jokes with the parties, tell them fables about the fishing, show them how to work the head, clean up when they puke.

I watch so that they don't fool with trying to readjust the star drag on Al's only reels. I change lures so they'll know we're doing everything we can to catch them more fish. I stand in the rolling cockpit from dawn to dusk when we have morning and afternoon charters. My index finger on my right hand has a permanent slice cut across the side of the middle knuckle where the leader always ends up when I reach over the transom to grab and hold it while I gaff the fish, or yank them into the boat if they're under ten pounds.

If we aren't catching fish, I tell the charter it's only a matter of time; when we do get into fish, I work fast and I make the parties work fast—the more fish they reel in, the more we'll have to throw onto the dock. And the bigger our pile, the more likely we are to pick up a charter for the next day, or the day after.

The thighs of my cotton twill pants are silver and stinking with scales. When we're into a school of small stripers or bluefish, I swing the fish between my legs, then yank the hook from the fish's jaws, toss the lure and line back overboard, then drop the fish in the live well, turn and strip off the line while the passenger holds the rod. That's all they have to do, sit in the chair with the rod butt in the gimbal, turn the crank when the fish hooks itself. Our gear is twice as heavy as it needs to be, the rods are as stiff as steel beams, the leaders are sixty-pound for ten-pound fish. Al doesn't even slow down for one fish; if we get two on, he eases up. He'll maneuver a bit when we are hit with a tripleheader; he turns around and begins yelling at me, telling me who to move where so the lines won't get tangled and we won't lose our fish.

Fish. That's what this enterprise is about. These charters, these parties, these men and women and children may tell themselves they are off to Montauk for an adventure, for a day on the water, for a look at the lovely blue sky, for a whiff of salt air and some relaxation—a break from the assembly line, a day off from behind the meat counter, a night away from the restaurant kitchen—but they all kid themselves. Once they get aboard, it's fish they are after. If they see fish going silver over the transom of a nearby boat, they turn to me and say, "Hey, they're getting them over there."

They wait in their chairs, their hands trembling on the rods, waiting for that slamming, sudden thump that a big bass makes when it hits. The rod bends, the reel whines and the party goes bananas, yelling, forgetting what he is supposed to do, forgetting what I've told him. Half the time he yanks the hook right out of the striper's mouth; the lure comes aboard with a lip hanging from it.

There are a hundred Montauk charter boats like ours, or better, carrying an average of four to a party. If those four hundred folks don't catch ten fish apiece, it's a bad trip. At two trips a day, which is the average for charters, that's eight thousand bass and blues tossed on the planked docks at Montauk every day. I find myself not believing it, even though I'm gaffing, scaling, gutting, and filleting everything the *Skip Too* brings in.

The parties wait in their Dacron shirts and their sandals while a hundred mates like me slice, scrape, behead, and disembowel the forty or fifty fish we average on most days. The public docks at Montauk reek with the sweetness of fish guts; the bottom of the harbor is pale with the flayed and rotting carcasses tossed over after the fillets have been slashed away.

I become fish. Their scales are now my skin, their hearts and livers and gonads are squeezed into my clothing. Their muscular writhings at the end of their battles for freedom are permanent tremors in my forearms, thumping as I try to sleep, unable to forget the vitality of the creatures I have pulled up and over the *Skip Too*'s transom. Fish blood running from the gaff fills my Topsiders; once white, the sneakers turn pale pink, no matter how many times I wash them.

And as I hunch on the dock, my knife cutting through the flesh in my hand, flesh that is mine now as well as that of bass or bluefish, the parties hover, watching to make sure they get theirs, to make certain this mate doesn't slip a fish for himself into some hiding place. And when every fish is cleaned, the parties bring out the plastic sacks they buy at Tuma's and Gosman's and fill them full of wet and slippery fish flesh until, ready to head back to Queens or Brooklyn, they realize they cannot lift the bags alone. Three hundred pounds still weighs three hundred pounds.

I watch clumsy struggles to get the trip's catch into the trunks of the cars, where the fish will ride, steaming and cooking over the shimmering highways back to the sidewalk front yards. I watch four men from 37th Street put so many bluefish into the trunk of their Pontiac sedan that the back bumper and muffler scrape and squeal on the town dock parking lot as the car goes dragging out, leaving a long white scar in the tar, and a parallel stripe of bloody seawater that sloshes from the trunk as the Pontiac lurches off.

There is a ten-dollar tip in my bloody hand. Al counts his hundred-dollar charter price, gives me another ten dollars, and goes to buy some Coke for the next charter, due for the afternoon trip in a half hour.

I turn on the dockside hose as high as the faucet valve allows, haul the nozzle with me aboard the *Skip Too* and try to wash down the decks so cleanly that not a scale or a drop of blood will be left as witness to the morning off Montauk. The boat must be clean for each trip, as if nothing had occurred on the one before. All the charters want to believe they are the first, that this is their particular adventure.

For me, it is always the same.

GREENHORN

MICHAEL CROWLEY *makes the lucky break from working on the docks to working on the deck of a wooden halibut schooner—but the rewards for a greenhorn are tenuous.*

THE SNOUT OF the halibut schooner *Attu* slammed through the spume-creased roller, hung there a moment, and then dropped into the trough. Propelled by 120 tons of fir planking spiked to heavy oak frames, a diesel that straddled her keel, and ice and bait packed in her hold, the sixty-five-foot schooner would have buried herself in the back side of the frigid Alaska sea, but as the hull cut into the water, her shoulders caught her, stopped the descent, and exploded the water out from the hull.

I hung over the rail, my vomit mixed with the roller's dark froth as the sea hurried on to its inevitable collision with the Alaska mainland. Below, in the dark waters, the *Attu*'s big four-bladed bronze prop grabbed hold of the ocean and sent the schooner plowing onward—toward the next rearing wave.

In the foc's'le, Greg and Kenny were wedged into their bunks, anticipating and bracing for each drop into the void and the climb back up. Pinky and Russ were huddled over the galley table, engaged in an intense never-ending cribbage game, with bragging rights more than money at stake. Up in the wheelhouse, the stub of the skipper's cigarette burned the night, falling and rising in time with the boat's motion. This weather didn't bother them a lick. No matter how much or how quickly the old wooden hull rolled or plunged, not one of them even burped. At dinner, Dick the cook, had slung spaghetti on plates, then heaved a big pot of sauce on the galley table.

"Kid," Dick said, "you need food if you're goin' be any good on this slab. Course, if it don't settle just right in your gut, just take a piece of that bacon there," and he pointed to the shelf over the stove where a package of

37

bacon lay ready for the frying pan, "tie it on a string, soak it in this here grease," and he tilted the pot to me so I could see the inch or two of grease and oil on top of the sauce, "and then work it up and down your throat and . . ."

I never heard the end. I'd been looking out the companionway at the masts weaving crazily across the stars and moon; my stomach was starting to follow the motions of the wheelhouse as it swung from one group of stars to another. One look at the spaghetti sauce grease, and I was leaping for the ladder and then stumbling to the rail before painting the ocean with what little remained of the food I had in me.

It wasn't fair. There I was, damned near worthless for deck-work, yet the first time I had seen this crew, most of them could hardly stand. That was in the Pioneer Bar in Seward, Alaska.

For almost six weeks, I'd been driving a forklift at Seward Fisheries, hauling carts of halibut to be weighed after they'd been dumped out of the unloading net to have their heads sliced off by a stainless steel guillotine. After one long day, a bunch of us dock workers headed to town. At the bar, the plant foreman was looking at three guys in the corner. "God, we'll never get them unloaded in the morning," he said. It was half the crew of the *Attu*. Two of them were leaning against each other, struggling to keep from falling down while trying to hoist the third guy to his feet. He wasn't just drunk—he was passed-out-pissed-in-the-corner drunk, and before long, all three were stacked in a heap on the floor.

The next morning, the *Attu* only had about 35,000 pounds of halibut to unload, but it took as long to get the fish out of the hold as it would a boat with 100,000 pounds. Two of the crew from last night were in the hold, pulling halibut into the un-loading net. Every time a net load of fish was hoisted out of the hold and up to the dock, both of them flopped back into the slime, fish, and ice, asleep until a hail or an empty net was dropped on them. And when a load of fish was hauled to the scales, the skipper had to be awakened to verify the weights.

Despite their condition—obviously hardcase fishermen—I wondered what it would be like to be out on a boat like the *Attu* for weeks at a time. I wanted to find out, but then I hadn't the foggiest idea how to go about it.

I was a refugee from the lower 48, escaping San Francisco, the university, and the chaos and turmoil of the late sixties. Somewhere I still had an overcoat with buckshot holes in the back, courtesy of the Oakland County Sheriffs' Department after they'd swung, like a ragged Roman phalanx, around a corner, their mouths open, gulping for air, their eyes full of blood, anger, and adrenaline. They had leveled shotguns down the street, at the backs of fleeing students. Later in the day, I'd watched one of the sheriffs swing his shotgun up to a rooftop along Berkeley's Telegraphic Avenue and blast the life out of a kid who had maybe—and maybe not—hurled a rock at the street below.

I had seen too many figures slide through the alleys and back streets, one stumble ahead of a beating or a bad drug deal. Sidestepped too many piles of dog shit on the sidewalks. Pushed through too many panhandlers' outstretched hands. Finally I did what others have done for generations when they didn't fit in—fled to the wilderness for strength and rejuvenation.

There was no more wilderness to the West, so it was north to Alaska. In the late spring of 1968, I stood in a line at the San Francisco airport, a backpack and suitcase at my feet, a ticket in my hand, less than $100 in my pocket, working hard to ignore the airport signs that read DO NOT GO TO ALASKA EXPECTING TO FIND WORK. THERE ISN'T ANY.

Once I got there, despite the airport signs, I was lucky. Petersburg Fisheries had chosen that spring to pump a lot of money into Seward Fisheries to draw boats to its docks that would otherwise have gone to Kodiak or Prince Rupert to unload. Within a couple of days I had a job, and soon I started asking every skipper who unloaded fish if there wasn't a chance aboard his boat. "Sorry, kid. Won't take any greenhorns," was the response again and again: None of them wanted a greenhorn. One skipper did say: "Kid. Maybe you'd make the good man, but forget it. Save your money. Someday go on one of those nice cruise ships. Then you can say you've been on the sea."

That same week, halibut schooners came in to unload after the first trip of the season. After that, no other type of boat interested me. With a long, lean hull, two masts and a small wheelhouse aft, the halibut schooner still had the lines of the old sailing boats. In fact, none were built after 1927, and most came from yards around Ballard, Washington. They were shaped with adzes, slicks, steam-powered ship saws, and the brute force and ingenuity of squarehead ship carpenters and designers.

At one time, my brother and I had pitched sleeping bags and backpacks onto the floor of a Southern Pacific boxcar as it was hauling out of the Oakland freight yard. We had rattled north to Vancouver, British Columbia, and then east across the foot of Canada to Halifax and Lunenburg, Nova Scotia, in search of old sailing codfishermen, from the time of the *Bluenose* and the *Gertrude Theabaud*.

Standing there on the Seward docks, I knew this was the closest I'd ever get to the old sailing schooners. These halibut schooners felt like kin—distant kin to be sure, with modern diesels bolted down over the keel and sails long gone from the masts— but kin nevertheless.

One afternoon, some of the gang from the docks pulled up at the house and cried out: "Hey, Crowley, the *Attu* can't find its cook. They'll take you if you want to go!" I didn't hesitate a second. For the first time I'll see the sea from somewhere other than a distance, I thought, my pulse racing. I didn't have the proper clothes or gear for fishing—no foul-weather gear, no thick-soled boots, no "wristers" that protected your shirtsleeves and forearms, no wool pants or long underwear, which I knew most wore even in the summer. But some of the crew pitched in and gave me wristers; a guy at the cannery gave me his stream waders and a set of rainwear that was good for an afternoon of lake fly-fishing. It wasn't much, but I would have worn anything.

It wasn't long before that dream seemed short-lived. Steaming out of Resurrection Bay, Donny, who was one of the most easygoing skippers you'd ever meet, had a rush of guilt at leaving the cook behind. A short discussion took place in the pilothouse, then the wheel spun hard over, the throttle pegged, and the *Attu* headed back to find its cook. And my fate now was—hell, I didn't know what.

The *Attu* tied up and the crew piled into two beat-up cabs and headed into town. The bars were the first place to check. Then inquiries were made of several select women, and finally Dick was found in a restaurant, unconcerned—as if it wasn't the first time—over the possibility that he'd almost missed a fishing trip. Once more the *Attu* headed out of Resurrection Bay. And I was still aboard. After Dick's retrieval, Donny was obviously uncomfortable having a greenhorn aboard, but he told me, "It wouldn't be fair not to take you. You can go. And if you're worth it, you'll get a quarter share this trip. After that we'll see how you do," he said, noncommital. I knew that to mean that the crew would vote on the size of my share based on how I did. A quarter share was generous, I felt—some greenhorns only got oilskins and boots on their first trip. But hell, I would have gone for nothing, even had I known I'd be hanging over the railing half the way across the Gulf of Alaska.

Not far out in the gulf, Donny pointed the bow on a course to take her outside of Kodiak Island, where we would start fishing. Locked inside the schooner's hull for the next three weeks were five fishermen and me, along with $700 worth of groceries, and 6,000 gallons of fuel to feed the *Attu*'s big Caterpillar diesel. Beneath the main deck's hatch were ten and a half tons of flake ice and 8,500 pounds of frozen bait: 3,500 pounds of salmon, 2,000 pounds of octopus, 2,000 pounds of cod, and 1,000 pounds of herring.

The wind was picking up and stood right on her snout as the schooner cut through the chop. On the foredeck, spray whipped past our faces as we stared off to westward.

"You keep an eye open," Russ said solemnly. "Soon as you see the first halibut come to the surface, holler out."

I nodded.

"See, when halibut start swimming to the top, well, then you know you're in a good spot to set your gear," Dick added.

They stood and watched with me for a minute, then went below.

I had only been up there about five minutes when I heard the laughter roll out of the foc's'cle. I realized that I'd been had. Halibut are bottom feeders, as I soon learned, and they spend their life on the ocean floor, not swimming about on the surface. Sheepishly I went below to get my deserved ribbing.

About one that morning, Greg woke me.

"It's time to bait up."

"Now it starts," muttered Pinky, one of the few things I'd heard him say that wasn't laced with four-letter words and references to female anatomy.

"Sixty skates," Donny called out from the wheelhouse. That

was a lot of gear in the water. A skate is a single nylon line usually about 300 fathoms, with a hook attached every 20 feet or so. From out of the hold came salmon, octopus, and herring, enough to bait over 6,000 hooks. My job was chopping bait—the very bottom rung of the ladder that leads up to a full share. Russ showed me how to cut up the bait without chopping off my hand or fingers. The frozen octopus goes on a big round block of wood that sits on the hatch. Then, using a meat cleaver, the octopus is cut into chunks about three inches by an inch and a half. What makes chopping bait potentially treacherous, especially for a new guy, is the continual pitching and rolling of the deck. Bring the cleaver down just as the bow slams into a head sea, and fingers are part of the bait.

To get ahead, Russ was also chopping bait, while the rest of the crew started baiting the skates. The crew wouldn't let me bait—not until near the end of the trip. It would be a long time before I would bait a skate. As Pinky would periodically remind me, "The only time greenhorns don't screw things up is when they're asleep. And since we don't get much of that, we're just trying to protect you from yourself."

Six or seven hours later, the last of the skates were tied up. The flagpoles and buoy lines were all in place; the anchors were rigged, and the bags ready to go over the side.

"As soon as we eat, we're setting the gear," says Donny.

The cook's got a breakfast of eggs, sausage, pancakes, juice, potatoes, and coffee. This is the first complete meal I've been able to put down since we left Seward three days ago.

It took three hours to set the gear. We put six strings of ten skates each in sixty-fathom water. The strings were set over a small ridge, parallel to each other with a three-minute birth between them. Six hours after we set, we started picking up the first string.

Donny swung the *Attu*'s bow into the wind to pick up the

flagpole while Greg filed the end of the gaff hook to a sharp point. Coming alongside the flagpole, Russ and Greg heaved it aboard and wound the buoy line around the gurdy's sheave. (The gurdy, a stand-up affair, with a horizontal sheave, is the winch that hauls the groundline aboard.)

Once the buoy line came aboard, Russ sat down on an old metal tractor seat at the far edge of the hatch, placed a skate bottom on the deck, and began to coil the groundline. When he finished one skate, he carried it aft and rebaited it while someone else coiled down the next skate.

Greg worked the roller, a small aluminum drum that acts as a lead to the gurdy and over which the groundline passes. The roller man's job is the most demanding and important job on deck. He has to gaff the fish and bring them aboard and make sure the line doesn't part on the bottom. At the same time, he has to watch out for flying hooks. A few years ago, a hook caught up in a plank, then snapped free and lodged in Donny's eye, robbing him of half his sight.

"Hey! Hey!" Greg cried. "Fish coming! Fish coming!"

As the *Attu* rolled down to the water, Greg snapped off the gurdy and in the same motion struck at the ocean with his gaff. There was a flurry of water.

"Gimme a hand," Greg cried, his body pumping up and down, then left and right as the fish struggled to escape the gaff and hook. Russ jumped next to him, swinging his own gaff. They both pulled hard, each with a foot braced against the gunnel, backs straining, until they heaved a dark, wide shape above the rail. One final effort and the fish came over the side.

"It's about one-fifty, I'd say," Greg offered as he slipped the hook from the halibut's mouth. Russ swung a heavy wooden club, stunning the fish. It flapped its massive tail once before Russ slung it onto the hatch. He slipped his knife inside the belly flap, and in two or three quick motions, he cut the gills free, sliced open the belly, and removed the stomach and guts. Last, the sweet meat and blood line was scraped out, and the fish was dropped into the hold, ready to be iced.

While all this was happening, I was still chopping bait, wondering when—or if—I'd be able to go to the roller and bring in a fish like that. It seemed so strange that this crew, which could barely function when I first saw them, now worked so smoothly together at sea, each knowing exactly what was expected of them. Now, I was the odd man out, the one viewed with skepticism and suspicion. I knew it would be a long time before that changed.

All the while, the *Attu* moved smoothly over the long, easy swells of a distant storm.

At 6 A.M. twenty-nine hours later, the original sixty skates had been hauled and Donny called a halt. In between strings, we reset all but a few skates. We'd start hauling again in three hours—it was our first break. I didn't even take the time to dip into the hot chocolate Dick made. After washing away the salt caking my face and eyes, I stripped out of my oilskins and boots and rolled into the bunk. Thank god it was the bottom bunk, because I didn't think I had the energy to climb into a top bunk. I'd heard of some fishermen who don't even bother to shed their oilskins when they sleep, so they're ready to go as soon as someone wakes them.

That's how it went for three weeks: for every eighteen to thirty hours of work, we got three or four hours of sleep. Hook after skate after skate after hook, night and day until I lost track of how many days we had been out. I became an expert at quick catnaps. Standing up, sitting down, I could doze for thirty seconds or two minutes and wake up and feel refreshed, at least for a short period of time. I was continually wet and cold. The sportfishing boots I was wearing leaked through a multitude of tiny hook punctures and knife holes. The oilskins were equally porous. My daydreaming was no longer of cars, women, parties, or even the end of this trip, but owning a stout pair of rubber boots with felt liners and real honest-to-god fisherman's oilskins. The only thing that kept us going was food, and there was plenty of that. Every meal was a several-course affair, but there was only ten to fifteen minutes to wolf the food down and follow it up with coffee before you were back on deck.

There was occasional relief from the long hours on deck when we made a run to another fishing spot or when a big enough storm moved in. One long run meant nearly eight hours in the bunk. Another time it blew 70–80 mph and we did nothing but jog to a flagpole for the day and a half it took the storm to blow through.

That was my first storm, and when I went for my wheel watch they told me only to "keep 'er into the wind" and to hand-steer her because the iron mike couldn't keep up with the boat's motions. It was a rain-blown dark night that had turned the Gulf of Alaska into a swirling, tumbling wasteland with marauding seas slamming against the hull and filling the deck. For the first time in my life, I knew real fear as I felt the *Attu* sink and then rise, trying to shake herself free of boarding seas. I wanted someone with me up in the wheelhouse who knew what the hell they were doing, but I stuck it out alone, spraddle-legged behind the wheel, fighting my own anxieties and the heaving vessel, gripping the spokes of the wooden wheel probably as hard as they'd ever been gripped.

After that introduction to Alaska weather, I found a quiet kind of reassurance in standing behind the big wheel and checking the course on the binnacle compass, armed on each side with painted cast-iron spheres. Well, here I am, I thought. For the rest of my life I'll be able to say I went longlining on a halibut schooner in the Gulf of Alaska. I knew not many would be able to match that.

When it came time to wake the next man for his wheel turn, I'd swing a quick look around the horizon to locate any boats, climb the three steps out of the wheelhouse, and scurry across the main deck to the foc's'le and galley, timing the run to make sure I didn't get doused by a wave in the process. Push open the companionway doors and drop into the foc's'le, a wedgeshaped cavernous space lit by a small light bulb. Farther forward were two sets of bunks, seven feet by shoulder width, about right for a coffin. On the port side were two more bunks. Some of the bunks were strung with curtains smudged with dirt and fish blood. Behind those curtains was the only privacy a crewman had for three to four weeks at a time. For most it was a room away from home. For others, like an old Norwegian halibut fisherman who told me, "Kid, a woman's place is ashore. A man's place is on the boat," it was home itself.

One morning after breakfast, just before we started to haul in the skates, Donny climbed out of the foc's'cle and announced in a loud voice, "We're going to shake the gear as it comes aboard." Everyone sighed with relief. We were going to take the old bait off the hooks, tie up the skates, and go in.

Once all the skates were stacked on the stern and we started washing down the boat, the *Attu* headed up Shelikof Straits, then went through Ouzinkie Narrows and across Monashka Bay on its way to Kodiak. Up in the foc's'cle, the crew took turns at the porcelain sink that drained into a bucket. They poured hot water into the bowl to wash up and shave, then splashed on cologne to mask the stench of three weeks of sweat, halibut slime, and blood. Going into Ouzinkie Narrows, I threw the same underwear I'd worn for three weeks over the stern: the mark of a completed halibut trip.

Once ashore, I took the several hundred bucks I got for my quarter share and bought myself a good pair of rubber boots, oilskins, wool pants, and a wool shirt. I wasn't a fisherman yet, but at least I could dress like one.

After a couple of days' lay-up, we headed out on back-to-back trips, stocked up with bait, fuel, and food. This time, I was determined to move up to half share, but I knew I had to do more than chop bait and dress fish, which I had started to do the previous trip. After about a week, Donny took me aside and said, "Okay, Mike, why don't you try coiling a skate?"

It didn't look that hard; he even slowed the gurdy down to make it easier, but I was nothing but thumbs. Everyone else aboard laid the groundline down in neat coils about eighteen inches in diameter, with the hooks laid out on the coiled line. Day after day I tried to coil like the rest of the crew, but all I accomplished was to cover most of the foredeck with a snarl of line and hooks. Russ said it was dangerous to even be near me when I was coiling. "Get caught up in that eagle's nest, and you'll never get out," he said. Finally I started to doubt myself. The fear of failure raised its snout, and all the self-assurance I'd started to gain slid away. The romantic image of being able to earn my way at sea, to be accepted at full share, had come up against reality, and reality was winning. For the first time I started to think of myself as clumsy, uncoordinated, and ignorant.

Every waking and sleeping moment I thought about coiling, going over it in my mind, trying to visualize how to hold the line, how to reach for the hook, and all the while afraid I'd never get it down. At the end of the trip, I knew Donny would say:

"Sorry, Mike, it's just not working out." Or maybe they wouldn't even wait till we got to shore. I'd heard about the greenhorn that turned out to be such a misfit that the crew put him in the fish hold for a few hours and then sent him to his bunk for the last two weeks of the trip. He was allowed out only to use the head and could only eat when everyone else was in their bunks for their three or four hours of sleep.

My coiling and snarls stalked me relentlessly. In one dream, the groundline and hooks were coming through the hatch and into my bunk. I began to coil it, but no matter how hard I tried, I was only creating a bigger snarl. In the midst of my torment, I was woken up by Russ: "Hey, Mike. What the hell?"

I came out of my slumber and both Russ and Pinky were staring at me, shaking their heads and laughing. I had been coiling the electrical wire that ran over my bunk to the reading light. I'd ripped it off the wall and was trying to coil it down over my chest.

By the time we'd finished the trip, I had gotten the hang of coiling. It wasn't pretty, but it was passable. At least the crew didn't leave what they were doing and gather around the hatch and comment about my abilities.

I'd also been given a half share, though in terms of money, it didn't mean that much. Fishing had been lousy. We'd been out forty-five days and hadn't made expenses. My half share entitled me to pay fourteen dollars back to the boat for the last trip's food. But I wasn't worried about money. Until we went fishing again, it didn't cost anything to sleep on the boat, and there was plenty of grub in the lockers.

PIECES OF
THE WIND

WENDY ERD, *who has setnetted for
salmon in Bristol Bay, near Pilot
Point, calls up the wind, evoking the
land, the native culture, the work on
the water she is forced to leave after
twelve years.*

S TORIES OF PILOT Point begin and end with wind. Wind so steady that when it quits, you look up suddenly as though someone's missing.

For five days a southeaster's been blowing twenty-five or thirty knots out of the mouth of the river. In Bristol Bay, everything vertical is an instrument for the wind. The hinges on our outhouse door creak, the abandoned truck at the airstrip clatters its open door, even the bent blades of grass sing. A gray ceiling's clamped down and I can barely see the middle sandbar that's emerged beyond our moored skiffs. This wind works with the outgoing tide, smoothing down the chop. On the flood the real face of the storm will show, when the incoming current will stack waves against wind. We need westerlies to push salmon into the nets on our side of the Ugashik River.

Last year, my husband, Peter, and I spun our index fingers counterclockwise in the air the way Esther had taught us. A Yupik Eskimo from Manokotak, she knows the native traditions for imploring the weather.

"Turn the wind," she'd said.

Whenever we remembered we'd implore the weather, and in a few days' time a screamer set of onshore waves and driving horizontal rain set in and seemed to last for weeks. Way more than we'd bargained for.

Esther passed us heading down to her beach site on her four-wheeler. Her four children, bundled in raingear, clung on behind her.

"Esther," Peter said, "it doesn't seem to work." He

showed her his own method, the slow downward strokes of his fingers he'd used to calm the storm.

"No." she said. "That's rain."

Five guys cluster around the two-horse outboard. The tiny cowling, no bigger than a lunch box, lies on the ground, and from the net-mending rack, I hear them grappling with a mechanical problem, manpower heavily outweighing the horsepower. I start humming the song I sing to myself: "Men, men, men, men, how does it work, let's make it work." Nut-and-bolt thought. I rarely have it. When we got a new truck I was happy it was red.

I spend my summers in a 16×20–foot cabin with five men. A capsule of testosterone. We're here to luck out our living commercial fishing. I straggle out in the middle of the night in long johns and eat oatmeal with the crew. I let my appearance go. We stare bleary-eyed out into the slanting rain before we slump off into the darkness to check our nets. I tuck my hair into a blue cap, smear Bag Balm on my hands, and stride off lugging a five-gallon can of gas. We drag our rubber raft through the calf-deep mud and then jump in on the edge of the tide. I pull-start the recently tuned two-horse motor and lump over the waves to dock alongside our moored skiff in the roaring, six-knot current. I'm exhilarated. I've stepped into a man's world and for a moment I'm at the helm.

Two miles downriver from our fishcamp, the Ugashik sweeps by a few dozen sand-etched houses clustered on a bluff. Below the village of Pilot Point, on the beach, Pete Hansen's hunkered over his up-ended four-wheeler, protected from the blowing sand by his plywood shack and his shop full of enough junk to cobble anything together. He squats between broken trucks, a wringer washer, and an old wooden salting tierce from the abandoned cannery. His eyes are narrowed with seventy years of squinting into the sun and wind. He's rigging a screwdriver for a pull-cord handle. Our dog, Bob, wag-tails his way in close. "I hate *dogs,* hello, Bob." Pete, gruff as far in as you could dig a pocketknife in old ironwood.

"What the hell are you doing on my barge? Someone's always screwing with my stuff," he'd yelled at us our first morning in Pilot Point twelve years ago when he found our tent pitched on his abandoned scow in Dago Creek. We'd sought refuge there, hoping we'd sleep above a brown bear's reach. Then each morning afterward, he'd arrive in the fog in his yellow Helly Hansen raingear and invite us to ride in his four-wheeler's trailer five miles back to his shack for rotgut coffee and warmth.

He pushes his wheeler upright. "Now, got to get the *Tyune* going." He looks past us to his old Bristol Bay boat, beached as a whale on cribbing in the sand. He'll patch her together for just one more season.

At night, there are ghosts in the abandoned cannery, Chinamen rising up from their laundry chores at China Lake, fishermen wisping in on the fog. At the base of the green bluff below the village, throwing shadows across Pete Hansen's shack, history sprawls in a huge complex of corrugated red tin: warehouses, crew quarters, canning rooms, net lofts, and the mess hall with its MUG UP sign over a boarded-up door. We creep into the sprawling catacombs of memory by inching our way through a broken six-pane window. The crunch of glass underfoot echoes up two stories to the tall ceiling beams; fir 2×12s fifty feet long that Alaska Packers shipped in by schooner in the 1890s when the river still ran deep by the dock out front, before the mud filled in and shut the whole place down. We're trespassing on both property and time.

Upstairs, wire-mesh lockers sag open, cages that once over-wintered fishermen's gear now drain old cotton web, soggy life rings, rusted Coleman stoves. In one corner wooden corks are scattered like tiny torpedoes in the dust. The stories of the fishermen hang in the air like moonlight through dusted glass. The wind lifts a loose piece of roof tin and bangs it over and over with just the same rhythm as the river; water and wind relentless, silting over men and history and fortunes made and lost again.

Peter and I love to be the first to fly in by bush plane to fishcamp early in June before our neighbors arrive. They roar and buzz and bang their setnet camps into readiness. In the pre-season stillness we can hear the birds. Loons on the pocket lakes, sandhill cranes gargling over, and ptarmigan on the tundra ridges behind our cabin who call, "come 'ere, come 'ere, come 'ere," then sing out, "go back, go back, go back," if we walk too near.

Yesterday, we heard an orphaned baby seal crying in Alex's old cannery retort, a huge metal barrel he uses to stabilize his bank against the ever-changing course of the river. The seal had squirmed its way to the top of the beach and found shelter inside, where its sorry sound was amplified. "Mom," it sounded like to me.

Johnny Ball had dragged the seal by its hind flippers down to the mud edge of the river, trying to save it, but it wiggled high up on the sand again until its small dark body was powdered and dry. You could see where the four-wheeler tracks had slowed and spun circles around it. As usual, none of us had the heart to shoot it, though that would have been the kindest act.

Nefutti was born in Ugashik, the next village upriver, an hour's skiff ride on a calm day. Once, as a young boy, he went on a hunting trip with his uncle. While they were gone, the flu epidemic of 1918 swallowed his village of Ugashik whole, like the gulp of some dark and foreign leviathan.

Our first years fishing, before he grew ill, he'd putt up the beach from the village on his four-wheeler and come in our cabin for tea. No cookies. He'd shake his head, "No teeth."

We'd bring our first king salmon of the season to Nefutti and his wife, Figli. They couldn't wade the low-tide mud to check their subsistence nets. Eighty years had worn and bent them like wind-stunted alders on the tundra.

"Hey, Nefutti, we brought you a king we found in our net."

"Mmm."

"Nefutti, looks like you hurt your leg, are you okay?"

"Fell off my four-wheeler." He laughs.

"You need any help? It must be hard to get around."

"No."

"Boy, it's sure been windy on the beach. Chewing away at the mud. Maybe it won't be so deep this year. Bugs aren't out yet, though. Not much showing up in our nets. You think the fish will come again this year?"

"Yep."

"Well, take care, we've got to go haul some water and get to the post office before Jan shuts it. Hope you enjoy the king. We'll stop by again when we get a chance."

"Okay."

Catie came by to challenge our setnet camp against hers in a speed knot-tying contest. On a piece of soft lay line we were to tie one double keg knot, then a clove hitch finished with a bowline. I tied the first set by habit, but then I couldn't tie a bowline upside-down, that part of my mind temporarily seized up. Sometimes, I can't conceptualize the physical world that is so crucial out here.

This year for the first time in eleven years I'm not fishing with Peter. We split our crew into old, young, and rookies and Peter and I each run a boat at our own sites.

A few days ago I couldn't judge when to tell my bowman to throw the anchor so I could run the skiff for the bank without catching and snarling the line in the prop. I'm desperate then to see clearly.

"Now," I shout, and know it's wrong even though I'm captain.

The anchor line pays out starboard into the current. My deckhand watches as we drift close but too far off the bank for him to leap out.

"Sorry," I say for the third time, humble. "Pull it in."

On the fifth try, it is perfect. I ram the bank, my deckhand jumps out and sets a stern anchor. This year I will learn from my own mistakes. I study the indicators of wind and tide and set my bearings on a course of self-confidence.

It's Sunday, so Esther says we have to say a prayer before we pick the herbs. She kneels on the damp tundra moss and asks forgiveness in a quiet voice. The fish haven't come. It's July 14 and the river's surface is still unbroken. No jumpers. No silver splash to announce their tremendous push. Remembering her grandmother's wisdom, Esther stopped by our cabin.

"Eee," she says, "We must burn labrador tea leaves and scatter the ash on the tidelines. Then they will come."

Both her inherited knowledge and the cycle of returning salmon that we pray for are ancient. She laughs a lot and I hold on to her waist and ride behind her as she bumps her four-wheeler across the rolling tundra. Esther says we have to dry the herbs quickly, so we use a propane torch. Later, at my cabin, I scorch a coffeepot of gathered herbs. The smell is mentholated and of the rich wet earth. In midsummer's twilight I walk along the tide line and throw the scant ash. The next morning the river sings and squirms with salmon.

· · ·

For years, I refused to run a skiff. My husband charged the brown swirling water, paying out the net, shouting directions. I worked the bow, pulling in buoys and lines, anchors and chain until my forearms bulged. Peter coaxed me to try the physically easier but more critical job as captain, steering one of our twenty-four-foot open boats, but at a demanding moment, I'd lose all awareness of left from right and walk away, and begging him to take the tiller handle back. "Motor panic," he'd say, shaking his head.

Today salmon swarm the river. From the few hundred I see jumping, I know a great silver wall battles the dropping tide. The murky water is thick with finning fish. One bumps into my rubber boots. A million spawners have pushed up the Ugashik on peak days like this, days we've earned a third of our year's income. I can't afford to make mistakes. I watch Peter head upriver with his crew. "You'll do great." He waves and disappears into the glint of sun on water.

"Five minutes," my crewman in the bow counts down until we can officially set our net, wound and stacked in the stern beside me. All along the riverbank, six hundred feet apart, other setnetters rev their motors, waiting. Something steadies me then, the years I've watched Peter, the times I've practiced, the faith I see in this young guy's eyes.

"How much time?"

"One minute." The river ticks past.

"Now!"

I gun the motor and net pours out of the boat, white corks popping over the stern in perfect punctuation, yes, yes, yes. In less than a minute, the last line whips out, chasing the web. *"Throw the anchor!"* I holler. *"Snap on the buoy!"*

We make a perfect set; three hundred feet of webbed fence stretch from shore and strain the river. Spray explodes in a frenzy where fish battle the mesh. The hard foam corks tug under water with the immediate weight of our catch. I wheel the skiff around like a rodeo girl into the incoming tide and steer for the net.

"Ride 'em!" shouts my crew.

With an economy of motion we work the next feverish hours, pulling in web, untangling gilled fish, sending the emptied net over. Pull and pick, grunt, pull and pick. Not talking. Intent. As fast as the cleaned net hits the water it thrashes with freshly tangled fish.

I leave my crewman picking into a small holding boat and deliver the first wallowing five-thousand-pound load by myself. The conditions are perfect for this turn of confidence, the water muddy silk as I pull alongside our tender a mile upstream. I idle in, leap across six brailed bags of shining fish, and throw the bowline to the tender man on deck.

"You all right?" he asks.

"Sure." My smile cracks the salt, fish blood, and scales dried on my cheeks. I am better than I can remember.

I unload and pull away empty, letting the current turn the boat's bow downstream. I feel the pride men must often feel, my hand on the tiller, the late sun catching the outboard's spray, converting the dark river to diamonds.

Below their surfaces, life in Pilot Point and the river pass with the same murkiness, falling away as they replenish. When we come back to the village each June, we brace ourselves to ask who age, alcohol, or the river itself has taken.

I saw Desee at the airstrip filling up her four-wheeler with gas. She wore a Russian Orthodox pin on her down jacket, and I asked her why their cross has a crooked lower stave and an extra cross above the Christian bar.

"The upper cross is for his crown, you know, 'King of kings,' " she said. "The lower tilted bar, well, that's what Christ's feet were nailed to, and when he died, his weight shifted and it tilted to the right."

"Grim," I said.

"Yeah, but it reminds us of his sacrifice."

On the way home to our cabin up the beach, hauling a fifty-gallon drum of water in the four-wheeler trailer, I drove past the church's cemetery high on the hill in the village. The wooden orthodox crosses lean north, as though listening, the white paint sand-etched off the wood. Now, after many summers, I know three buried here. Old Nefutti, young Loren, who fell drunk off a fishing boat on his twenty-first birthday, and Anna Tracy, who told us she watched Japanese bombs fall on Unalaska.

As much as I tug, my hand will not fold to fit through the stiff neoprene tube I wear to support my aching wrist. I've pulled thousands of fish from our nets, and now, left alone, my swollen fingers curl around an invisible salmon. Salt and fish scales sparkle to the floor in the Coleman light. It is 2:00 A.M., nearly slack tide, and time to check our nets. Silent shadows, each of us bends automatically into damp waders, life jackets, and cold boots. The intensity of the season has pulled us into itself. We cannot remember in the dim hours of dawn and dusk whether we are beginning or ending another day. We will wake, though, when we walk out into the night and face the river and the wind again.

When the kinnikinnick turns scarlet and the first few silvers thrash in our nets, the women and children from the village drive their pickups and four-wheelers down the back ridge and spend all day picking the tasteless coarse black berry they will mix with Crisco and sugar and call agooduk. The red salmon push is over, half the setnet cabins are shuttered. Between the Ugashik river and distant Mt. Pulik, the women's parkas are bright circles of color on the endless tundra.

No one in the village knows this is our last season in Pilot Point except old Johnny Ball. We haven't the heart to say so. After twelve years of frenzied fish picking, two bones in Peter's right thumb are worn flat and grind at each other. Fishing in Bristol Bay has become more competitive, more contentious. We've had to fish apart at times. Peter takes one skiff and goes to fish the outside beach where the ocean breaks, while I stay with my net inside the river. I watch the swells build at night, the dark roll in, peering out the window until I finally see the halo of his halogen light growing brighter on the horizon of the emptying river. He is slow, pushing the current, coming home.

The night before our plane comes, we ride into the village to say good-bye. Johnny's father-in-law, Alex, only a few years older than Johnny, lets us in, barely. He opens the door just a crack and peers out, "Yes?" John Ball behind him hollers out, "Come in, come in," over the yammering of their three poodles and both TVs.

We are unlikely friends and the best of friends. At seventy-five, Johnny is a Seventh-Day Adventist who'd love to convert us and doesn't. Peter and I are children of the sixties, not a reverent bone between us.

"One last game of crib?" he asks Peter. "Be there," he hollers at his cards. He shakes his head at a bad cut. "First your money, then your clothes," he says.

After twelve years I hear these quips in my sleep. We've brought back the scrimshawed cribbage board he loaned us years ago so he could skunk Peter at our cabin when he wasn't tending his net that stretched next to mine. We don't talk about the future. Just move the pegs around. But when we get up to leave he shakes our hands a long time. Thick-throated, I bundle up quickly and push out his door. Clamped behind Peter on the

Honda, we roar down the hill past the church's silhouette and skirt the shuttered cannery.

The wind lifts the sand and my eyes tear until my face is wet. Even with my eyes closed, I can see the river darkening and feel the chill of August creeping in.

HURLED TO
THE SHARK

LESLIE LEYLAND FIELDS *relates her
first year setnetting salmon off an
island in Alaska as a twenty-year-old
newlywed, trying to find her balance
and her humanity in a world where all
the rules are broken.*

TODAY IS PUT-OUT, the day we stretch and drop our nets back into the water, the day we load them from the racks on the beach where we have stood for four days, stopping only for sleep and food, to mend the holes punched by sea lions swatting their lunch from the net, from sharks who have rolled themselves nearly end over end, like a cocoon, their skin sanding vents through our nets as huge as their bulk. I am grim already. Already because it is only my first season, 1978, and yet I know exactly what will happen in the day and night ahead. I have done this four times by now, which makes me still a nervous greenhorn, since Duncan, his two brothers, and his father have been fishing here, off a tiny island off Kodiak Island, Alaska, for twenty years.

Now I stand in the beached skiff as it sits sideways, loading each of the eight nets into the skiffs. We are clawing the net, our hands like rakes, pulling the green webbing from the racks over the sand and up and over the skiff sides. My husband, Duncan, is pulling the leads, the heaviest weight; Wallace, his younger brother, is pulling the corks, the most awkward job; and I am in the middle where the fine thread of web will fall in a silken pile. The nets must be stacked precisely in the skiffs so they will drop clean into the water, spin out over the stern without a knot to pull a boot, or one of us, after it.

All the nets are loaded now, eight nets then, in three skiffs. We step out of the last skiff, and I glance behind me as I leave the beach, our little battleships loaded and ready.

These are setnets, attached to shore, which makes them

more or less stationary. The net is fixed—it is the fish that move. Each net extends out anywhere from 50 to 150 fathoms. We catch fish not only by encircling them and scooping them up, as the seiners do, but by waiting and hoping that as they journey home to the streambed to spawn, they will not notice the green ocean-colored web strung out in front of them, meshes sized to snag on their gills and body as they try to pass through. Our job, then, is to come along in a skiff, pull up the net, and extract each salmon by hand. Our hands, like a violinist's or world-class pianist's, are our precision tools. Not machines, or nets, traps, pots, or any kind of technology—just our hands. Wallace told me one day, as an aside, "Do you realize that we're fishing the same way people have for hundreds of years, excepting the outboard, of course?" Yes. Our machinery is the same as theirs: backs, shoulders, and hands.

The nets are loaded now. It's time to go. We head up to the porch, where the gear hangs on rows of hooks. I wear nearly the same outfit as the others. The wool socks on first, two pairs, pulled up over my Levi jeans, an old pair I found in the attic of my parents-in-law's cabin. A wool plaid shirt, and over it two hooded sweatshirts, then the black rubber hip boots that were too big, the Helly Hanson dark green rain pants, the same brand rain coat, an extra I found hanging in the gear shed. My black hair is a hip-length braid I stuff up under a white-brimmed cap, then white cotton gloves for my hands. The gloves absorb water like a sponge and do little to keep our hands warm, but they give traction on slippery fish. It is hopeless to try and pick fish with bare hands. The uniform adds twenty pounds to my 115 and feels as though it doubles my bulk, but already I am used to it.

· · ·

I like this uniform better than the one I had worn the previous four summers back at home in New Hampshire—a stiff orange polyester dress with an orange-and-white plaid apron that buttoned down the front, hair in the same braid but pinned up, and if Howard Johnson's was worried about inspection, a hair net to complete the ensemble. My uniform was often stained with brown gravy, or strawberry sauce from a sundae, a patch of mashed potatoes from the tray I saved from a near dump. It was hideous, of course, but glamour was not the lure of waitressing. Tips were, which meant money to go to college and money to keep my 1964 station wagon in gas. A single year separates me from that world; a single year separates me from being a teenager, and a single year separates me from being a girl. The month after I turned twenty, I married. I would be there at Howard Johnson's this very summer had I not married Duncan. I am now three thousand miles away, and I do not even know that former world yet as memory, not good or bad or anything—it has simply vanished.

I am the last to gear up. I run down the grass yard, onto the sand, leap into the skiff and we are off, the five of us, all looking alike in the same raingear, out to skiffs all painted red, white, and black. Because of our uniformity, not only our clothes but our gear, the skiffs, the cabins all painted red and white, it feels like an industry, an enterprise so much larger than the facts at hand: a core of three brothers, a sixty-four-year-old father, seven skiffs, and nine nets, and now me, a twenty-year-old East Coast woman-girl. For a moment I see us, Weston in the stern running the kicker, eyes squinted in concentration as he maps out the afternoon and evening. Duncan solemn as he watches the water. Wallace, just seventeen, with the same air as his brothers, and their father, DeWitt. And me, my face no different, not because

I am strategizing, as they are—who puts out what nets, in what order, will the northeast get worse?—but because I have taken this world on like a face, except it goes deep already. I am one of them, I think; then no, I am not, but I will be, if I can.

It takes nearly three hours to get the nets in the water. Then it happens, what all of this is for—the fish. Sometimes, as soon as the net is wet behind us, we see silver lifting it back up out of the water, a furious thrash of anger as three, four, a group of salmon hit together. And we stop, no matter what we're doing, smile at one another at the instant logic and mathematics of it—yes, a year of ordering supplies, a month of fourteen-hour workdays for this moment, for these salmon behind us and at our feet.

If the fish keep hitting that night, and they are this night, we pick. I would like to go ashore and be done for the day. What perfect closure, move on from one task to the next, a night's sleep in between. But we don't work that way. The time clock for fishing follows Alaska's summer sun; in May and June, night and day are twins, one a slightly paler version of the other. We nap in the day and work in the night; pick fish in the day, pick fish at night; these nets, these fish, are no respecter of person or sleep or fatigue.

So then, now comes the beginning of the rest of the work. We've been out six hours now, it's nine o'clock. We've missed dinner and we're hungry. I have to pee, and so does Duncan and his father.

"Well, I guess I gotta shake the dew off my lily," DeWitt intones in a homey father's voice, his Oklahoma accent still traceable, though he left during the Dust Bowl of the early thirties.

I smile at Duncan, he smiles indulgently and I turn around. I like this, that we can live together this way. When they're done, it's my turn. "Let me off on that rock over there, Duncan." I point to a cove with a shelf of rock jutting out. If we were alone, I would go right there in the skiff in a bucket. It's not quick, with layers of raingear and life jackets and wet gloves on, but it is nothing to me, just a necessity that has nothing to do with dignity or culture or the loss of.

While I am getting the luxury of my own private rock for today, Duncan and DeWitt pull out the candy bars and pop.

"What do you want, Leslie, a Hershey's or a Uno?" Duncan asks, holding both up. He's sitting on the seat in the stern, with a root beer beside him.

"Hershey's, of course," I say as I reach for it. "Ugh!! How can you eat those things! They're just chocolate-covered Crisco." I roll my eyes as he takes an exaggerated bite. It shocks me, still, the consumption of sugar and fat here. I take the offered Hershey's with a faint twinge. On shore, I would never consider eating a candy bar or drinking a pop, but it's different out on the water. When I can see for two hundred miles, when more than half a mile of net filled with kelp, grass, and fish that have swum thousands of miles wait for our hands only, when the work subsumes even time itself, how is a candy bar significant in an economy like this? I unwrap my Hershey's and pop my Coke.

We sit there, the three of us, our skiff tied to the net, slapping the water gently. Duncan and I are sitting together as we eat, our rubberized and raingeared legs pressing against each other on the seat. Duncan leans over and gives me a kiss, leaving a wet spot on my face where his nose dripped. He's got a couple of scales on his cheek, and a smudge of fish blood on his forehead. I've got something dried on my jawline; my gloves are a blend of blood and gurry. I'm not feeling romantic. He's yelled at me three times already this put-out. I know later he'll explain that a job's got to be done no matter who it is, wife or crew or anyone. Then I'll complain that he treats me like a crewman and he'll say, Well, you are. Then I'll say no, I'm your wife and you can't step in and out of marriage just because you're climbing in and out of a skiff, and so it will go. I did not expect the skiff to be run democratically, but neither did I expect such a pronounced hierarchy. I'm not sure what to do about this, how to establish in this geography the kind of balance and equity we have in the other parts of our lives.

By the time we get to the next set, the Outside, we call it, because it sits straight into the Shelikof Strait and is unprotected, the wind has picked up, a northeast, blowing now maybe 20. The forecast is for NE 35. It has happened in minutes, which means the 35 could stew over us in minutes as well. I never knew weather anywhere could change as fast as it does here. "Please Lord, let us finish and go in before it blows harder," I offer silently as a wish-prayer. The wind hits my face under the brim of my hat, spray lashes us now from both sides. "Get ready to grab the net!" Duncan yells to me above the wind. He is running hard up to the net against the wind. He'll slow and aim the bow at the net and just before it hits, he'll go into neutral, then reverse to swing the stern around so we are parallel to the net. My job is to lean over the side, grab the net in the water as soon as I can, and then hold on no matter what happens. In calm weather, and if the tide is not running too strong, this is not a difficult maneuver, but now. . . . I pull my cap tighter and lower my head, lean out poised for the net as we approach, the water white around us and just a roar and howling in my ears. All of me is focused on that cork, there. We speed toward it, my hand is out, I'm leaning almost over the side—now! My arm pounces, makes a swipe—I missed! Again, lean a little farther, arm into the water now past my elbow, can't get it! The net is too tight, like a steel bar. It won't pull to me at all. I straighten, look apologetically at

Duncan, who doesn't change his expression. He wheels the skiff around in the wind, readies for another approach, and I know I've broken a rule, the rule that you get it the first time, not the second or third, especially when it's blowing. I will do it this time. I have to.

Duncan turns the skiff again for another try. I want to scream at him, "Why is this so important?? Can't we just leave it until the weather calms?" But I know the answer. I glance back. He stands darkly resolute, as if there is no storm blasting around us, the only upright and seemingly untouched object in my entire vista. I can find no island of calm within me, just storm inside and out. This time, I vow, I will hang on until my arms pull out of their sockets, if need be. It seems a small sacrifice. Once again, the head-down approach straight into the wind, my arm out, my stomach hard on the skiff edge as my fulcrum. A breaking wave catches me on the face and shoulder; an icy stream finds my neck and trails down my back as I hang like a tortured figurehead, poised, and then "Got it!" I yell behind me, then the second arm joins the first, and two-armed, ready to hang on till death, I wait for the maneuver, and it works. Duncan angles the stern over to the net, he leans in a flash and has the net, and together with one mighty pull we lift it over the side and into our skiff. I am exhausted, immensely relieved, and the pick for this net begins.

We work three more nets after this one until near dark. I am so tired I can hardly stand. Duncan is tired, too, but he doesn't complain. No one ever complains. For some reason I want someone to, as if that would help somehow.

I am not completely shocked by this world of work. Growing up, my family restored old colonial houses. We moved in first, and then tried to live around the work. By the time I was five, we had moved five times, from one town to another in New

Hampshire, from one house with a hand pump in it for the kitchen sink and no indoor plumbing, my mother with four of us under the age of five then. Then we moved again, outcasts in a country-club town, down a back road in a big yellow colonial. It was two hundred years old and the worse for its age. We lived there for five years, my mother managing six of us now, and working on the house every moment she could. She replaced the floors, using wooden pegs as nails, as in the early colonial houses. She scraped layers of old wallpaper and replastered and repapered every room in the twelve-room house, hoping she could sell it for a profit. By herself, and with such help as we gave, she completely rebuilt the house. During those five years, somehow she was able to buy a series of small derelict houses in other towns. On weekends we went there to those, painting, scraping, tearing up floorboards, replacing windows. When the Amherst house sold for a profit, it was begun, the cycle that defined our lives growing up.

The most derelict house of all was the house near the end of a maze of back roads in another town. Our first task was to jack the house up and replace a rotten sill, which my mother had discovered to her dismay when tearing up the old floor. For a week we had no kitchen floor and balanced about on joists, with the dirt cellar underneath us. For months after, the outside wall was only partially repaired, since we had run out of money already. There were holes in the walls as it snowed. We sat around our only heat, a woodstove in the kitchen, with blankets wrapped around our heads. Over my high school years, on weekends and when we got home from school we worked under mother's charge and changed all the windows in the house, tore off a front porch, knocked down walls built later to add more rooms, tore off the plaster that sealed off the three original fireplaces, scraped and steamed off seven layers of wallpaper, laid new wood floors, put up Sheetrock, taped and painted—the house was restored gradually, with little joy or even relief. Each of those four years, as winter approached, the work slowed, then stopped as the inside temperature dropped. The house had no insulation. We never had enough money to put in a furnace, so our single heat source remained a single woodstove. We slept under piles of sleeping bags, took hot bricks from the stove up to bed with us on the coldest nights, wore hats, mittens, scarves, two pairs of socks, and buried ourselves underneath our covers every night with just our noses sticking out.

Summers and falls moved our work back outside. On weekends, we moved into the woods on our own land, where we chainsawed down maples, birch, oak, sawed and stacked them into an old truck, then to our shed, working from morning until the summer light faded. On sunny days, when the fields were dry and the grass long, my mother joined us out in the hayfield hand-mowing and raking a winter supply of feed for our ten milking goats. We didn't have a tractor, and had no money to buy one no matter what the vintage, so my younger brother Todd and older brother, Scott, rigged up a Leyland special, the engine and hood of our mother's old Mercedes with a back half of a wood wagon attached. We hand-scythed the hay, then returned later to fork it up into our "tractor." We laughed at our contraption and were glad we lived so far out. No one would see it. If they did, perhaps they would begin to guess the truth. It served as the perfect symbol for our lives. Outside we wore the veneer of the middle and upper class: my mother drove a black Mercedes; our dog was not a spaniel or a mutt but a Russian wolfhound; we lived in a gorgeous-appearing house. Yet, the reality: The Mercedes was eight years old, haggled down to less than three thousand dollars; our house was below freezing five months of the year; our food was carefully doled out; and we spent much of our time, when our friends were playing, in the house, in the fields and woods, working.

Finally the nets are judged done enough for the night. Weston and Wallace come up beside us in their skiff, both looking tired, but wearing the same expression I see on Duncan. They decide the mechanics of who will take what skiff to the tender to deliver, and I am hoping they will not need me. I won't ask to go ashore, though. "You can go in," Duncan finally says to me in my ear. "I know it was a tough one, but you did great. You really worked hard. Thanks, Leslie."

At the beginning of the season I might have protested, but in these weeks I have become grateful for any concessions Duncan makes for me, but at the same time, I feel weak and guilty that I need them. I never needed them before. I was the one out of a hundred ninth-grade girls who could climb the gym rope to the ceiling in six seconds, beating everyone else. In tenth grade, I could still beat some of the guys in arm wrestling. I could match my three brothers on most tasks. Why couldn't I work as hard and long as these men?

I slide out of the skiff, trudge through the black night water up to the beach to the warehouse where we sleep. The wind has not abated any, and though it is sucking sound in the opposite direction, I can hear the skiffs straining under their loads, still going in the dark, just arriving at the tender. I have no energy left to pity them; indeed I do not, for haven't they grown up with this? Doesn't Duncan profess love for this? Then up the ladder and into our attic loft, a tiny room we built last month, just big enough to stand up in the middle, with just enough room for a bed, a chair, and a wood stove. It is cold in there without heat, and the tin roof is banging, and something else is whistling with the wind, but I don't care. I climb under the three sleeping bags and sleep. It is 12:30 A.M.

When our nets aren't working us, we work the nets. On closures, when Fish and Game closes fishing for a few days to let the salmon up the streams to spawn, we untie the nets and pull them up, this time using not the kicker to unravel them, but our arms, dragging them up from the ocean floor, heavy with kelp sometimes, sometimes fresh fish just hit. The nets have to be out of the water, not a shred remaining, by 9:00 P.M. To keep everyone honest, Fish and Game flies over regularly. Take-ups are just as intense as put-outs, with one ameliorating factor. The speed is our own, not motorized, and so within our control. We are fast. We pull up one-hundred-fathom nets regularly in twelve minutes going all out, hardly stopping for breath, hand over hand as fast as hands can move in web, as fast as arms can pull a heavy lead line from the ocean floor to the skiff bottom. The take-up of a single net is a like the four-hundred-yard dash. Not a sprint, because you couldn't poop out halfway and then just walk the rest. And even if you pace the first net perfectly, so that you make it to the end, there still were three more nets to go. We are always up against the clock, and timing and pacing are everything. We work together like finely oiled machines, and take unspoken pride in that. I do as well. That three people can work in such concert, aiming so singlemindedly toward this one task, and that it is done so proficiently regardless of the forces against us: the numbers of fish in the net, the size of the sea under us, the pull of the wind at our faces, our own level of fatigue, and still, almost no matter what, when the last piece of web slid into the boat, it is 9:00 P.M. precisely.

Toward the end of that summer, we had visitors, new fishermen from a site about four miles away from us. There were three of them. The youngest, a college student, bragged to me when we were in the room alone that they had pulled up their net in, and he paused for dramatic effect—forty-five minutes! I smiled politely, said, "Wow, that's fast," and laughed proudly inside. I had signed on with the best.

Of all the work, mending net was the easiest, therefore the best. With a pair of delicate sewing scissors hung from mending twine around my neck, a white plastic needle in my hand, I could mend as fast as anyone, but no matter the pace, it was all solace. Net-mending days meant rest for my shoulders and arms, especially the left shoulder that had started to hyper-extend lifting the slightest weight—picking too many fish and pulling too many taut lines. Though there was always pressure to get the nets done for the next opening, still, there was a relaxing rhythm to it, and the ground was solid under my feet. The scenery was magnificent, as always. I hadn't tired of the swoop of ocean around our little island, of the mountains and volcanic spires of the Alaska Peninsula off to the south and west that trailed off into their own horizon, of the tides that flooded and drained with such constant drama. On rainy, windy days, there was little pleasure in it; we endured the wet and cold that stiffened our hands and slowed our work to a numbed proficiency. Sunny days, though, when they came, were inspiring, filling us with air charged with the warmth of light, heating the chill from us, the moist that lingered always in our clothes, our bones.

Best of all, beyond and above the weather and scenery, though, was the conversation. Starved for communication other than that forged by the necessity of labor, this was mind time, spirit time, communion. We all craved it. I longed most for women-talk, poet-talk. My sister-in-law Beverly and I would maneuver ourselves inconspicuously to the same net, to face each other, working toward each other as much as possible. We waited days for this.

"Bev, I read this incredible poem last night. It's called 'The Web,' by Karl Shapiro." I am cutting out web from a huge hole and keep my eyes on my fingers.

"Really?" Bev answers with interest, and a spark in her eyes. "How'd you have time to do that? Can you remember any of it?" She is finishing off a three-holer, with a deft snip from her scissor necklace, and she is done, now pulling through the web toward me, searching for other holes.

"I've got it here in my pocket. Wait." I look around, see everyone on the other nets intent on their own work. We've got until tomorrow to finish all eight nets, and we're only on the third one now. This is no time for poetry. But the card is not there—wrong pair of pants.

"I don't have it with me now, Bev," I say, disappointed. "But it's about a man who has lost his leg—an amputee—it loses something in my translation, but he's saying that no matter how his body is destroyed, his spirit will not be. The last stanza is a prayer to God, 'That if Thou take me angrily in hand / And hurl me to the shark, I shall not die!'"

We are silent. I say it again, this time aiming my words above the wind: "'That if Thou take me angrily in hand / And hurl me to the shark, I shall not die!'"

We both stop our work for an instant. I look around quickly to make sure no one is listening, then I am back to my patch and Bev has found a sea-lion hole. Bev looks up at me. Our eyes meet.

"Doesn't that remind you of the Book of Job? Remember what he said after he's lost everything—his family, his goods, his house . . ." I say finally, breaking the moment.

Bev nods. "'Though He slay me / Yet will I trust Him,'" she quotes.

I sigh deeply. This verse scares me profoundly, and yet it gives comfort, too. "Have you written anything this week?" I ask, though now I am counting the number of knots in the hole I've just cut out for the patch. "Hold it, don't answer, I've got to count: sixteen, seventeen . . . " Under my breath as I finger each knot, then, "Okay, twenty-three by sixteen. Just a minute. Don't say anything until I get my patch web."

"Okay." Bev laughs as she moves to another section of the net. This net, unimaginatively named the Seventh, is a mess, torn up by rocks and sea lions.

I am back, my patch web hung off my shoulder. "What have you written?" I ask, guessing she has written something. With her two toddlers, one of whom seldom sleeps, living in a half-built house, hauling her water the farthest of anyone and a husband always out fishing, Bev suffered more than the usual island claustrophobia, and I knew finding time to write was even harder for her than it was for me. Yet she had to write, just as I did.

"I've started a poem I think I'll call 'God's Whirlwind,' " Bev says quietly. She starts in on another small hole. "Remember Elijah, how he stood waiting for God to speak—"

"And the windstorm came," I interrupted, remembering, "and God wasn't in the wind, and then what happens?"

"After the wind came, then there was a fire, and God wasn't in the fire. Then, after it was quiet, and God spoke in the quiet in a very small voice. Elijah expected God to speak through some great display of power and drama, but He didn't that time. Just when we think we know God," Bev stopped mending and looked up, "he surprises us, again."

I'm coming back up the second side of my patch. I look quickly up at Bev. "Maybe He wanted to make sure Elijah was still listening." We watch each other's face, knowing all we are not saying, then quickly look down at our hands, still mending.

One morning, near the end of July, it happened, the run of

pink salmon forecast by Fish and Game came running, and so did we. Fifteen million were forecast, and when we stumbled up the hill for breakfast, Duncan looked out in his usual visual check of the nets visible from shore, then said, "Hey, where's the hook of the third? We've either got a shark in it or it's sunk with fish!" It was sunk with fish. And the derby began. We had fished and caught healthy amounts of salmon up until then, enough to keep us tired and reasonably sure of making our tuition payments that next year, but we hadn't made enough for rent and living expenses. I had hoped for the flood of fish along with everyone else, but now, as my heart fluttered and my stomach turned, as though I were about to go on stage, I wondered, if we haven't been catching many fish yet, what will it be like when we do? And then the answer: What I thought I knew about hard work became a Romper Room memory. There were pink salmon swarming all over Kodiak Island, filling the seiners' nets, sinking ours, the ones that got away choking the spawning streams. We stood in our skiffs in salmon up to our ankles, then our calves, then our knees, walking in them, falling on them as we still bent to pull the net in for more. Three weeks of days and nights nearly indistinguishable from one another, eating and sleeping around the fish, lunch twelve hours after breakfast, Duncan and his brothers' arms going dead-numb at night, their hands locking with carpal tunnel, my hands so sore and bleeding in the deep cracks between my fingers I wrap them with surgical tape before putting on the cotton gloves. . . .

When the season was over, late in September, we flew from our island back to Kodiak. The first Sunday back in town, I stood beside Duncan in church, singing hymns, my eyes closed and face uplifted. After four months at fishcamp, the congregational voices washed over me like milk. At the end of the service, a family friend strode across the aisle to greet us.

"Duncan! Leslie! How did your season go?" he boomed, his hand extended to Duncan. I knew he was a business executive for a local native corporation. We had been invited over to his house once for a potluck, where I had heard his latest fishing stories—he fished a short subsistence net one day each summer to stock his freezer.

"Oh, we got a few fish," Duncan said, smiling a bit wanly. We were both still shell-shocked.

"A few fish, I bet!" he grinned knowingly. Then he turned to me. "Leslie, you pick any fish?"

"A few," I said, in the same killer understatement, too tired to care about accuracy or making a good impression.

"Did you? Well, let's see your hands! You know, you can tell a lot by someone's hands," he says, smiling a wink at Duncan.

I held my right hand out, palm up, looking away. He placed one hand beneath to steady it, with the other he pulled lightly on my fingers, then brushed his fingertips over what was left of the skin. He looked up at me quickly. "Yeah, I guess you did pick a few."

"She picked more than that," Duncan said, putting his arm around my shoulder proudly and squeezing.

I smiled blandly at them both, unsure of what to say, only knowing that I had survived, that there were now eight other months before me to return to college and live a different life, and choosing then to believe that though the seasons would circle around again and chase me back to that island every summer for the rest of my life, surely I would live, again.

CLIMBING
THE LADDER

ROBERT FRITCHEY *leaves graduate school for the Louisiana bayous to make a living with his own hands. He starts at the bottom—pursuing the dinosaurlike garfish.*

I T WAS AN AUGUST evening in 1980, and my first time
out with John Freeman, who was better known in these
parts as "Garfish John." Fortunately he hadn't earned that
handle through any resemblance to the alligator gar, but
rather from having spent countless nights in pursuit of
this prehistoric creature.

The work suited John, who'd gotten a bad break growing up back in Oregon: He and some teenage buddies
swiped a car for a joy ride, but the fun ended soon after
they crossed the state line. After eight years in the federal
pen, John had come out gentle, reclusive, his best friends
Budweiser, Pall Mall, the night.

Unlike most of Louisiana's fishermen, who picked up
their trade from their daddies, John had been lured to the
state by oilfield work, and later fell into fishing.

"I first got into gar-fishin' fifteen years ago," he'd told
me. "Worked for a fisherman out in west Lou'siana as a
skinner. He paid me eight cents a pound, and I was really
makin' money."

Anchored in a shallow bay in the coastal marsh, we
had just set the nets and were passing the time in John's
high-sided open skiff, smoking cigarettes and brewing
dark-roasted coffee on the Coleman stove.

John's nets were unusual: Called flag nets, they were
made simply by hanging gillnet webbing from a typical
cork line, and that's it, skip the leadline. Without any
leadline to stretch the net to the bottom, the heavy nylon
webbing waved seductively in the water. Conventional
wisdom says the more weight on your net the more fish
you catch, but garfish aren't conventional. They can grow
as long as an alligator but they've got tiny gills, and in

hot weather these reptilian fish will drown if they can't get to the surface to gulp in some extra air. Flag nets let them do so.

We'd staked ours to the bank and run them straight out to intercept the fish as they cruised along the shoreline. In the rosy afterglow of the fallen sun, the ominous whine of hungry salt-marsh mosquitoes grew louder. While I sprayed down with the OFF, I asked John how it looked.

"Looks good. Tide's comin' in. They'll come in on that to hunt this shallow water. Anytime now."

As if to punctuate his statement, the first gar hit. Searching for a mullet or other prey, the great fish had stealthily eased in on the tide. Encountering one of the nets, it had slipped its pointed beak through a mesh, kept moving, and as the webbing tightened around its body, the predator panicked. Without the weight of a lead line to restrain it, the five-foot-long fish came straight out of the water, slashing its head side to side like a marlin. As it beat the water to a froth, John, with his eyes shining above his dense gray beard, lit another Pall Mall.

Later, under the stars, the explosive splashes grabbed our attention and we'd stare in amazement at the eerie white fireworks the erupting fish set off as they startled the luminous plankton that filled the subtropical water.

"Holy shit!"

I knew even before we sold our catch in the morning: "I can do this."

As had John, I was coming into commercial fishing from the outside. My father and grandfather hadn't been net fishermen, but doctors, and until just two years before, it was pretty much a cinch that I'd be following in their footsteps. Instead, after earning a master's degree in tropical medicine and medical parasitology at LSU's med school, I spun out. And a convergence of events steered me away from the bookish indoor life that I'd been leading for so long to the robust outdoor life that I'd been missing.

While in grad school I married a fantastic woman who'd grown up in a big Catholic family. Like a nest of baby blue jays, she and her many siblings had clamored for attention. Or so I rationalized as I was increasingly berated for the lack of time I shared with her. But I was more self-sufficient to start with, and in the midst of a tough program of research and courses with books the size of cinder blocks, our cramped New Orleans apartment became a pressure cooker.

As my three-year program drew to a close, the pressure only increased. There were written exams, an oral grilling, and a scientific thesis that, in order to please my perfectionist mentor, ran into eleven drafts.

The awarding of my degree coincided with our separation, which preceded our divorce. So much for love at first sight.

With a heap of debts, I took a job in Belle Chasse, across the river from New Orleans. Engineer's Road parallels the Intracoastal Waterway, and on the narrow strip of dusty land between lie one oilfield construction operation after another.

I started at one, as a roustabout. We worked outdoors, twelve months a year, ten or twelve hours a day, and I began to harden up, physically and emotionally.

After the first year, my former mentor at LSU encouraged me to come back to school for either an M.D. or a Ph.D. But I'd already come too far. After all those days in the sun and the wind, in jeans and Wellingtons, cutting and welding steel, chewing Red Man and smoking Camels, the thought of lab coats, exams, and fluorescent lights tightened my gut.

I knew I wasn't going back, but where I was going, I didn't know. I was still shell-shocked when my father invited me on a fly-fishing trip to Maine. Dad was a great sportfisherman who traveled the world to catch fish and, like any good father, he'd encouraged his kids to excel at his own avocation. Of course, he never imagined that I'd cross the line to fish for money and, at the time, neither did I.

Our guide, Verdel "Casey" LeCasse, canoed us down the West Branch of the Penobscot, to a tent that he'd set up beforehand. We spent a week there in crisp September, with the foliage ablaze, and caught all the landlocked salmon we wanted. But for me, the trip turned out to be more than just a pleasant outdoor experience.

Casey was of French Canadian descent, compact and strong as an ox. He'd worked for years as a lumberjack and as he split logs for the fire, he flicked his wrists just as his razor-sharp ax touched the wood, which sent the two slabs flying. Whether shooting a fly line, cooking over the fire, fixing the outboard, or poling against the current, he was exceptionally capable.

During the summer he took clients fishing. During the fall there was hunting and during the winter he trapped or laid low. From where I was at the time, it looked pretty good.

Before the trip was over, I'd decided to become a fishing guide.

From the confines of graduate school my best friend Frank Cogswell, a former Marine, and I had spent hours perusing sportfishing books and magazines. With money that we earned as guinea pigs in drug studies, we'd put together a twenty-year-old flatboat, a ten-year-old engine, and a homemade trailer that enabled us to get down to the marsh, away from our books and the city.

While I worked construction, Frank worked on his Ph.D., and we continued to fish together, slowly learning about the marsh. After two years of hard labor, I'd paid off my marriage-era debts, and started to gear up. I bought out Frank's share in our little rig, and then, with every check, I'd buy a tent, a water cooler, a fishing outfit, ice chests. . . .

The plan was to move onto the marsh until I became competent enough to slide down to Belize and open a sportfishing camp. The idea wasn't as harebrained as it might seem—I'd fished all my life and, through my studies, had plenty of experience in the tropics.

In May of 1980, in the American tradition of renovating one's soul by immersion in the wilderness, I bailed out of New Orleans and set up camp on a small marshland ridge.

In those days, you could sell the fish that you caught with a rod and reel. If it wasn't quite legal, nobody cared because, in coastal Louisiana, fish are abundant and, back then, fishing effort was a lot less than it is now. Nevertheless, with my food and living expenses now linked to the fish I caught, I soon found out that I wasn't as great an angler as I thought I was.

Trapping crabs didn't take the know-how of catching fish, and by June, I'd begun to salvage abandoned crab traps that shrimpers had caught in their nets and tossed on the bank.

I started with about a dozen and, without enough money to fill the six-gallon gasoline can, I'd run the engine to the upwind side of my line, shut it down, and run the traps with oars. I was close enough to the edge one day that when a raggedy rope gave way just as I was about to grab one of my traps, I nearly cried.

It was a big day when I first filled the fuel tank to the brim, and my daily income started to inch up from $16.00 to $25.00 to $37.00. Finally, with a loan from my brother, I bought enough wire to make fifty brand-new traps, and prospered through the summer.

Then, at the fishhouse, I met John, who asked me if I wanted to go out with him one night. I jumped at the chance and, after fishing with him for a few nights, he left to go to Baton Rouge for a weekend. He let me use his nets and I made more that night than I'd made in a week of running crab traps. And it was a heck of a lot more exciting.

After fishing with John for a spell, I'd learned enough to break out on my own. From my small tent, I'd graduated to a tar-papered trapping camp, deep in the marsh. Working from there, I got into the rhythm of setnetting, of laying down the nets in the evening, and then, at around ten o'clock, screaming out in the little flatboat to clear them of that first charge of fish that had moved into the shallows at twilight. With the moon and stars as my light, I'd wrestle the gars into the boat and with a rusty screwdriver untangle the twine from their needle-sharp teeth. With the bottom of the flatboat strewn with the now-docile fish, I'd crank up the old eighteen-horse Evinrude and shoot for the camp.

As I raced down the curving bayous in the night, the boat's cresting wake glowed cool white and, like asteroids, luminous jellyfish, big as baseballs, streamed behind.

After tying up by a crude table planted at the water's edge, and with a hand under each gill cover, I'd sling the heavy fish up onto the table with a grunt and go to work.

Cajuns call the gar *"poisson armée"* because the fish is armored with flinty scales. Sparks flew as I hacked away a thin strip of the hide, clearing an entrance for my razor-sharp beef skinner. With a few strokes of the curved blade, the heavy hide dropped away to leave a solid chunk of bloody meat as long as an alligator tail.

In the yellowish glow of the hissing Coleman lantern, I chopped and grunted, sliced and butchered, sharing the night with the country's truckers as we worked to WWL's Charlie Douglas and the Road Gang, "He stopped lovin' her today. . . ."

After a rest, at around 3:00 A.M., I'd make another run. And then at dawn, it was back again, to pick up the nets.

With the catch neatly iced down and myself scrubbed up, there was always a satisfying breakfast of fried eggs, bacon, and sometimes a pan-sized sheepshead or flounder, fried crispy, all washed down with yet more of the dark-roasted coffee that fueled the whole operation.

After running the catch into town, I'd come back late in the morning with fresh supplies and a pocketful of cash. Lulled by the Gulf breezes drifting through the screened doors and windows, I'd snooze most of the day and wake up late in the afternoon, eager to do it again.

The freedom and the natural beauty of commercial fishing, with its challenges that were almost immediately rewarded, entangled me. After thirty years—two-thirds of which had been spent in school—life had begun.

And the allure of a career in recreational fishing faded.

It didn't take long to realize that there was a hierarchy in fishing. And that the backbreaking and gory alligator gar fishery wasn't very high up. As I'd unload my catch by the fishhouse dock, balancing myself in my bobbing aluminum boat, I'd watch as the real fishermen would slide up in their solid, homemade skiffs.

Kicking his big outboard into reverse, the captain would bring the skiff to a smooth halt by the entrance to the fishhouse. While his deckhand tied off the boat, he'd slide back the cover of his homemade fishbox. As a fishhouse worker lined up the heavy wire baskets along the dock, the fishermen would reach into the icy slush and start pulling out their catch.

Using the fishes' cold-stiffened tails as handles, they'd flick their wrists to send each one cartwheeling across the dock to slam the rim of the basket with a jangle and then drop in. After unloading their day's catch, still in their slicker pants, they'd use a hook to drag the baskets across the concrete floor to the tables inside. Each taking a handle of the hundred-pound basket, they'd dump the fish onto the tables. Saying little, and with blades flashing, they would soon have their day's catch gutted, washed, and back in the baskets, ready to be weighed in.

As they lit fresh cigarettes and cleaned up with the hose, they'd keep an eye on the scales. Then, after collecting their money, they'd crank up, slip their lines with a cowboyish tug, and ease off to tank up at the fuel dock next door.

These were redfish. Solid like bass, they averaged a little better than five pounds. I enjoyed watching the fishhouse workers as they carefully packed them into the heavily waxed cardboard cartons that would carry the reds to New Orleans. To keep the water from the melting ice from collecting within them, the workers arranged each fish upright, as if they were still swimming.

Looking down upon their dull, olive-brown backs, surrounded by the fresh ice, you could see how difficult it would be for a bird to pick out the fish when, as young, they rested over the muddy bottom of their marshland nursery. Down their sides, the fish turned the brown of winter marsh grass and then metallic copper and bronze. Against the bleached white belly, the fins were orange red. Just before the broad tail, on each side, there was a black spot, nickel-sized, surrounded by a pale halo. Finally, on the sides of their heads—gold.

I'd pick up an occasional redfish in my gar nets. They like to follow the bank and sometimes there would be a single or a pair in the net, just as it came off the shore.

Once in a while, usually after a cool front, a net would produce more than usual. The next evening I'd cluster my nets in that location and it would sometimes work in a small-time way. But, for the time being, redfish would remain *lagniappe*, a little something extra, a couple of easy dollars that might pay the gas.

To many people, the red's marshland habitat appears a feature-less prairie, a maze of knee-high grass and water. Though it might all look the same to us, it doesn't to the fish, which hang out in preferred locations.

I didn't know it at the time, but to find them you had to ride the marsh and look for them. To do that, you needed a boat, you had to know what to look for, and when you found them, you needed a net to wrap them up.

Though I was fishing, I wasn't yet a fisherman: How to leave the house in the morning and return in the afternoon with a box of reds and your day made was a complete mystery to me. It would remain so, until I hooked up with another teacher.

Andrew Cheramie didn't keep a lot of stock in his Leeville store. For his canned goods, Andrew would hit the sales at the stores up the bayou. He kept a couple spools of rope and a little hard-ware in the back, but his main business was making up sand-wiches for the lunchtime crowd of oilfield and shrimp-shed workers. He also had a Laundromat.

You had to take a little cut through the marsh to pull up at the back. I'd wait in one of the chairs out on the front porch, which overlooked LA 1. Between the traffic down the road and up the stairs, there was plenty going on. But often there would also be a fellow across the street, working by his shed.

One day he came over and sat beside me. He was a big Cajun, something you don't see every day here, where the men are mostly French. When he sat down on the milk crate, his knees stuck up to his chest.

His name was Edville Cheramie but he went by "Pagaie," which is French for paddle. Pagaie fished and he traded. And luckily for me, he'd just traded away his fishing boat.

Pagaie was from a Golden Meadow clan that had woodworking and fishing "in the blood." He'd spent most of his sixty-two years fishing for redfish and, for him, building a boat was nothing. The problem was to buy the materials.

Before long, we'd made a pact: We'd fish together, using my gear and his knowledge. When he looked me in the eye and asked, "Do you know what it is—to fish?" I knew I was in for a ride, and in it for good.

PAYIN' YOUR DUES IN TOGIAK

JOEL GAY *plays a jazz riff on "the stuporous waiting followed by minutes of panic" that characterizes Alaska's most infamous herring fishery.*

You can't always get what you want . . .

—ROLLING STONES

TOGIAK–IT'S 9:30 P.M., and we be jammin' now. Half an hour to show time, 'til we finally get to rock 'n' roll. We've been hanging on the hook for almost three weeks, anxiously anticipating the arrival of mega-schools of Pacific herring. Now the wait is almost over. The crew of the *High C* is wound up, focused, intent, intense. We're jazzed. We're gonna rock. This is our year. We can feel it, we can smell it, we can almost touch it. We're due. We're gonna catch some fish. A lotta fish. Way lotta fish. We're gonna do it. We're gonna be it. Top dogs, big guns, herring honchos, the ever-lovin' rockin'-rollin' baddest of 'em all, the 1992 Togiak highliners!! Yeah! Yeah! Yeaaaaaahhhhhhh!

"Whoa, Doc, pull your chute!"

"What? Oh yeah, standing by. . . ."

Guess my personal stereo was a little loud. Yeah, I'm excited. It's just that I've heard so much about Togiak, and we've been waiting so long, and so many fish are expected—we have to make a killing. Skippy and the other two crewmen have had some big hauls, but not recently. They're due. Overdue. That's how herring highliners see the world—you can't score big at ever' stop on the circuit, and not ever' year. But it adds up, it evens out, and this is the year for the *High C*.

This is my first trip to Togiak. Heard all about it, seen friends come back with big grins and fat wallets, but I'm the new kid on the block. Still, I'm thinking a little beginner's luck is in order. Nothing exceptional. Hundred tons. Maybe 150. The fish have been small all over the state, which means we could get six hundred dollars a ton. Yeah, nice little shot.

First thing, I buy a Stratocaster. Sweetest electric guitar in the world. I can almost feel its curvaceous heft, the screaming power of three pickups screwed tight to a solid maple body. Ebony neck, whammy bar. I'm ready. I've done the acoustic thing, Dylan, Peter, Paul and Mary. Now I wanna rock. I wanna play the blues, bend some strings, Stevie Ray, B. B. King. Lord-a-mercy, sting me!

I don't know if hanging out in Togiak qualifies as "payin' your dues," but it should. Flew to Dillingham with Dane, our skiffman, thinking we'd be home pronto. "We've got it down," Skippy told us, "start to finish, ten days." But, nooooooo, it wasn't spring in Dillingham, it was winter, eighteen degrees, ice still forming. Had to buy a new jacket for forty-five dollars. They don't cut you any slack in Dillingham.

Herring fishing often requires days of stuporous waiting followed by minutes of panic. So Miles, the other deckhand, and I brought our trumpets. We go way back, playing together in the hills above town. Not that they wouldn't let us play downtown, you understand, but rather that our special and unique blend of musical genres transcends the stifling restrictions of traditional harmonic delineation.

After hearing us, Dane kept his earplugs handy and Skippy urged us to keep our mutes in until we were launched. But hey, when music is your life, there's no holding back. We do it all, Sousa, Santana, "Star-Spangled Banner," "Mickey Mouse Club," Dixieland, reggae, blues. We bad.

Just when we had located free showers and got chummy with Ricardo, the Pizza King of Dillingham, word filtered down that herring were seen in Hagemeister Strait. Afraid we'd miss the fish, we loaded the seine in a rush, stowed the groceries, and set out to Nushagak Bay.

The rest of Alaska is wild, but you're really heading for the edge of the map when your bow is pointed toward Togiak. When you think of Dillingham as "the big city" and the only thing between you and Tokyo is Dutch Harbor, you're out there. At Cape Constantine we hit six-foot seas that exploded on our stubby little bow and rained back down onto us like diamond teardrops backlit by the sun. Off in the distance whales spy-hopped—black pillars emerging briefly from a shimmering blue desert and then just as quickly gone. We passed huge factory trawlers quietly dragging for yellowfin sole, all business and monstrously hungry compared to the giddy fleet of thirty-two-footers parading past.

The western sky flooded red at sunset, then black, and we were enveloped in that world known only to mariners, defined by the cabin walls, the muffled roar of the diesel, the green glow of the instrument panel, and the polyrhythmic bobbing of the boat. After a big bowl of Skippy's garlic soup, I went out and barfed.

We anchored around midnight in the floating city that develops every spring in Nunavachuk Bay, just east of Togiak. Morning found us surrounded by one hundred or more seiners, tenders, and processing ships. Skiffs ran around like bicycle messengers in a marine metropolis. Airplanes and choppers zoomed in and out. Everywhere you went, exhaust stacks bellowed and belched. After a lovely walk on the beach we drove over to Togiak Bay, where life wasn't quite so hectic.

Togiak. The name trips off the tongue lightly, whether you've been there or not. It conjures images of, what—Alaska wilderness calendar beauty? A five-thousand-year-old Native commercial fishery? Sorry, the correct answer is "D. None of the above."

There are no trees in Togiak, and in May the beach is littered with brown and gray ice. There is no dock. All the houses look like they were built in Bellingham and barged in, and the cars, snow machines, and three-wheelers appear to have come to Togiak to die. "Our Store" has traditional woven grass baskets and frozen pizza. The only thing that seems vaguely old is the road, which twists around downtown Togiak as if recalling the days it was a footpath.

We anchor across the bay in the mud flats off Togiak Fisheries Inc. with three dozen other boats, rafting in twos, threes, and fours. Rafting up makes life more interesting when the tide is out. Each raft is a little city, with two or three times the population of a single boat. But when the tide comes in it's a zoo—boats churning mud in hopes of staying off the raft next door, skippers yelling, crewmen fending off errant vessels.

That's about the only excitement, however. For the next two weeks, we watch springtime come to western Alaska. Birds. Ice floes. Some follow the playoffs on big-screen TV in the cannery. Miles and I run daily on the beach and play duets, Dane reads a lot with his earplugs in, Skippy flies home. Our big thrill is watching two guys walk to shore through knee-deep mud. Sad, but funny as hell.

We sleep late, eat a lot, read, play cards, and lounge. And every day, without fail, we talk about how much money we're gonna make. It's what herring fishing is all about. The possibility of making the big score, hitting the jackpot. Recounting stories of six-hundred-ton sets, sets so big the purse rings break. The stories weave their way into your subconscious, and soon you start to think two hundred tons is entirely possible. Hey, someone has to do it, why not us?

Miles says a fat paycheck will let him pursue his sculpture, and not fish salmon this summer. Dane wants to upgrade his setnet operation. Skippy has everything he needs. After a Stratocaster and amp, new skis, and packing my retirement fund, my list is fairly short. We try not to be overconfident, but with a crack crew like ours and the Alaska Department of Fish and Game projecting a catch of fifteen thousand tons, how can we not make money?

After nearly three weeks of preparation and waiting, the first herring appear on the grounds, and soon we're prowling the shore, the last of the hunter-gatherers. We fish at ten tonight. We've looked around in Eagle Bay and Metervik, but now we're back in Nunavachuk. Tall bluffs on the west end cast long black shadows on the water, but we're on the east side, basking in the last rays of sunshine. Mistake No. 1.

As Skippy drives around, Miles and I inspect the deck. Pelican hook lubed? Check. Cleats covered? Check. Towline, wind line, breast line in order? Check. We see buddies from home, and laugh at how jealous they'll be when we catch two hundred tons. "Maybe we better leave enough for another opening," Miles jokes. This period is just twenty minutes, which everyone interprets to mean "the first of several." Mistake No. 2.

Being the superstitious type, I silently apologize to the herring gods for my greed. We don't need two hundred tons, really. Forty would be fine. Actually, just enough to pay expenses. And a Strat. And an amp. That's not asking too much, is it? Mistake No. 3.

Fifteen minutes to go and we find ourselves among two dozen seiners. Not Bristol Bay "gill-seiners," but the real thing. Crow's nests, seine trays. Each one has probably made one hundred sets this year. We made three, this morning. Mistake No. 4.

Five minutes. The aromas of diesel, gasoline, and testosterone fill the air. An enormous school of herring—eight hundred tons? One thousand?—fills this end of the bay, and everyone seems to expect a chunk. Skippers jockey for position, idling and charging, forward and reverse, while skiffmen hang on for dear life.

One minute. The roar is deafening, the tension palpable, the focus so intense you'd think this was war. Someone charges through the school in frustration. Airplanes circle tightly over-head. Every engine is redlined, every skipper armed. One skiff cuts loose, then another, and suddenly everything is in motion. Flying corks, churning water, Skippy is yelling, Miles is yelling, I'm yelling. . . .

Mistakes 5 through 29 occur very quickly, though it's like a dream to me now. I remember the skiff hitting another boat, letting the net go too early and then hauling back five fathoms of gear by hand, something about a rock, and then suddenly we find ourselves alongside a tender. It's dark now. We seem to be floating in the void, a netherworld created by halogen deck lights and a gently lapping sea.

A tenderwoman with hot pink hair and a nose ring suggests maybe we ought not to deliver. Something along the lines of, "It's not big enough." We do, though—just under nine tons. There's a three-fathom hole in the net where the other 191 tons must have escaped. Next set, we say.

But there is none. The next morning, Fish and Game an-nounces that the fleet caught nineteen thousands tons. That's it. No more. See you next year.

The crew of the *High C* is in shock. My personal share, the total sum of my earnings for the last month, is less than one ton. The Stratocaster silently fades away. I don't know whether to laugh or cry.

In twenty-four hours, I'm flying back to Anchorage. Back to family, responsibility, obligation. No more fantasies. No more dreaming. Back to reality. I peruse the want ads. For some reason I skip "Help Wanted" and go first to "Musical Instruments," where my heart stops. "Stratoscaster, good condition, with amp and case. $300."

"No way," I mutter, "it's too good a deal." Must be a mistake. Maybe $600. Even $500 would be a steal. But $300? I'll bet it was gone the first day. At the airport I don't even call.

Instead I drive straight to the Fly-by-Night Club, slam down a couple of beers, and listen to a killer Chicago blues guitarist. The lights, the sound, the people with their fancy clothes and neat haircuts—it makes Togiak seem a million miles away, and I catch myself wondering which one is real. The chilling sensation of ice scraping the hull just an inch away from your head, the stinging Arctic wind, the haunting cries of a jillion migrating birds, the helicopters and Japanese buyers, the millions of dollars invested in fish eggs—is that real? Or are these acrylic fingernails and spray-paint coiffeurs, these five-hundred-dollar suit coats and Italian shoes real? Beats me.

The next morning, I can't stand it any longer and I call. "Yeah," the guy says, "I still got it." I race over to his darkened apartment and there it is. My Strat. Red as Madonna's lipstick, begging to be fondled. I hand him a stack of twenties and practically run out the door, afraid he'll realize his error or I'll realize mine.

Two months later I see Skippy in town. I've haven't called him because I honestly believe I owe him money—I'm sure we spent more on groceries and fuel than we grossed. But he's a helluva nice guy and says, "Hey, I got a check for you."

"No kidding?"

"Yeah," he says, and smiles wide. "Three hundred bucks. Whadya gonna do with it?"

MUG-UP

LINDA GREENLAW *was the only female swordboat captain on the East Coast. In this most personal chapter of* The Hungry Ocean, *she re-creates the forces in her childhood that drew her to a life at sea.*

I AM A WOMAN. I am a fisherman. As I have said, I am not a fisherwoman, fisherlady, or fishergirl. If anything else, I am a thirty-seven-year-old tomboy. It is a word I have never outgrown. Neither abused nor neglected, I am the product of a blissful and unique childhood . . . a rare claim these days. Like all young children, I believed wholeheartedly in the words of my mother and father. It was only natural that I took seriously the assertions of my parents that I could do whatever I like with my life, become anything I wanted. Although the advice was well intentioned, my parents never dreamed that it might come back to haunt them when I decided that what I liked, and wanted to become, was a fisherman.

I woke up one morning, at the age of twelve, to the smell of low tide. The scent of seaweed and tidal pools crept through my open bedroom window and tiptoed around the room, not overpowering, but arousing interest. Usually awakening to the faint smell of pine and the rush of wind in the trees, that day I was intrigued with the thick, musty odor of sun-baked salt and mussel-covered rocks. My ears strained to pick up the slight sloshing of the tide as it swept in and out around the low-water-mark rocks and ledges. It seemed strange that having been surrounded by the ocean my entire life, this was the first time I noticed the screeching of the gulls and the drone of a diesel-powered lobster boat nearby. I approached my bedroom window and, leaning on the sill, looked out to sea. The surface of the water sparkled, every ripple reflecting the color of the sun like millions of golden sequins. Dark and shaded, my usual playground of the woods behind our house never knew this type of brilliance.

The woods were comfortable. I knew every gnarled root and fragrant bayberry bush like the back of my own hand, and although I loved them, their total familiarity left me with no new challenges. Most of the fun had gone out of building forts and stalking squirrels with slingshots. There was something mysterious about the sea, something alluring. This day I would leave my slingshot and Swiss army knife on the back porch and, rather than head for the deep woods, I would wander down to the shore in Robinson Cove.

From the rocky beach beside my grandfather's dock I could see all the way across Penobscot Bay to the island of Vinalhaven. Looking to the south, I could see Brimstone, a small lump of an island, and Saddleback Ledge, a stark rock with the lone structure of a lighthouse tower. I had been around these islands dozens of times aboard my dad's boat, but had never found them quite as interesting as they were this morning.

I watched a lobster boat glide through the water and approach the cove from Isle au Haut's main harbor. As the boat passed the spindle between our island and Kimball Island I could see the name *Danita* on the bow in large black letters. The *Danita* entered the cove and slowed to a drift. I watched as the captain reached over the side with a short gaff hook and pulled a yellow-and-red buoy from the water to the boat. Next he ran the line trailing from the buoy through a block that hung on the end of a short davit mounted on the outside bulkhead of his boat's small house. He drew the line from the block into the steel plates of his hydraulic pot hauler. Seconds later a wooden lobster trap broke the surface and came to rest against the hull of the *Danita*. The captain yanked the trap onto the gunwale of the boat and slid it aft a bit, where his helper opened it up.

The helper in the stern of the boat appeared to be a boy not much bigger than myself. The boy picked the lobsters from the trap, tossing the small ones back into the water and placing the larger ones on a table beside him. He then baited the trap, and turned to the table where he had placed the big lobsters. While the boy measured the lobsters and stretched rubber bands around their claws, the captain shifted the boat's engine back into gear and pushed the trap over the side and into the water, allowing the line to pay out over the rail of the boat. The buoy splashed in behind the trap and line, and the boat turned and headed toward the lighthouse. The captain waved in my direction with a smile. I was thrilled and surprised with the wave, and waved back with enthusiasm that shook my chunky frame. Just then I was startled by a voice behind me. "Hi, Captain Jack!"

The familiar voice carried across the cove to the *Danita*. I turned and looked to see two small figures waving their arms at the boat. My younger brother and sister, five year-old twins, sat perched on top of a ledge like a couple of sea gulls. I climbed up the ledge and joined the twins, the three of us watching the *Danita* make her way to the next yellow-and-red buoy. "Do you know them?" I asked, my gaze fixed on the hauling of the next trap.

"Yup. They got three keepers out of that last trap. Only had two yesterday," answered my little sister, Bif. Bif, short for Elizabeth, was the talkative one of the twins and usually answered for both herself and our brother, Charlie. Charlie nodded his blond curly head as if confirming Bif's lobster tally, his bright blue eyes intensely watching the picking of the second trap. "Wow, looks like four good ones this time! Didn't they only get one there yesterday?" Bif asked of Charlie.

Still nodding and staring, Charlie answered in his usual one syllable. We watched as the trap was baited and pushed back into the water, disappearing in the wake behind the boat. The *Danita* turned and went around the point of land where Point

Robinson Lighthouse stood, leaving behind a puff of white exhaust and a wake that quietly rolled its way to the shore at our feet.

With the boat now out of our view, Bif focused on me. "That was Jack MacDonald and his Danny. You know, Danny from the softball games? Jack waves to us every day, and we count lobsters. He catches a lot more than the other lobstermen," she explained.

"A lot more," Charlie echoed as he made his way down the ledge and onto the beach, where he found a small tidal pool. Charlie crouched at the edge of the pool and stared into it as if he were seeing all the way to China. After thorough examination he looked up at Bif and me with a grin and reported, "Four crabs! Eleven periwinkles!" He stood now and peered down the beach, focusing on a much larger tidal pool. Hopping from rock to rock, Charlie made his way to the bigger pool and, wading in up to his knees, began his count again.

Below me on the beach, Bif was struggling with a bunch of mussels. She pulled mussels away from the rocks where they had attached themselves. As she freed them from their tangled mess she laid them singly on a flat rock beside her. As the top of the rock filled with mussels I asked, "Does Mom know you two are down here alone?"

"We're not alone, we're with you. She said for you to keep an eye on us and don't let us get our sneakers wet again," Bif answered, pulling another dark blue shell from between two stones and laying it with the others.

I laughed, looking at Charlie, who was now up to his waist in the salt water. "I guess it's a little late for the sneakers."

Bif shifted her attention from the mussels to Charlie and shouted, "You better get out of that water. Mom's gonna be mad."

Charlie said "Yup" and climbed out of the giant puddle. He

sloshed and dripped his way back up the rocky beach, joining Bif by the pile of mussels. Grabbing a stone about the size of a baseball, Charlie began smashing the blue shells Bif had so carefully laid out. Fully expecting Bif to scream or run home to tattle, I watched in amazement as she picked up one of the squashed mussels to feel the gooey yellow mush insides with the fingers of both hands.

"What are you doing?" I asked, surprised that my usually squeamish little sister would touch the guts of anything.

"Looking for pearls. We found two yesterday. Makes sixteen all together."

"Yup. Sixteen," echoed Charlie as he broke open the last of the shells.

While the twins busied themselves with their rituals and counting games, my attention returned to the water outside the cove. I looked as far to seaward as I could, beyond the islands, out into the middle of the bay. I was sure there was something out there for me; I could feel it. There were many things to see, but they were all just over the horizon, just beyond my sight. I squinted and strained to see farther, but it was no use. I knew instinctively that the ocean had stories to tell me; all I needed to do was listen. Intrigued, I searched the beach at my feet and found a shell that had been vacated by a hermit crab. Putting the shell to my ear, I listened to the empty, hollow, ringing sound. There was a pattern to the ringing that reminded me of the surf on the ledges when the wind blows. There was something else, though, something faint and far out to sea.

Clasping the shell to my ear and scanning the horizon across the bay, I found myself lost in a most vivid daydream. I imagined boats and fish and faraway islands. I harpooned whales, jigged for cod, and sailed clear across the Atlantic Ocean before my dream was interrupted by the tide coming in around me.

The twins had already found some higher ground up the beach and were scratching their names into a small patch of wet sand with sticks. Unwilling to let my daydream evaporate, I asked, "Anyone want to go fishing?"

"I do," answered Charlie, dropping his driftwood pencil.

"Me, too! Aren't you going to play in the woods today?" asked Bif.

"No." I smiled. "Today I'm going to sea."

And go to sea I did, every chance I got for the next twenty years. Rarely did a day leave me ashore. I rowed until I inherited an antique outboard motor; I putted around the cove in the skiff until I had courage enough to "borrow" my Dad's forty-foot powerboat, at an age when most kids contemplate stealing the family car. I fished, mostly with hook and line, for mackerel and pollock, and experimented with nets and makeshift harpoons. Fishing my way through college, I made my first Grand Banks trip at the age of nineteen aboard the *Walter Leeman*. My primary job was looking, and although I disliked the galley chores, I liked the money. It wasn't until a fellow crew member hit the bunk with a back injury that I was allowed to work the deck, work I enjoyed for years. While harpooning, I was spotting the majority of the fish before Alden or any of my shipmates, and because I was experienced at running my dad's boat, I became the *Walter Leeman*'s helmsman.

By the time I graduated from college I had outlasted the original crew members I had started with, most of whom moved on to boats of their own, and so I became first mate by attrition. Promising my parents that I would postpone law school for just one year, I became a full-time fisherman. One year turned into sixteen. After I had been working as mate aboard the *Walter Leeman* for four years, Alden bought a second boat, the *Gloria Dawn*, and gave me my first opportunity as captain. I learned the bulk of what I know about at-sea emergency repairs and catching swordfish in my three years at the wheel of the *Gloria Dawn*; it was an expensive education in many ways, and it nearly put Alden in the poorhouse. I have fished on a number of different boats involved in a number of different fisheries, learning something from each and every experience; I am still learning today.

Being a woman hasn't been a big deal. I never anticipated problems stemming from being female, and never encountered any. I have been surprised, even embarrassed, by the number of people who are genuinely amazed that a woman might be capable of running a fishing boat. Frankly, I'm amazed that they're amazed. People, women in particular, are generally disappointed when they learn that I have not suffered unduly from being the only woman in what they perceive to be a man's world. I might be thick-skinned—or just too damn busy working to worry about what others might think of me.

WORKING BELOW
THE WATERLINE

SETH HARKNESS *trades a hammer
and a land job for an urchin rake and
an undersea job site as he enters
the urchin-diving fishery off an
island in Maine.*

RARELY IN MY LIFE have I been in the right place at the right time and realized it. At least once it seemed true. In 1993, the summer after college, I moved to a Maine island tethered to the rest of America by a narrow bridge. It's a beautiful piece of granite, spruce-clad and hemmed by the sea, and at the time this was reason enough for me to be there. For a short while, unencumbered by a job, I mostly drove back roads and looked at the water. Later, I took what work I could find and began commuting two hours a day to hammer nails for seven dollars an hour. We often built near the water, and sometimes on lunch break I'd swim in the cold ocean.

After a month, I asked for a dollar raise and got fifty cents instead. There had to be a better way, I was sure, but I didn't know what. With the first frosts in September, the island emptied of the tourists and foreign cars that had crowded Main Street all summer. In October I noticed a new set of vehicles lining Main Street, mostly rusty pickups carrying dive tanks that clanged in back as they rounded corners. *Urchin season again,* said people in town, shaking their heads. *Used to be you never saw anybody you didn't know around here this time of year.*

Once I began looking, signs of the urchin harvest were everywhere. Some days the narrow street was more congested than it had been in summer. Trucks parked halfway on lawns and blocked driveways. I saw dive gear hanging out to dry on the balconies at the seaside hotel. Another carpenter told me a bunch of urchin fishermen came into the cafe where his girlfriend waitressed. She said they drank chocolate milk and paid with hundred-dollar bills. On a day without wind, a dive day, it seemed like an overturned world—more people spent their day below water than above.

A new hurried energy took hold of me like a fever. It wasn't so much a decision to become an urchin diver, as a recognition that this—right here, right now—was an opportunity I couldn't let pass. I'd never before had a chance to be so independent: to be outside, to work for myself, and to make a decent living, all of which seemed possible as a fisherman. Everyone had heard the rumors, surely exaggerated, of big money in urchin diving. *So many urchins down there, first thing you have to clear a place for your knees. A thousand bucks a day. Some days, anyway, some divers.* Most jobs seemed to offer either flexibility or money or neither. Here, maybe, was a chance to have both, to be free.

Within a week, I quit my carpentry job and took the plunge. I sent off for an urchin license and searched the classifieds for a used set of dive gear. This was in the midst of a long string of fine fall days. At some level I realized, but didn't stop to consider, that divers are in fact outside and under water all winter in the North Atlantic, water that wouldn't melt an ice cube for weeks at a time.

The small economic explosion which allowed me to trade my hammer for an urchin rake was like an ocean wave that originated in Japan and ultimately crashed on the coast of Maine. Though to lobstermen they have long been "whore's eggs," a spiny nuisance that invades their traps and sticks their hands, the Japanese hold urchins in higher esteem. Sea urchin roe, or *uni,* has been a delicacy in Japan for centuries. The sweet tangerine-colored roe, touted as an aphrodisiac, has an incomparable, some would say incomparably dreadful, taste: imagine edible perfume. As their own stocks diminished, the Japanese began aggressively importing urchins from other coasts, including Chile, California, and eventually Maine.

By a cruel twist of biology, urchin fishing is best done in the coldest months. Urchins build roe in winter, reaching their most desirable state around February, and spawn in the spring. Fishing in summer, though comfortable, would mean harvesting empty shells. But cold water didn't deter nearly two thousand people, mostly single men, from scrambling into the wide-open Maine urchin fishery before the state eventually stopped printing licenses. Anybody could get started by buying a license, dive gear, and a few garden rakes, the preferred harvesting tool. In between the lobster license plates on the fish pier there were now vehicles from California, Virginia, and New York. Around town I heard divers speaking Cambodian, Bulgarian, and Oklahoman.

Some divers had been to law school and some had been to prison. There were men who liked to drink whiskey and fire bullets into the night sky, and men with five children, a mortgage, and a regular pew. There were those who only wanted to make a winter's income in a place where the economy hibernates in winter, and others who came cross country for the big chance, the new start and the bending of the rules they had always hoped to find. What we all shared, if anything, was the fact that we had discovered or stumbled into an opportunity under the water that looked better than anything we had going on land. But first, we ex-carpenters, ex-mechanics, and ex-cons had to learn to fish.

I rolled backward off the inflatable skiff, catching a glimpse of an inverted horizon with water over sky before I splashed into the ocean. Since it was only my second urchin dive (the first was from the beach with a rope tied to my waist), it was still a matter of blind trust to leave the boat.

"Breathe," Tony said in his Slavic accent, "that's the most important."

His instructions may have been obvious, but they gave me

needed peace of mind. Not only totes of urchins, but also a body
had come over the fish pier in recent months. At least six divers
drowned in the first years of the fishery; they had gotten tangled
in their own lines or run out of air or panicked. None were in
more than thirty feet of water when they died. Almost all were
urchin diving for the first or second time. The deaths had made
the news and even my out-of-state grandmother had heard of
them. She had recently called, horrified, to ask me what I was
doing with my life.

Breathe, I reminded myself, I can do that.

Tony and I had met a few days earlier on the fish pier. He
owned the fourteen-foot inflatable, and inflate it we did, frequently, since it had experienced many spiny urchins. As had
Tony's knuckles, which were knobby and oversized. He wasn't
new to the business, and he was a confident diver, maybe overconfident. For several months he had been diving alone from his
small boat. One time he surfaced, looked around—no boat in
sight. He floated on the waves a while, then, from the crest of
the higher waves, spotted his skiff, a dot out on the horizon.
Luckily, a nearby lobsterman reconnected the bobbing diver and
the drifting skiff. Now I was his tender, following him in the
skiff, and in return he was teaching me the basics of urchin diving. After he finished a couple tanks, we'd switch roles and he'd
tend for me.

My lungs anticipated a long drink of salt water. I braced for a
cold stream to pour down my neck. Instead I was shockingly
comfortable in the water. I pushed a valve, air bubbled out of
my rubber dry suit, and I slipped below the boat. A calm came
over me, just the opposite of my feelings up above. The same
gear that felt cumbersome and turtlelike up there—the fifty
pounds of lead around my waist and ankles, the air tank on my
back, the stiff dry suit with the tight neck seal that felt like a

birthing process to put on—was now weightless and natural. Beneath the dry suit I wore fleecy long underwear; it was December and I was swimming in my pajamas in the North Atlantic. At fifty degrees, the water wasn't uncomfortable. A flip of my fins and I swam down into the green murk. The outboard made a crunch as Tony shifted into gear to follow my bubbles.

Twenty feet down I touched the ledge and soon began to see that I was simply another link in the food chain. All around me other creatures, armored and busy, were trying to make their living in the same way I intended to do. Lobsters, magnified by my mask, snapped their claws and retreated backward when I interrupted their feeding. Crabs scuttled past without any curiosity in their little eyes. Schools of small pollock fed in the cloud of dust behind me. And, sure enough, dotted across the ledge and continuing down into deeper water was a pasture of my own prey. I took to raking them with the same single-mindedness with which the rest of these underwater creatures were working.

I soon realized, though, that these were the airball urchins, marked by their pale-green shells and long brittle spines, that Tony had warned me about. They live below the kelp on a near-starvation diet and, consequently, have little or no roe. Buyers hate them and pay accordingly. Harvesting urchins wasn't quite so simple as raking anything that looked green. I swam up the ledge, a little closer to the sun, where the jungle of kelp began. A breaststroke motion separated the rubbery kelp, and I squirmed into the seaweed jungle in search of better-fed urchins.

In my hands I carried the tools of the trade, which were simple enough. One neoprene mitt clutched an urchin rake, a three-pronged garden cultivator with a fat wrap of duct tape around the handle for a better grip. And in the other hand I held a mesh bag tied to a line, in turn tied to a buoy, which trailed above me at the surface. Picking slowly through the kelp, I occasionally saw heavy urchins bristling with short, dense spines. Feeling like a jewel thief, I pried them from the rock and with a sweep of my arm sent them tumbling into the bag.

Had I stuffed a bag, I would have hauled down on the line and relied on Tony to place an empty bag over my buoy. We eventually learned to anticipate each other's actions based on small clues. Big explosions of bubbles indicated the diver was frantically raking a patch of urchins and would soon need a bag. Polite little bobbing motions of the buoy translated to, "Another bag, please." Giant jerking motions obviously said, "I'm waiting! I need it! NOW!" Sometimes Tony's bubbles trailed off to a small fizz. I asked him about it and he placed his palms together and rested them against his temple. "Sometimes I take a nap," he said.

But one bag was enough for me, unfortunately. Spotting a few urchins in a crack in the ledge, I was certain I'd found the start of a green valley. But inevitably this vein and all the others like it dried up and I was back to fighting my way through the forest of kelp. Lost in the kelp, I sometimes circled around and discovered my own scratch marks on the ledge where I had already harvested. When I grew distracted or discouraged, I'd squander time and air by breaking a few urchins and feeding them to wary lobsters. Tony had filled three bags on his last tank. Mine remained half empty.

We were an improbable pair, Tony and I, but not completely unlike. He had escaped from Bulgaria before they opened the gates. In a previous career he had been a weight lifter in the circus and once had broken his ankle when he had stepped in an elephant's footprint while balancing a woman on his shoulders. Now, to save money and because he chose his company sparingly, he lived in a small capsule of a trailer hauled back into the woods in the middle of the island. "In America everything is money, money, money," he frequently said. He smoked anxiously and constantly worried that his truck was going to break down, which it often did. His dream, as he told me, was to buy a small piece of land. He would let out a deep breath after mentioning this, as if there would never be worries once he had his land.

In a way I had all the advantages he didn't: I had a place to stay on the island at my parents' summer cabin. I spoke the language, if not the local dialect. But in other ways our circumstances were not so different. I also had empty pockets and an unreliable vehicle. Our cabin had no running water, and when it snowed I walked down the winding dirt road towing my groceries and water jugs on a sled behind me. We both had ample room for upward mobility. And to much of the besieged local population, many of whom were born and will likely die on the island, and who had spent their lives fishing there, every strange face was equally foreign. One time an older lobsterman, with whom I'd spoken frequently, pointed to me as I stood with Tony and some of his Bulgarian friends. "You speak better English than the rest of them," he said. "I'm from New Hampshire," I explained. *We speak English there,* I thought but didn't say.

Soon the needle on my pressure gauge had fallen into the red and each breath came with an effort. I dropped my rake in the bag, clipped it shut, and a shot of air in my suit lifted me, slowly, toward the blurry blue sky, which came into sharp focus when I broke the surface. Tony idled over and hoisted my weight belt and tank and looked skeptically at my partial bag of urchins. I raised myself, threw a knee over the side, and flopped back into the skiff. A breeze had begun to corrugate the water. To my surprise, late afternoon light reddened the granite shore of a nearby island. I'd been down an hour, though it felt like minutes. Fortunately we hadn't gone far out into the bay. In those days there were still urchins close to the harbor, and I wedged myself between the bags of urchins and the dive gear for the choppy ride back to town. It was time to sell our urchins, which could be more work than catching them in the first place.

In urchining, the day's measure is ultimately how many pounds you can load on a scale. And the price for each of those pounds. But unlike say, lobsters, where you can see what you are selling at a glance and the price is the price, not open for discussion, selling urchins is always a negotiation. This is because with urchins nobody knows exactly what they are buying or selling, and the market soars and crashes more than a manic depressive.

Urchin buyers are generally either very skeptical people or they are unemployed. Buyers are ultimately buying just the urchin roe, which they can only judge for color and fullness by breaking the shell and examining its contents. But, like the market itself, urchins are wildly inconsistent: full, empty, golden roe and black roe all from the same spot on the same ledge. Buyers can't break every urchin so they typically crack a few in each tote, then the buyer points to the poor urchins, the diver to the better ones, and the haggling begins.

"Skinny, skinny. Eighty cents—that's the best I can do."

"You kidding? This stuff's killer. All day I was picking in the kelp. Yesterday you paid me eighty cents. That *was* garbage. Look at these—if that's an eighty-cent urchin, you're the Pope."

"That would explain all the charity I do—like buying your eggs yesterday. What's on the bottom? Let's flip one."

"Go ahead, I like to put my best work on the bottom. But you know what could happen. Those other guys might see those good eggs and offer me a buck. And I won't say no."

"But you always sell to me."

"Not if you're always going to give me eighty cents."

"Ninety?"

"Yeah, you can steal them for ninety, I guess."

"Don't tell the rest of the mob—they'll all want the big price."

In later seasons I began to see patterns in the market that weren't obvious to me in the beginning. The Japanese emperor's birthday on December 23 eventually became one of my favorite holidays. This and the New Year's season, I later learned, bring the highest prices of the year. This is when up to eight trucks sometimes park at the pier, buyers waiting to pounce on each arriving dive boat and bidding against each other in a frenzy of open-air capitalism. This is when the brown paper wrappers with which banks tie hundred-dollar bills into bundles of a thousand sometimes blow around as street litter. In November and February and March there are often long slumps when buyers don't answer their phones and won't be seen on the pier for weeks at a time. Occasionally a load of urchins lands back in the water or the woods. The totally unpredictable can also be expected. An earthquake and a food poisoning scare in Japan have both sent the market reeling for months. More than once, just before selling my urchins, a cell phone has rung—a flood of urchins from Nova Scotia or Siberia has hit the market—and the price falls like a dropped weight belt.

By the time Tony and I reached the pier, boats were already rafted three and four deep, many overloaded with tall stacks of totes and scuppers deep underwater. These were real boats with cabins and diesel engines and rumbling exhaust systems. It might be hours and long past dark before we could sell. Flames rose from a barbecue on the stern of one boat where the crew had settled in for a long wait. Many of these boats lined up along the overstrained pier read Portland, ME, across the stern. They had steamed a hundred miles east in search of better catches. I may have just been getting started in this fishery, but for others it was already declining. Around Portland, where the fishery had started about four years before, urchins were already scarce. As a newcomer myself I had no right to feel territorial, but I did. Within a few years, though, I'd be migrating east myself.

Tony, always an opportunist, spotted a gap between two larger boats and we hoisted our totes onto the dock. After the inevitable bargaining, we sold for a dollar a pound. Despite landing possibly the shortest stack of totes on the pier, I had a good feeling about this new career. Earning nearly a day's carpentry wages in an hour of diving of course agreed with me, but there was also a satisfaction in not selling my hours or my days, but something I had harvested.

Over the next month Tony and I took his skiff as far as we dared out into the bay. Tony picked the dive spots. It took some time to develop my eye for urchins. Though he continued to insist that he did some of his best sleeping underwater, Tony usually caught twice what I did. "Look for them," he said when I asked him how he did it. My eyes weren't closed down there. What did he mean *look for them*?

I thought of a friend of mine who has been digging clams for more than twenty-five years. Occasionally I join him and, working right beside him with the same size hoe, he will be tossing clams into a half-full bucket while I haven't yet covered the bottom of mine. He calls it his "clam radar." Maybe he has an extra sense for bivalves, but more likely I think he has an understanding of their habits and habitat based on careful observations. Slowly, I was learning the same things about urchins. I noticed how they preferred the south sides of ledges, clustering together along the base of rocks or in crevices. How they hated mud and sand, but liked rocks in sand. Direct sunlight distressed them and they often found shade beneath an umbrella of kelp. My stack of totes began to grow taller.

Urchin diving requires spending an unusual, maybe unhealthy, amount of time alone and under water. What do you think about down there all day, several people asked me. At first I didn't know how to answer this. Other than the background noise in most people's minds, thoughts about ex-girlfriends, bits of songs—what did I think about? Something, surely. Then one day I watched a blue heron feeding at the shoreline, completely concentrated on the ground before it. Yes, I realized, that's what I think when I'm diving. Learning to see urchins, for better or worse, is partly a matter of learning to ignore everything else. I began to see urchins with a predator's eyes. Once I saw some beautiful urchins in an aquarium and felt my blood begin to race.

When I began fishing, I also began measuring my life by boats. In the seven seasons I've been diving for urchins, I've owned a progression of them, leading up to a reasonably seaworthy boat today. Generally, esthetics weren't a top consideration in the urchin fleet. Price was. One old rotten urchin boat had a bicycle lashed to the top of its flying bridge, as if the owner planned to pedal away if his boat was sinking. Another was simply called *Red Slab*. Tattered blue tarps were the signature accessory of the urchin fleet. Most had winter enclosures of unpainted plywood and right angles that showed no respect for the original lines of the boat.

The first winter winds to blow down from Quebec prompted Tony and me to begin looking for a better boat. Clearly an open skiff wasn't meant for this weather. Another option was to dive from somebody else's boat and pay that person 40 percent of our catch, as most divers did. But Tony hadn't risked his life escaping a communist country in order to give up almost half his earnings. And I preferred working with someone to working for someone. "We're not brothers," Tony said, "but close." But even brothers can fail at sharing a boat.

Two lobstermen, brothers, once shared a boat and then had a falling out and now run their own boats. Today, they won't speak or even look at each other. If one is unloading at the dock, the other won't enter the harbor. He will circle around instead until his brother has finished and then avoid eye contact as they pass. I don't know exactly what happened between them, or if they know themselves, but conflicts on boats are more intense than ones on land, and often more trivial. The argument that convinced me Tony and I couldn't work together was about a dust cap on a scuba regulator, but its causes had more to do with sharing only half a language between us and the clash of two stubborn personalities. It wasn't an angry parting, but we both knew it: We were on our own again. And so I wound up working for quite possibly the most inexperienced and inept captain in town—myself. Which meant I needed my own boat.

Another combing of the classifieds yielded all the boat I could afford, in other words not much. It was a twenty-one-foot aluminum Starcraft factory-made in Indiana. A small cabin offered shelter from the wind and spray. It was definitely more a picnic boat for Midwestern reservoirs than a saltwater fishing boat. A peculiar musty smell filled the bow, where the former owner and his dog had lived at times. Initially the two bilge pumps struck me as an admirable concern for safety. Later, I discovered they were a necessity since the boat was porous with loose rivets. I'd regularly dive beneath the boat with putty that set under water and plug the holes. A rough passage across the bay and they'd spring open again.

In a hurry to start fishing, I was proceeding stern first. I had a boat but no mooring. I tied up to one of the urchin buyer's floats, where I thought my boat could sit for a few days until I secured a mooring. This might have been a safe bet in July, but in late December I was playing very bad odds. The next night, out of the southwest, from which our harbor has no protection, came a punishing wind. Wind and rain lashed the house and kept me awake, as did worry for my boat.

After midnight I went down to the harbor and experienced a sensation in my stomach I'd never known—my boat was sinking. It had snapped a stern line and swung around so that instead of heaving beside the float it was pounding against its sharp corner, each collision placing a new dent in the bow until one of the blows would soon puncture it like a can of soup. The bow rose high out of the water, showing bottom paint before slamming into the dock. I grabbed a life jacket and, clinging to the rain-slick dock with one hand, held it across the corner of the float as a bumper. The boat reared up, and I was sure would come crashing down on me. The stern line was the key. I needed to reattach it, but couldn't do that without letting the bow pound again. Awful thoughts came to me. Would I have to stay on the heaving float all night? Should I maybe have gone to law school after all? The wind and waves were tireless. I considered, briefly, walking away and going back to bed.

Out in the harbor I could see the upward-pointing bow of one lobster boat that had sunk at its mooring. Worse, a new fiberglass lobster boat, the *Sea Spray*, had parted its mooring and washed onto the rocks, where it grated with a hollow scraping sound. Soon the headlights of several trucks converged on this boat, and I could see someone wading out through the surf. Next the cabin lights flicked on and the diesel roared and spewed black smoke. The *Sea Spray* backed down off the rocks and set out at full throttle across the storming harbor toward the shipyard, racing against the water that was surely flooding through its keel. Nobody had walked away from that boat. I held on.

For me, help that night came in the form of a posse of kids who were out wandering in the storm. They saw my predicament and helped by finding some used tires, which I tied to the float as bumpers. Together we secured the stern to the float again and stopped the pounding. In the morning the wind had died completely and boats pointed in different directions at their moorings. But there were still the dents in the bow of my boat and green paint on the rocks where the *Sea Spray* had grounded. As things turned out, the night I thought I'd lose my boat, I found a tender. I hired one of the kids a few days later and we went fishing.

Soon it was a couple of weeks into a particularly frigid January, the weather radio calling for day after day of gale warnings. The ranks of divers began to thin out. Some migrated away like the lobsters and returned in the spring; others decided urchining wasn't whatever they had hoped and quit completely. An underwater welder from Seattle who started in the fishery felt as comfortable in the cold water as a seal, but fishing didn't sit right with him. "I feel sorry for the urchins," he confessed to me. "Sometimes, when nobody's looking, I put some back." He returned to Seattle and to welding before the winter was over.

In the January cold things froze that I didn't realize could freeze. The harbor, for one. A small icebreaker appeared to clear the main thoroughfare. There were frozen scuba regulators and gas lines and bilge pumps and tank valves and outboard motor throttles. At home my toothpaste froze. Neoprene hoods froze and sometimes I had to jam a crunchy hood down over my head. Boats returned to the harbor shellacked in frozen spray with only a small circle free of ice on the pilothouse window. Still, Tony continued fishing from his open skiff, arriving back at the pier with a blue cast to his face and ice on his dry suit.

Underwater there was a vacant feel, like a boardwalk in winter, since the lobsters, crabs, and pollock had all departed for deeper, warmer water. It was hard not to suspect they were wiser than me on days when I waded down my snowy drive, chipped the ice out of my skiff, and prepared to go swimming. After an initial shock to my hands and face on jumping into the water, there was a period of what seemed like warmth until, slowly, I began to sense how unfit my warm-blooded, uninsulated body was in this cold sea. Either I would have to heat it, or it would cool me, which is of course what began to happen as the cold seeped in from all sides until it met in the middle, convulsing me in a gigantic shiver. The biting cold was undeniable, but I also learned that it could be a state of mind. When the sunlight fell on my back underwater, I always felt warmer, though the temperature was no different.

At night and in the morning I listened to the slightly hypnotic marine weather report, and planned my life according to the wind and waves. *From Rockland, Maine, to the Merrimack River out to twenty-five nautical miles: gale warning in effect. . . . This afternoon winds becoming south and increasing to twenty to thirty knots and shifting to the southwest by morning. . . . Average seas ten to fourteen feet.* Even with a forecast like this, the day might begin still and windless. Then it became a judgment call whether to go or not. Especially if other boats went out, I felt anxious being on land. I'd only relax if, later in the day, the wind began to blow and shake the trees. Friends from the city sometimes called and woke me on a Friday or Saturday night when I'd turned in early because of a forecast for calm seas the next day. They couldn't imagine a work schedule set by the wind rather than the day of the week.

A few particular trees outside my window became my wind gauge. A slight swaying of branches here meant surf pounding on the exposed rocks where we dove. Waves like these toss a diver around like a leaf in the wind. They're even worse for the tender, who has to navigate between breaking surf and sharp rocks in an open skiff. Almost every diver has at one time or another surfaced from a dive to the sight of a dripping, miserable tender standing on a ledge beside an overturned skiff. These are the experiences that convince you, and your tender, to stay home the next time the trees are swaying.

No wind was a problem too this time of year, because then the sea ice formed overnight, usually just a skim, but sometimes thick enough to freeze the boats solidly to the ocean. An eerie stillness filled the harbor on these days. Mornings when the air was much colder than the water, vapors of sea smoke rose from the ocean in an inverted fog. Oddly, it looked like the water was about to boil. I envied the people working in the post office at a federally mandated sixty-eight degrees. And there was a time, sometime in February, where I no longer noticed or cared to notice the view of the ocean from my parents' cabin.

One place that was always warm, even hot at times, were the meetings where scientists, government managers, and fishermen tried to decide what to do with this runaway fishery. At one meeting, a public hearing, over three hundred divers arrived, mostly to shout down a proposal that would have drastically cut back the fishing season. A long line formed behind the microphone. There was much talk of welfare and hungry children if these changes went through. And yet, around the docks, everyone complained they couldn't find urchins like they used to. It's not that urchin fishermen were completely incapable of cooperation, just close to it. Once I saw one boat towing another out in the morning, and back in the afternoon. The captain of the broken boat didn't want to miss a day of fishing just because his engine was useless. But a boat in distress was one thing, and a fishery in the same situation was apparently another.

One thing sure to warm me up under water was finding good urchins, but I rarely did so in this first fishing season. Morning and night, I unrolled my crumpled chart, "Approaches to Blue Hill Bay #13313," and studied it like a mysterious treasure map. But I had almost no feeling for the waters it represented. I hadn't yet seen enough rocks at extra-low tides; I hadn't yet noticed where the other boats did and didn't fish, and I hadn't yet overheard the right conversations. But what I lacked in experience, I tried to make up for with persistence. I dove everywhere, un-selective and equally unproductive, but slowly this strategy be-gan to pay off. I was learning where urchins don't live, which eventually points to where they do.

It wasn't until the next season, almost exactly a year after I started fishing, that I rolled into the water at yet another ledge, immediately felt the cold needle of water stab my knee in my by-now leaky suit, and then let out a yell that emerged as a pulse of bubbles and a thin sound in my own ears. It was a sight. Wider than a two-lane road and spaced like checkers, the urchins made a green swath around the rock. The nearby kelp appeared to have been gnawed by rodents. I didn't know where to start. Then I did, first clearing a place on the ledge for my knees.

We worked late that day, culling heaps of urchins until past sunset, which comes early in Maine in December. Then, with the boat low and slow in the water, I set out across the bay toward the blinking light of Mark Island, which marks the entrance to the thoroughfare and back to the harbor. Soon the light had drained out of the western sky completely, the first stars ap-peared overhead, and the orange light of my compass lit the small cabin. I had never run at night before, had never seen the black water blend with the night to surround the boat with dark-ness. All my references quickly diminished to two, the compass and the lighthouse, but with those two guides I was sure I could find my way back to town. Close behind me I could see the red-and-green running lights of my friend's boat. John and I had been fishing together that day and he was following me home. I lined my bow up with the blinking lighthouse and he lined up with me and we became a small caravan traveling across the dark water.

Not far out into the bay, I swerved to avoid a lobster buoy, which appeared suddenly before me in the night and sent my compass spinning. For a moment I lost my bearings and didn't know which way to steer. Mark Island light, which only blinks once every six seconds, wasn't immediately visible. I swerved around looking for the light and immediately began to feel uneasy without a clear heading. When the lighthouse did finally flash, off in the corner of my window, I could breathe again. Just to be sure, I counted seconds until the next flash. It lit up right on number six and I locked on to the light, determined to keep my bow pointed directly for it until it had guided me safely home.

My compass had settled back to normal, but it now read a different bearing than it had before I lost the light. About sixty degrees different. But it was an old compass and like just about everything else about the boat, I didn't trust it. The lighthouse flashed reassuringly again in front of me every six seconds. That I could trust. At least my outboard was running well; there was one thing I didn't need to worry about. The motor hummed along and water splashed beside the boat as we made a dogged course for the light. The trip out had been a quick one. With no load and flat seas, we had planed across the bay in no more than twenty-five minutes. Now, on our return, we plodded along with our heavy load in what felt like a trance, and the light didn't seem to be getting any closer than the stars; in fact it was difficult to be sure we were even moving. I wondered if I could be towing a lobster trap, and making only a knot or two. The engine droned on for what could have been twenty minutes, an hour, I didn't know. Then I did notice a change, or rather I became aware that something had been slowly changing for a while and I was only now recognizing it. The waves slapping against the hull sounded different and the boat had begun to roll beneath my feet. And the light was finally getting brighter. It seemed like a good thing that we were nearing home just as the seas had begun to kick up.

The shrill sound of a fog signal made me realize my mistake.

It wasn't the sound of Mark Island, which signals with a deep resounding foghorn. Instead it was a high-pitched tone like a digital alarm clock. We continued until we could make out the lighthouse itself, and my fears were confirmed. A granite tower sat on a jagged ledge. Waves broke with flashes of white against the dark rock. This was Saddleback Light, a lonely rock barely wide enough for a lighthouse that sits alone in deep water marking the entrance to the bay from the open ocean. Years ago, the keepers of this light used to carry out a little soil each spring to grow their vegetables on this bare ledge. Inevitably, this washed away in winter storms, when waves wash completely over the rock. The only resemblance between Saddleback Ledge and Mark Island is that they both blink on six-second intervals. Unbelievably, I had gone more than twice the distance to Mark Island, and in the wrong direction. The compass, if only I'd listened, had been telling me so all along. I ran back to check my gas tank and found I had only a couple inches of fuel in the nearly empty tank.

John arrived a few minutes later and examined our situation. "I thought you were going the wrong way," he said.

"Then, goddamn it, why did you follow me?" I said, angry with him and even more so with myself.

"You wouldn't want to be out here alone, would you?" He reached over and handed me some butterscotch candies, something he never seemed to be without. I still remember how good they tasted, especially compared to the taste of fear in my mouth.

As the swells rolled beneath us, John checked his fuel and found he didn't have much more than I did, definitely not enough to reach town. We set out for the little town of Isle au Haut, about six miles away on the north end of a long island. We ran close to this island in case we did run out of gas, even though this meant passing through the gauntlet of rocks and ledges lurking along this shore. I listened for the engine to splutter and wondered what I'd do if it did. Using all the gas we had between us, we did just reach town and then had to wake some unfortunate people to buy more gas to make it home. That night I fell into bed and the next day I didn't go near my boat. The day after that we unloaded the leftover urchins in the morning, went back out diving on the same ledge, and sold two days' catch in the afternoon.

This time I was sure to leave for home with daylight to spare. We had again loaded our boats, but we had also swum completely around the ledge so there wasn't any reason to return again. I had a feeling of pride and something else too on this ride home, with every inch of deck space buried in urchins. I had loaded my boat, which is after all what urchin fishermen are supposed to do, and behind that success there were more than enough failures and mistakes to make it feel earned. But I also suspected that having found one good spot, there was one less to find. Could all those thousands of pounds of urchins we had harvested reappear by next year, or the one after, or the one after that?

In the six seasons since I set out with Tony in his inflatable, I've avoided that question, like most divers, by constantly searching for new fishing spots. By buying a faster boat and working east, all the way to the Canadian border, I've usually been able to find some urchins, sometimes lots, enough to move out of the cabin and buy a house of my own. Urchins do seem to reappear, in some places, but not in the green carpets that we originally found them, and not as quickly as they are harvested again. That's why it's no trouble parking on Main Street anymore. Less than half the divers who originally flooded into urchining are still fishing. Tony hasn't appeared in town for about a year; I've heard he's back in Bulgaria. Driving on the island, I recently noticed one former urchin boat, which had always returned to the pier low in the water, now sitting in the pasture on a poultry farm, turkeys perched along it from bow to stern.

On the last day of the last urchin season, I was fishing on a barren offshore island that my charts list as American territory, although there is a lighthouse here manned by Canadians and flying a maple leaf flag. It's disputed territory, about one hundred miles east of Penobscot Bay. There were several other boats I recognized from the pier this day. All of us had come east in search of better fishing. Out across the water, we could see the dark cliffs of Grand Manan and a scattering of offshore ledges. There were urchins over there, no doubt, and I'm sure every other diver felt as tempted as I did, but here was a limit we couldn't cross—the international border. Though we may all have been self-taught fishermen, we've gotten good at finding urchins. What we haven't found, though, is some notion of when we've found enough. So here we were, having fished our way to the end of the line. It reminded me of the night I ended up on Saddleback Ledge. The signals were there, but we've been choosing to see what we wanted to see. Suddenly, it was hard not to think that we should have paid attention to the compass.

Of course nobody took the last urchin that day. There are still some spots out there, and boats will be back fishing next season. But mine may not be among them. My boat is for sale. I don't like contributing to the depletion of the urchins, but I can't honestly say that's the whole reason. Since I've been catching less recently, I've been thinking a little more, and I've realized something. When I first moved to Maine and began diving I was primarily looking for freedom. Somewhere along the line that changed, and I began looking for urchins instead. They're not the same, I'm sure of it.

A DAY IN
THE LIFE

NANCY LORD, *who has setnet for*
salmon in Cook Inlet, Alaska, for
twenty-four seasons, depicts a day
in the skiff.

I WAKE BEFORE THE ALARM, as I always do on fishing mornings. Nights before fishing, I'm never really asleep but only waiting, monitoring the wind and water. For hours already, I've listened to the creek trickle and the songbirds warble. Now I sit up and look outside. The skiff—which I always check first—is still on the mooring, slack on its line and milk-cow tame. In the northeast sky, behind layers of low clouds, the sun glows with an oyster-shell light. The water lies as flat and dull as a pewter plate, its edge solid against the shore. It's my kind of fishing day. It might also be a very good one. We're in the third week of July, and the sockeye run should be close to its peak.

Ken stirs. "Wicked surf," he teases. He knows I've worried all night that the weather might change. He's never in his life worried about something he couldn't affect, and he prides himself on his ability to fall asleep the second he puts his head down and to sleep through the ragingest storm.

I get up and dress, then make myself a bowl of instant oatmeal. I learned a long time ago that if I didn't eat before going out to fish, something would happen that would keep me from eating until way past the point of low-blood-sugar grouchiness. It's one of the laws of fishing, like another I generally obey: take raingear or it'll be sure to rain. Ken, however, doesn't need to eat. He waits until the last minute to get out of bed and throw his clothes on.

Chest waders, flotation vest, raingear, hat, glasses, gloves, lunch box. I run down my mental checklist. Make sure Ken has his knife. We go out the door.

The tide is still coming in, an easy tide to set on. It's a good day of tides, all in all—large enough to move fish but not so large that the water will suck out as we watch or leave our low-water sets in rock piles. We carry our nets to the water's edge; then we carry the rowboat down, and Ken rows for the skiff.

Ken motors in and we load the nets. He does leads and I do corks, piling them into the center and port bins so they'll set out neatly over the stem, in order. We work quickly and silently, except when I ask, "This one?" before grabbing a new end and Ken grunts in response. Most inlet setnetters divide their allowed gear into three thirty-five-fathom nets—indeed, that's the rule for most areas—but we fish more nets of shorter lengths, as short as ten fathoms. Throughout the day we move, switch, replace, and tie these together, depending on location, stage of tide, height of tide, wind, waves, current, time in the season, and how things are going. Ken's the master at devising these fishing plans, and I'm the crew that follows directions and just sometimes suggests we move a net sooner or let one soak a little longer.

No fishing day is the same as any other, and we always think we can be a little smarter about how we fish, work harder, and catch more salmon.

Ken ties one end of the cork line to the setline at the high-tide mark and climbs back into the boat; I pull us out along the setline; Ken lowers and starts the motor, and at exactly 7:00 A.M. we set our first net. Leads and corks tumble out over the stem as I watch for snarls, and then, when we reach the end of the net, I wrap a bite around the setline and tie the net off.

We both turn expectantly to see what's happening behind us—whether fish are hitting the net, whether this will be a fishy day. I continue to watch behind us for splashes as we speed to the next set, but the corkline lies in a perfect gentle crescent against the current.

Our first sets go like clockwork, right down the beach. I love fishing when it's like this—the smooth, voiceless teamwork, the echoing clank of orderly corks over the stem, the practiced feel in my hands. I don't think so much as I am. The body knows; the memory is in my fingers, my shoulders, the knees that brace me. My physical self knows the grip of line, the quick tightening, the double hitch pulled over itself. If I stopped to think about what I do, I would surely fumble.

The nets are out, and I stoop to scrape seaweed and sand from the bare boat bottom. I'm sweating inside neoprene; the sun, breaking through the clouds, has lit the fireweed and monkey flowers on the hillside into a blaze. *The red salmon come when the fireweed blooms.* So they say; so the old-timers said about the sock-eyes, the money fish. We are ever hopeful.

To a fisherman, every fishing day is like Christmas, every net like presents to be opened. We never know what surprises we might find, only that there'll be something there and that it just might be, this time, the stuff of our dreams. That's why we fish on days when we catch just ten fish, and in storms, and on those days when nothing seems to go right, because the only thing predictable about fishing is that we won't catch anything if we don't have web in the water.

This morning our nets are not, however, loading up with fish. Ken blames the weather. It's too good; we need a storm to move fish up the inlet and in against our shore.

We start back through the nets, pulling leads and corks between us across the boat. Ken snaps loose a silver, worth just half a sockeye. The next fish is a silver, too. I slip a finger under one gill to peel away web and then shake the other side free. Every fish is its own puzzle to pull through, spin out of a twist, unbag, ungill, shake off. After years of practice the hands know, but my brain still clicks through its calculations, seeing the patterns. Ken looks glum, but at least we've got fish in the boat. This is another maxim among fishermen: We have to have one fish before we can have ten, and we have to have ten before we can have one hundred. We pull more net and Ken grabs for our first sockeye. "Now that's a beauty," he says.

The fish, still fighting fresh, leaps around the center bin as though it would throw itself from the boat. It smacks against the aluminum, splashes water, dances on its tail, and comes to rest against one of the still-twitching silvers. It is, in fact, a very good-looking fish, with a rounded body and a dainty-featured face, marred only by the gillnet's score across its head. It's the color of distant water, a soft gray-blue that deepens over its back into a metallic, nearly cobalt shine. Mirrory scales divide into contour lines like shifting plates of antique, tarnished mail.

The fish flops again, spattering blood that's hemorrhaging in thick, tomato-bright clots from its gills.

Wherever this ocean fish was headed, it was a long way from beginning its transformation to spawner. In another week or so we'll begin to catch an occasional wasted-looking sockeye, as flat as if it had been driven over by a truck and rose-colored, with a monstrous green head and hooked snout, all the better to scare its competitors once it reaches its spawning grounds. One will spill eggs like jewels into the boat, and we'll wonder if it lost its way home.

The fish makes a last flop and then lies quietly, its mouth working open and shut as though it's gasping for breath.

I'm well aware that some people think this cruel—killing fish like this, killing anything. They forget—or they never understood—that killing is part of how we live, the fish as well as the fisherman, the fish eater as well as the most committed vegan. Something dies that another may live. To me, the morality lies somewhere else—in what happens after the killing. When salmon are caught as "bycatch" in other fisheries and discarded overboard, or when someone takes a fish but leaves it on the bank or in his freezer to get freezer-burned, that's when behavior must be faulted.

These days, I frequently find myself examining that most basic of Dena'ina beliefs—that all things have wills and give or withhold themselves by choice, depending on whether a person shows respect or is insulting and wasteful. Among Peter Kalifornsky's Dena'ina belief stories is one about a young man who didn't listen to his elders about the proper treatment of animals. He left bones lying all around, and he killed mice cruelly and threw their bodies away. Other mice spoiled his meat, chewed up what was in his traps, and scampered over him in his sleep. At last he dreamed of going to the place where the animals wait to be reborn, and there he saw the ones whose bones had been walked over. They were horribly disfigured by his mistreatment and unable to return to human space.

Such lesson stories clearly helped enforce what the Dena'ina considered proper behavior and served the culture well in the long run. Would that our own laws and practices worked so well to feed people within a conservation framework.

What's a better end for a salmon—being chewed on by a seal, rotting to a slow death after spawning, or flopping into a fishing boat? From a salmon's point of view, the question has no meaning. The salmon's brain can't consider the options. The salmon doesn't think; it reacts. Nor does it feel pain as we know pain, not with its simple nervous system. The sockeye in the boat isn't gasping. It only looks that way to people, who know what it feels like to them to struggle for breath.

In the belief that a quick death is a humane one, sport fishermen often club their catch on the head. We knock only the lively kings with the back of the gaff, to keep them from bruising themselves—or us—as they thrash. The smaller fish are difficult to club without damaging their flesh, and they fade away quickly as it is. In any case, most fish we bring into the boat are already dead; once they're in the net, the web caught in their gills prevents them from working water through properly to extract oxygen. In fishermen's language, the fish "drown."

The best way to handle a fish—to be quick and to ensure good quality for whoever's going to eat it—is immediately to slit it gill to gill and drain out the blood and then place it on ice. Some commercial fisheries have moved in this direction, and the better care brings a higher price. Change is slow, though, in those fisheries that have traditionally dealt more in volume than in quality. Our processors still want salmon untouched by a knife, and they won't bring us ice.

We do the best we can. We don't step on our fish. We don't let them go dry on the beach or get beaten into noodles in the surf. We keep them out of the sun.

Our count now is up to eight—four sockeyes, four silvers. There's the sockeye with the metallic shine and another that's smaller and greener, the silver with a thick tail and two lankier ones that took like twins. These are the fish in a "mixed-stock fishery," where salmon headed for a variety of large and small, glacial and clear, fast- and slow-running rivers and lake systems mingle before turning right or left and separating out. Bluebacks belong to one river, bullet shapes to another. That's the beauty and the essential genius of salmon: the custom design that matches each separate stock to color and stream flow, the natural conditions in their different home waters. As the big kings evolved to dig spawning beds below the scoured depths of powerful rivers, the sleekest sockeyes perfected their ability to move through shallows, the strongest to throw themselves up falls, and the greenest to blend into mossy depths.

I soak a piece of burlap over the side and cover the fish, a little brown mound in the center of the boat. Across the inlet, the sky is streaked with rain. The time is 7:40.

"How many?" Ken shouts as he cuts the motor. This is one of our games—to guess the number of fish in a net. Ken has not only much better eyesight than I do but also an uncanny ability to predict what lies under the surface of the thick flour-roux water.

I always make a conservative guess. That way, when there are more, I feel lucky to have them. "Three," I say, leaning from the bow to grab the cork line. I already see two heads.

Ken guesses six.

There's a silver along the lead line right away, and then the next pull of net brings in a big, headless sockeye, all gnashed red meat and dripping eggs. Ken curses and we both look around.

The seal's right there, just fifty feet off the outside buoy, bobbing up to get a better look at us. The way it stretches from the water makes it look as though it's standing on something solid, on tiptoe. Ken and I both yell, and I grab an aluminum post and bang it three times against the boat. I always think this should sound to a seal like gunfire, but it never seems to have much effect. This seal—a harbor seal, the most plentiful of Alaska's seals—merely ducks under and reappears seconds later a little farther downstream. "Go away," I yell as I might at a dog loitering around a picnic table.

The seal lowers itself to whisker level and stays where it is, watching us. It has a bowling-ball head, dark and shiny, and saucer eyes. Most people think seals are cute; they would have a completely different opinion if seals had hard, little eyes and ferocious fangs—if a seal looked, for example, anything like a bat. Seals, in our modern classification system, are closely related to Bambi, and everybody loves Bambi. As a culture we Americans have Bambified ourselves away from any real understanding of individual species and their importance in the ecological picture.

Sometimes, grudgingly, I, too, will admit to being taken with fawns, bunnies, puppies, the baby seal that once swam to our boat wailing and still wearing its umbilicus—all soft and cuddly animals, cartoon creatures with fluttering eyelashes. *Bambi* was the very first movie I was taken to as a child, and I was struck to the soul with empathy. It was many years before I came to understand that there could be cultural systems even within my own country with beliefs different from and as strong as any I grew up with. This understanding came to me with pinprick clarity the day a Native woman told me about the time *Bambi* played in her village: when Bambi and Bambi's mother came on the screen, all the boys in the audience raised their arms as if to shoot.

At least cartoons were recognized as cartoons then. A more recent movie, about a seal named Andre, stars as Andre not a seal at all but a young sea lion. Every few years we spot a sea lion in the inlet, and even from a distance—with most of the animal underwater—it's easy enough to distinguish it from a seal. Much larger, more brown than gray, a sea lion swims and rolls along the surface, tossing its flippers. It has a pointed, dog-like face and visible ears. Out of the water, it has longer limbs and an altogether different, more upright shape. Perhaps it was the sea lion's superior posture that attracted Hollywood, or perhaps they're easier than seals to train or have some other cinematic advantage; I don't know. Hollywood didn't care about correctly depicting a marine mammal, and most viewers, more familiar with E.T. and the Little Mermaid than with either seals or sea lions, didn't have a clue.

Ken keeps an eye on the seal as he works to free the mangled fish. With the head gone, there's no good way to grip it, and the web is tight in the flesh and tangled with bones.

It's not that we begrudge the seals having a meal; it's just that we think they ought to get it on their own. We can only guess how many gilled fish they steal from us. Often there's little evidence—just an empty or near-empty net. Their usual technique is to grab fish by the heads and pull them cleanly through, though sometimes they tear the heads off salmon that are too fat to slide through the web, and rarely, like vandals or epicurean wastrels, they swim along a net and bite out just the sweet bellies.

Ken finally frees the fish and it drops into the boat with a lifeless thud, like a sack of wet sugar. Since we can't sell it, we'll take it home for ourselves. The seal has ducked out of sight, on its way, we imagine, to our next net. We rush to beat it there, though we know our slapping around in a tin boat is no competition to a creature born to the water and shaped like a torpedo. At most, we can try to keep our nets picked clean, to avoid leaving fish dangling like so many buffet items.

Seals—though in recent years they've grown both more numerous and bolder along our beach—have, of course, been a part of the life here for as long as anyone knows. The traditional Dena'ina relied on them for their skins, meat, oil, bladders—all their various parts, down to their whiskers. It took twenty seals to make one large skin boat.

After Americans brought the canned salmon industry to Alaska, seals, despised for eating fish that could otherwise be caught by fishermen, were systematically slaughtered. For most of the past hundred years the government paid a bounty on their noses and even, for a time in the 1950s, dynamited seals at the mouths of salmon rivers. At the peak of bounty hunting in the 1960s, 70,000 seals were taken in a single year. Not until 1972 were seals protected; the federal Marine Mammal Protection Act prohibits the hunting of seals and other marine mammals except by Natives for subsistence purposes.

Today, although seals are notoriously hard to count, biologists estimate there are about 250,000 harbor seals statewide, a population considered healthy. Alarm has arisen only recently over apparent sharp declines in the Gulf of Alaska and the Bering Sea. Those two areas are, perhaps not coincidentally, the locations of aggressive harvesting of bottom fish by factory trawlers.

When we began fishing, we rarely had problems with seals raiding our nets. Most seals in the area kept to the south of us, to the clearer water of the river sloughs and the easy hauling out along the bars. Whether population growth has pushed them north or they've simply learned how to find an easy meal, I don't know. I imagine the sound of our outboard calls seals to our nets in the same way the grind of an electric can opener calls a hungry dog to a kitchen.

Not too many years ago, Alfred and Ann Topkok, Natives originally from the coast near Nome, fished a few miles north of us. We sometimes saw Alfred boat past our camp as he went to hunt seals, and when we visited them at their camp Ann showed us baby booties she sewed from the spotted silver pup skins.

Alfred and Ann are gone now, and the local seals are probably less hunted today than since before the Dena'ina first arrived on these beaches. Perhaps they are also as fearless as any seals, ever.

When the tide's high, it's time to move nets.

We tear over the flat water at full throttle, the shore alongside us a narrow band, the water everywhere high and capacious, swirling in muddy boils. Darkening clouds make a patchwork of the wide sky. I lift my chin and breathe deeply of the rushing air, lick my lips clean of salt and splashed gurry. We pass under a low-flying flock of gulls, and for a time we neither gain nor lose on them but keep their exact pace, floating with them in the same ethereal dimension. We stare at each other, the birds and I. Their wings sweep up and down. I could be a feather, a barb of a feather, one of the one million fluted and hooked barbules of a single feather. I could be the floating lightness of down.

This, too, is a part of fishing.

We take a break and go ashore, clipping our bowline to a net. The sun has broken through and beams down warm on the sand, rumpled with old bear prints above the tide line. I shed my gloves and vest, peel neoprene to the waist, open the lunch box, and take a long drink of water. I make myself comfortable against a rock and unwrap a Fluffernutter sandwich, an obscenely high-fat, high-sugar, sticky concoction of peanut butter and marshmallow cream. Ken and I both ate these as children and somehow came back to them for fishing foods even though the thought of eating one in any other circumstance makes me gag.

I've taken just two bites before Ken spots a seal at one of our nets and we rush back out. We pick fish, and then we sit on one net and then another, waiting for more fish, watching for seals. The water's so still we can both see and hear salmon moving past—jumpers behind us, a finner leaving a ripple, small fish squirting through our nets. The jumpers leap elegantly into the light; like dancers or basketball players, they defy gravity to hang in the air, stop time. We watch one launch itself several times, closer, closer, closer to a net, and then we don't see it again. Another, instead of slipping back tail first or landing on its side, traces a high arc, like a diver springing from a board to make a clean, headfirst entry into a pool.

Why fish jump is one of those questions that may forever entertain us with possible answers. Surely one good reason is to escape predators—in this case, the seals that continue to pop up around us. Some biologists, noting more comely females than humpbacked mates among pink salmon jumpers, believe that at least some jumping has to do with females trying to loosen their eggs. I think it's entirely possible that fish may appreciate, on some level, the sensation of leaving the water, of feeling air ruffling through their gills and the blast of all that white light on their eyeballs.

Off to the south, a skiff at Kustatan glides out toward the rising bar. As we pick one fish, two more hit the net, kicking up splashes of water. Ken shouts, "They're really popping now." This is what our former neighbor Lou used to say before he quit fishing and we bought his sites, and it's become part of both our lexicon and our folklore, our ritualistic good-luck chant.

The tide goes out. We pull nets from the beach and reset them between offshore anchors. When we return to pick the first of them, I've only just lifted the cork line and begun to gather web when a huge, purple face floats up out of the murk.

"King!" The word squeaks through my teeth. We rarely see king salmon after the beginning of July. Ken squeezes into the bow, and I let my side of the net go as he studies the way the fish lies against the net and begins to bunch web around it. Kings are too large to gill, and when they don't simply bounce off a net they often only rest up against it or are snagged by a single tooth. They can be gone in a flash.

Ken loves nothing in fishing more than catching king salmon, and he is at his most intense at this moment. This is his art. He works quickly, delicately, wrapping web around the passive fish and then grabbing for the bundle.

The fish comes alive. It thrashes with violent, tortuous twists of its body, spraying water ten feet high that falls on us in sheets. But Ken has hoisted it over the side, and it dumps into the boat to finish beating itself out among the little fish. It's not as large as its shapely head made it out to be—perhaps thirty-five pounds—but it's a fresh ocean fish, still gleaming, its spotted tail unfrayed. It's rounded like an old-fashioned pickle barrel. Near its tail, a couple of scaleless circles the size of nickels mark where lamprey eels caught a ride through a far sea.

On average, our kings are smaller than this, but they can reach Bunyanesque proportions. Earlier this summer, a sport fisherman across the inlet caught an eighty-nine-pounder. A catch like that on rod and reel must surely be a thrill, but the burgeoning sport fishery that's developed around kings threatens those who fish commercially. Across the inlet more than here, commercial seasons have been shortened—targeted to sockeyes and timed to avoid the early- and late-running king. In addition, fishermen there have begun their own campaign of releasing live kings from their nets; they hope this altruism will keep them from losing more fishing time. I try not to be overly pessimistic, but if history is any indicator, the battle over fish won't be won by the commercial side. There are many more of them than there are of us. Already the "sports" get the main allocation of silvers as well as the kings, and now they're casting into the political system for more sockeyes, our money fish.

We head for the scow to make a delivery and lighten the boat. As we motor past George and his crew, bent over a net, I slip my hands into our king's gills and hoist it high for them to admire—and envy. George pushes the air with his hands and yells across the water, "Throw it back! Throw it back!"

After we've tied up alongside the scow, Ken and I pitch our salmon. We grip them by their heads, tossing sockeyes into one tote, silvers into another. We keep our own silent counts. The fish drip slime; stiff and discolored now, they handle like sticks of firewood. Ken lifts the king last, steps up onto the scow, and drops it in on top of the sockeyes.

To our north, Mount Spurr towers whitely over the land. A volcano as raw as the beginning of time, Spurr belched ash and steam and nearly brought down a passenger jet just a couple of years back. Its Dena'ina name, which translates to One That Is Burning Inside, attests to its eruptive fame; of the four volcanoes in the region that have been active in my time, it's the only one whose traditional name refers specifically to its status as a volcano.

Today, as we chase fish in its shadow, scientists are poised on Spurr's rim with a NASA robot, the world's most sophisticated, designed for exploring Mars. The spiderlike machine, named *Dante II*, will descend into the crater on its computer-programmed legs and then beam up video and geochemical data to a satellite. I take a minute to marvel at the juxtaposition—fishermen on water as perilous as it's ever been, engaged in the same basic hunt for food that people have pursued since day one, and space technology on the mountain, as state of the art as it gets. What a world we live in, that can accommodate both in the same here and now.

The reason we chose setnetting over other fisheries in the beginning was largely for its simplicity: its basic, low-tech nature. All we really needed was a skiff, a net, and a couple of pairs of hands. When the world's oil was drained, we told ourselves, we would row our boat with oars; we would work with the tides. And yet, I'm surely no Luddite. I follow the space program with a keen interest in all its inventions and discoveries. I want to know about the farthest stars just as I want to know about the bottom of the ocean and the inside of a salmon's brain. If the "crater critter" designed for Mars can also totter down into an active volcano and add to our collective understanding about rocks and gases, that's gravy.

Rachel Carson wrote that the picture of the sea that existed at midcentury was "like a huge canvas on which the artist has indicated the general scheme of his grand design but on which large blank areas await the clarifying touch of his brush." That picture, surely, still has plenty of blank space. Why do fish jump?

Where do the belugas go when they leave the inlet? What's the reason for the sudden sharp decline in the numbers of seals and sea lions in the Gulf of Alaska? Only recently have marine biologists discovered that the deep ocean floor, long thought to be a biological desert, is in fact home to a diversity of species rivaling those thought to exist on the planet's land surface—somewhere between 10 and 100 million different species. Imagine the possibilities for undersea discoveries in light of the fact that an entire species of large terrestrial mammal—the goatlike *sao la* of Vietnam—escaped scientific notice until 1992. Although I don't doubt that someday humans and their machines will reside away from the earth's surface, I also believe with absolute certainty that no artificial creation or substitute world will ever be as infinitely interesting and lovely—not to mention munificent— as this one and only earth.

We motor past George again, and this time he holds up a fish. It's a pink salmon, we can tell even at a distance—skinny as a knife blade, weighing less than two pounds. If we were closer I'd hear George saying, "I caught one of them spotted-tail fishes, too."

At low water we move nets again, back around the point. These offshore sets we make with regular anchors, whose buoys have popped to the surface now that the tide's out and the current has eased. It takes my whole body to lift each anchor while Ken motors into the current; from the soles of my feet to my aching shoulders, every muscle pulls. For each set, I hook the anchor on the gunnel and tie off the outside end of the net to its buoy. We motor to shore; I hop out and fetch the onshore buoy and tie the inside end of the net to it. Then we motor out again, spilling net behind us. When the net is straight and tight, I drop the anchor over.

This time, though, we screw up. One of the nets catches on

itself, and a lump of corks and web flies out of the boat all at once. Ken slows and tugs on it, but it doesn't come free, and then the current swings us into rocks, where we bang the prop. We pull back on the net to try again, but as we back up with the motor in gear the net flags, and suddenly there's that abrupt clothy sound that's always like a kick to my gut. The prop has caught web and ground to a stop. Ken swears and slams his hand against the boat, then climbs onto the seat and balances over the transom to begin twisting and untwisting and peeling the tightly wound web from the prop. I'm grateful for the calm weather, that we're not caught in surf and having to hack away with a knife while the boat pitches.

All afternoon, seals continue to plague us. We pick nets and find only viscera or telltale catches in the web, and one very large new seal-shaped hole. We break sticks, throw back flounders, and shake out the aptly named jellyfish that roll in the net and fall to pieces like Jell-O taken too soon from a mold. We pause to eat again from our lunch box. I peel an orange with hands that smell as foul as the insides of my leaky rubber gloves. A seal surfaces well outside the net with a flopping fish in its mouth. It bobs high and looks as though it's juggling the fish as part of a circus act, though it must only be trying for a better grip. We continue to pick fish, one by one by one. We're catching more sockeyes than silvers and are glad of that.

Ken chants, "One fish, two fish, red fish, blue fish." I try to remember the words to a Russian peasant rhyme that counts dresses and sacks of flour and magpies. Gulls squabble over something in the rocks and are silenced when an eagle lands in their midst. Eagles are, above all, scavengers, which is one reason Ben Franklin didn't think they were particularly suited to represent our country. "He is a bird of bad moral character," Franklin wrote of the eagle after it was selected as our national symbol over his own favorite, the turkey: "Like those among men who live by sharping and robbing, he is generally poor and often very lousy." In places with clearer water, eagles are known to dive for fish, but here they rarely even circle the water when salmon are finning or jumping. We've never seen one catch its own fish, though we did once see one carry off a wiggling one.

When the tide comes in, we move our nets back up the beach.

At 6:30 we begin to pick up nets, and at 7:00 P.M. on the dot we pull the last piece of web from the water and head in to dump the whole pile on the beach. We deliver again to the scow, tossing our afternoon fish into our totes while George and his crew do the same into theirs. The tender will be by later, sometime during the night; we have only to leave our permit card and some outgoing mail in the "mailbox" tacked to one end of the scow.

While Ken fills our gas tanks from a barrel we keep on the scow, I pour water over the fish and fit the covers back on the totes. I summon a last spurt of energy to wash down the boat, coil lines, rinse the burlap and stretch it to dry. My legs are bruised and my shoulder creaks. The muscles in my hands are tight, and my little finger got squashed between an anchor and the skiff's rail. My chest aches from being pressed into the bow every time I lifted a cork line. I hurt with the hurt of a full day's work, hard work done well.

Before we leave the scow, I take a look into George's totes. We highboated him again, just barely. We have 262 fish for the day.

Back at the cabin, I strip off my fishing clothes and wash my face and arms. I scrub aluminum stain from my forearms until they're pink, and then I pick off fish scales with a fingernail. Each scale pops off like a brittle flake, leaving a circle on my skin like a slightly gathered pockmark. There's something satisfying in this picking of scales, even in finding a last, crisp scale days later on the back of my arm—better than gold stars, they're the medals that remind us how we live with fish.

"We work hard for our fish," I say to Ken. "We work harder for two hundred than we do for a thousand." It's been a long time since we caught anything near a thousand fish in one day, but it's true that when there are more fish to pick, we pick more and work our gear less. It's trying to maximize possibility that's so hard.

Ken yanks off his hip boots and drops them with heavy clunks in the center of the floor. He has mud on his cheeks and fish slime glistening in his beard, and his hair is so matted his scalp shows through. The back of his neck has darkened one more shade. He smiles a tired smile and says, "You can expect to find a little extra in your paycheck this week."

The leftover pizza warming in the oven has begun to fill the cabin with its burnt-cheese and tomato smell. Ken asks, "How many sets do you think we made?"

The individual pieces of the day are becoming a blur to me, but I know Ken recalls every set, every circumstance of every set, every pick of every set. He has a memory that can recall the play of a bridge hand six months earlier, and he carries a map in his head for every city he's ever visited and every road he's driven, just as he knows every contour of our beach and its every rock.

"How many?"

Ken lists our sets in order, holding up a finger for each. "Cove, Point, Emmet's, South Point, Eddyset with a short net, Eddyset with a full net, 12K, short net at Point, Eddyset deep, Lou's, Emmet's deep, Point deep, short net at Slide, full net at Slide, Rock, Campset, Emmet's, Cove. . . ."

Eighteen. The recitation is like poetry to me, but it's poetry I want only to wash over me at the bottom of deepest, absolutely motionless sleep. Eat, then sleep. The next fishing day is four days away.

UNDER
MONTAUK LIGHT

PETER MATTHIESSEN, *in this excerpt
from* Men's Lives, *gives a rare
autobiographical glimpse of his three
years of commercial fishing and
running a charter boat off Montauk,
New York.*

THAT SUMMER OF 1954, the charter season was well under way when the *Merlin* arrived. There was one slip left at the town dock, right across from one of the pioneer charter men, John Messbauer, and we soon found out why nobody had wanted it; the current was strong and the approach narrow, and the one way to back a single-engine boat into this berth was a sequence of swirling maneuvers at full throttle. Unless executed with precision, these maneuvers would strand the boat across the bows of neighboring boats, held fast by the current, while the customers wondered how their lives had been consigned to such lubberly hands. Before I got the hang of it, there was more than one humiliating episode, not helped by the embarrassment of my trusty mate, who would shrug, wince, and roll his eyes, pretending to the old salts along the dock that if only this greenhorn would let him take the helm, he could do much better.

At thirty-two feet, the *Merlin* was small by Montauk standards, and she lacked the customary flying bridge, not to mention upholstered fighting chairs, teak decks, and chrome. We had no old customers to depend on, and no big shiny cockpit to attract new ones, and Captain Al Ceslow on the *Skip II*, for whom John had worked as mate the previous summer, was the only man in the whole fleet of forty-five-odd boats who would offer advice or help of any kind. However, it was soon July, and fish and fishing parties both abounded (and were biting hard, said cynical Jimmy Reutershan, who was bluefishing out of Montauk in his Jersey skiff, and who believed strongly in lunar tide tables as a guide to the feeding habits of fish and man; he had noticed, he said, that *Homo sapiens*, wandering the docks with a glazed countenance, would suddenly stir into feeding frenzy, signing up boats with the same ferocity—and at the same stage of the tide—that *Pomatomus saltatrix* would strike into the lures around the Point).

And so, from the first, the *Merlin* did pretty well. We made up in eagerness and love of fishing what we lacked in experience of our new trade, we worked hard to find fish for our clients, and except on weekends, when we ran two six-hour trips each day, we sailed overtime without extra charge whenever the morning had been unproductive. Also, unlike many of the charter men, who seemed to feel that anglers of other races belonged on "barf barges"—the party or bottom-fishing boats—we welcomed anyone who came along. One day we sailed a party of Chinese laundrymen from up-Island, each one equipped with a full-sized galvanized garbage can. Their one recognizable utterance was "Babylon." Conveying to us through their Irish-American interpreter that trolling for hard-fighting and abundant bluefish did not interest them, they said that they wished to be taken to the three coal barges sunk southwest of the Point in a nor'easter, a well-known haunt of the black sea bass so highly esteemed in Chinese cookery. Once the hulks were located, they set out garbage cans along the cockpit and pinhooked sea bass with such skill (to cries of "Bobby-lon!") that every man topped off his garbage can. The half ton of sea bass that they took home more than paid the cost of the whole charter, while gladdening every Oriental heart in western Suffolk.

Another day, three Shinnecock Indian chiefs in quest of "giants" (they were soon off to Alaska, they declared, to shoot giant brown bear) took us all the way to Rosie's Hole off the coast of Rhode Island in vain pursuit of giant bluefin. Because of the fuel, the barrel of bunker chum bought at Ted's freezer, and the installation of the *Merlin*'s heavy tuna chair, the trip was expensive even for car dealers from Washington, D.C., where the three chiefs spent most of the year, passing themselves off as black men. The chiefs liked us because the other boats had refused their trade, and we liked them because they spent their money cheerfully, though they saw neither hide nor hair of giants.

No other boat got a bluefin that day either, and John and I were relieved as well as disappointed; in theory, we knew what to do once the huge fish took the mackerel bait that we drifted down the current (crank up the engine, cast off the buoy on the anchor, and chase after the exhilarated fish before it stripped the last line off the reel), but being inexperienced with giant tuna, we foresaw all sorts of possibilities for dangerous error. Big blue-fin may be ten feet long, and nearly a half ton in weight, and the speed and power of these fish are awesome. (In the *Merlin*'s former life in Ipswich Bay, a passenger had come too close to the blur of green line leaving the tub after a horse mackerel had been harpooned. The line whipped around his leg and snapped him overboard and down thirty feet under the sea before some-one grabbed a hatchet and whacked the line where it sizzled across the brass strip on the combing. Had that hatchet not been handy, and wits quick, the nosy passenger would have lost his life.)

Toward the end of the homeward journey across Block Island Sound, I encouraged the chiefs to stop on Shagwong Reef and pick up a few bluefish to take home for supper. The thwarted giant-killers had consoled themselves with gin on the long voy-age, and one man agreed to fish for blues if we would strap him into the big fighting chair and give him that thick tuna rod to work with, so that he could imagine what it must be like to deal masterfully with one of those monsters back at Rosie's Hole. When the strike came, it failed to bend even the rod tip, but the angler, cheered on by his friends, set the hook with a mighty backward heave into the fighting chair. "It's charging the boat!" his assistants yelled as something broke the surface; the only porgy in the *Merlin*'s history that ever went for a trolled bluefish lure had been snapped clear out of the water by that heave and skimmed through the air over the wake in a graceful flight that a flying fish might well have envied.

So much did all three chiefs enjoy this exciting fishing experience that they felt obliged to lie down in the cockpit, collapsed with laughter. "No mo' bluefishin'," they cried helplessly, waving us on. "Giant pogie's good enough!" Once ashore, they gave both of us giant tips, thanked us as "scholars and gentlemen" for a splendid outing, and went off merrily down the dock with their souvenir porgy. Next time they visited these parts, they said, they would bring their girlfriends down to meet us (which they did).

Not all our clients were such good sports as the three chiefs. A charter demands six hours at close quarters with company that is rarely of one's choice, and often there are two charters each day. While most of our people were cooperative and pleasant, others felt that their money entitled them to treat captain and mate as servants, and one ugly customer advised me even before the *Merlin* cleared the breakwater that he knew all about the charter men's tricks and cheating ways. I turned the boat around, intending to put him on the dock, but his upset friends made him apologize.

Another day the motor broke down on Shagwong Reef in clear, rough weather of a northwest wind. A cockpit full of queasy passengers wanted to know why I did not call the Coast Guard. The truth was that their captain, having had no time to go to New York and apply to the Coast Guard for a captain's license, was running a renegade boat, and was stalling for time until Al Ceslow in the *Skip II* could finish his morning charter and tow us in. One of the men, under the horrified gaze of his newlywed wife, actually panicked, shrieking at the other passengers that the captain's plan was to put this death craft on the

rocks; I had to grab him by the shirtfront and bang him up
against the cabinside to calm him down. (On another charter
boat one morning—we could hear the shouts and crashing right
over the radio-telephone—a disgruntled client had to be slugged
into submission, with the skipper bellowing for police assistance
at the dock.)

The *Merlin* was plagued by persistent hazing from two charter
boats that now and then would turn across our wake, out on the
Elbow, and cut off all four of our wire lines; no doubt other new
boats were welcomed in this way as well. Wire line, lures, and
leaders are expensive, and because wire line is balky stuff, it
often took most of an hour of good fishing tide to re-rig the lines
for the unhappy customers. The two big captains of these big
boats (both of them sons of earlier big captains who now ran big
enterprises on the docks) were successful charter men who had
nothing to fear from the small *Merlin*; often this pair trolled side
by side, chatting on radio-telephones from their flying bridges.
One day off Great Eastern Rock, heart pounding with mixed fear
and glee, and deaf to all oaths and shouts of warning, I spun
my wheel and cut across both of their fat sterns, taking all eight
of their wire lines at a single blow.

In the long stunned silence on all three boats, John Cole said
quietly, "Oh boy," and suggested a long detour to Connecticut.
"Those guys are going to be waiting for us on the dock," he said,
"and they are BIG." But there was no reception party, and our
lines were never cut again. Not long thereafter one of these skippers called the *Merlin* on "the blower," passing terse word in the
charter man's way that he was into fish: "See where we are, Cap,
down to the east'rd? Better come this way."

One day on the ocean side, working in close to the rocks west
of the Light, we picked up a striped bass on the inshore line and
a bluefish on the outside; we did this on three straight passes,
and probably could have done it again if we had not been late

for our afternoon charter and had to head in. So far as we knew, those three bass, and three more the next day from the same place, were the only stripers taken out of Montauk for nearly a fortnight in the bass dog days of late July. From that day on, we had to wait to fish this spot until the fleet went in at noon, because other boats began to tail us with binoculars, in the same way that the *Merlin* sometimes tailed Gus Pitts when the *Marie II* worked the striper holes along the beach, watching his mate strip out the wire to guess the depth at which Cap'n Gus was trolling, or glimpse what lure he was rigging to his rods.

On days when we had no charter, we went out handling for blues, heading west past Culloden Point and Fort Pond Bay to Water Fence, at the western boundary of the land acquired by the Proprietors of Montauk, where the cattle fence that once kept East Hampton's livestock on the Montauk pastures during the summer had extended out into the water; past the walking dunes, a sand flow at the old forest edge on the north side of Hither Hills; past Goff Point and the fallen chimney of the abandoned bunker factory at Hicks Island. East of Cartwright Shoal, the shallow waters teemed with small three-pound "tailor" bluefish that bit as fast as the hand lines were tossed overboard, and brought a good price on the market.

The *Merlin* was no longer a renegade boat (I got my license in late summer), and no one ignored her radio queries or disdained to call her; she had already built up a list of clients who wished to charter her again the following year. The bluefishing was strong and steady, and offshore the school tuna were so thick that by leaving one fish on the line while boating the other three, we could keep all four lines loaded almost continually until the box had overflowed. On some days, poor John, skidding around on the bloody deck, exhausted from pumping the strong tuna off the bottom for the weary customers, would send me wild-eyed signals to get the boat away from the goddamn fish, maybe show the clients a nice shark or ocean sunfish.

But there were days in that first summer when the *Merlin* sat idle at the dock, and in August the price of bluefish was so low that hand-lining would not make us a day's pay. Bass remained scarce in the dead of summer, and one morning when his boat was hauled out for repairs, we decided to show our friend Al Ceslow our secret striper spot on the ocean shore west of the Light.

In the days before, there had been offshore storms, and the big smooth swells collapsing on the coast would make it difficult to work close to the rocks. We also knew that Cap'n Gus, widely regarded as the best striped bass fisherman ever to sail under the Light, had put three boats on those rocks in his twenty years of hard experience. And so we rode in as close as we dared on the backs of the broad waves, letting the lures coast in on the white wash. We were not close enough, and tried to edge in closer, keeping an eye out for the big freak sea that would break offshore and wash us onto the rock shore under the cliffs. Unlike the established boats, we were not booked solid a full year in advance, and the loss of the *Merlin*—we could not yet afford insurance—would mean the end of our careers as charter boatmen, apart from endangering our lives.

The wave we feared rose up behind us, sucking the water off the inshore rocks, and as Al or John shouted, I spun the wheel and gave the *Merlin* her full throttle. With a heavy thud, our trusty boat struck into the midsection of a high, clear, cresting wave, and for one sickening moment, seemed to lose headway. Then the wave parted, two walls of green water rushed past the cockpit, over our heads, and the boat sprang up and outward, popping free. If we ever fished that spot again, I do not recall it.

Hurricane Carol, on the last day of August 1954, blew so hard at Montauk that I ran the *Merlin* at eight knots in her slip in order to ease the pressure on her lines. At high water, only the spile tops on the town dock were visible above the flood, which carried loose boats and capsized hulks down toward the breakwater. In leaping from the stern to fetch more lines or lend a hand with another boat, one could only pray that the town dock was still there.

The hurricane's eye passed over about noon, in an eerie silver light and sulfurous pall. Then the winds struck in again, subsiding only as our fuel ran low in midafternoon. By evening we felt free to leave for home, but could not get there; the storm seas, surging through the dunes, had reopened the old strait in a new channel into Napeague Harbor, knocking down one of the radio towers that transmitted to the ships at sea. Until late that night, when the tide turned and the sea subsided, we were stranded on Montauk, which was once again an island.

I was not sorry when the season was over and I ran my boat back west to Three Mile Harbor. To judge from the sour, contemptuous remarks that were traded back and forth on the radio-telephones, a lot of charter men were opportunists, out for an easy dollar that was not forthcoming. Almost all of us made good money between July 4 and Labor Day, but only the best boats in the fleet, with the longest lists of faithful customers (these were the charter captains we admired, the skilled and happy ones who loved to fish) could make it in the colder days of spring and autumn. The *Merlin* was not yet one of those boats, and we quit right after Labor Day, to make the most of the first weeks of the scallop season. It was a poor season that year, with so many scallops destroyed by Hurricane Carol.

The *Merlin*'s summer in 1955 was busy and successful, but I ended my second year of chartering with the same feeling. I chartered because it paid for my boat and I made a living out of doors in the season between haul-seining and scalloping; I scalloped and hauled seine because I liked the work, and liked the company of the commercial fishermen, the baymen.

One day in the late spring of 1956, on the *Merlin*'s radio, I picked up the wild shouts of a draggerman up around Noman's, south of Martha's Vineyard, beaming the news to anyone who cared that he was rich. Apparently his dragger had hove to overnight in the thick fog so prevalent in June, when the sea is still cold and the air much warmer, and at daybreak had found herself surrounded by a company of migrating swordfish, which lay dull as logs on the smooth surface. The striker harpooned thirty of the weary fish before the rest took alarm, and the dragger was now on her way into New Bedford to celebrate her extraordinary good fortune.

In those days most swordfish were taken by big draggers, which were fitted out with a spotting tower and a long harpoon stand, or pulpit, extending forward from the boat's bow. The "finning" fish with its dorsal and caudal fins like black curved knives slitting the surface was struck by a detachable brass dart or lily with tandem barbs, fitted to an eighteen-to-twenty–inch iron rod inserted in the tip of a long wood harpoon pole perhaps fourteen feet long. The lily, which pulls free of the iron when it is struck into the fish, remains fastened to several hundred feet of line coiled in a tub; this line is secured to a wood keg that is thrown over the side to mark the location of the fish and also tire it. The wild "green" fish cannot be horsed into the boat but must be tended carefully by hand, to be sure that the dart is not pulled free.

In previous summers, swordfish had been scarce, and I wanted a chance to strike one from the *Merlin*. On a certain slick calm day of June, Stewart Lester recalls, "We made a haul down Napeague and didn't do nothin' but the ocean was dead calm, so we decided to take your boat, go get us a swordfish. I think

Richard was with us; anyways, we went off southwest of the Point, and it wasn't too long before I seen a fin. Ol' Pete here"— he nudged my arms—"was at the wheel, but when I seen that fin and started forward to the pulpit, Pete hollers, 'Hell, no, Stewart, this is my boat and I'm gonna stick the first one!' "

Among the draggermen, there were a number of great sword-fish "strikers." Stewart's cousin, draggerman John Erickson, Jr., says that the best of them rarely or never missed with the har-poon, even when the fish was well below the surface. One miss out of ten might be accounted for by the fish flaring off at the last second, but as Elisha Ammon liked to say, "If you miss two out of ten, you get off the pulpit, let somebody else try it." Even men like these, who made a mystique of swordfishing (Johnnie Erickson's record for these waters was nine in a single day, al-though he has taken twice that number off Nova Scotia), were very nervous on the boat's approach, which required as much skill and precision as the strike itself.

And so I was wound tight with expectation as I ran forward to the pulpit, freed the long harpoon lashed across its rails, and stared ahead at the two curved blades tracing a thin slit on the water. The beautiful fish was of moderate size, less than two hundred pounds, a swift and graceful distillation of blue-silver sea (larger fish are darker, and look brown). Its round eye, a few inches beneath the shining surface, appeared huge. I was still staring when the night-blue fish shivered and shot away, leaving only the deep sun rays in the sea.

Years later, recalling this bad moment, Stewart grinned. "If that had been my old man, now, you would have got nowhere near that pulpit. That time with my Uncle Bill when my dad beat somebody to the harpoon by sliding down the guy wire from the spotting tower, there was a turnbuckle at the bottom where the cable wasn't spliced, and he ran four or five of them wires right through them burned hands. Blood all over the boat,

I heard, but he never noticed, not until after he had struck that fish. Anyway, I took the wheel, put you right on that fish, too, but you never struck him, never even let go of the pole; you just stared at him, and you know why? You seen the eye. My old man taught me never to look at the eye, just at the dorsal fin, because right alongside the fin is where you strike him. That fish rolled his eye out and he fixed you, and you ain't the first. Nobody believes how big that eye is, and by the time they get over the surprise, the bow is past him and that fish is gone."

By 1956, Pete Scott and John Cole had despaired of making a living as commercial fishermen; both departed the South Fork for jobs that might take better advantage of their education. That spring I hauled seine with Ted, Stewart, and Milt, and sometimes Capt. Frank's son Lewis Lester, or whoever else might fill in on the crew. When there was no weather on the beach, I sailed an occasional charter out of Three Mile Harbor, and that summer, rather than hunt up a new mate, I avoided the dogfight at Montauk, where too many boats, fouling one another's lines around the Point, had taken most of the fun out of the fishing. I sailed out of Montauk only once, in late July, when the *Merlin* was hired by a man named Peter Gimbel, who did not show up. I took his friends out anyway, and upon returning, we learned that Gimbel had left for Nantucket the night before. He was the first diver on the wreck of the *Andrea Doria*, which had just been sunk by another ship on the Nantucket Shoals.

Running without a mate out of Three Mile Harbor, I worked the rip over the sunken sand spit between Gardiners Island and the Ruin, which in those days was still used for bombing practice. More than once, the amateur airmen of the National Guard scared hell out of my unsuspecting clients, missing their target by a mile. That year the blowfish and the kingfish (a small relative of the weakfish) were still thick—both would disappear a few years later—and sometimes I ran bottom-fishing parties to

Crow Shoal and Pigeon Reef, using skimmers that I harvested with tongs from the west side of the Three Mile Harbor break-water. Most of my parties came aboard at the Town Commercial Dock near the harbor inlet, and coming up the channel from the head of the harbor, I sometimes picked up small striped bass by trolling a white bucktail in my wake.

On occasion I ferried workmen out to Gardiners Island, or ornithologists who wished to band the ospreys. The great sea hawks were so numerous in those days that their huge stick nests, built higher every year, were constructed all along the up-per beach along the southwest shore and across the channel on Cartwright Shoal as well. The first black skimmers that I ever saw on the South Fork were already established on the little island across from the Commercial Dock, and the first oyster-catchers were nesting on Gardiners Island. (The last-known Lab-rador duck, or sand-shoal duck, pied black and white like the swift old squaw, was shot down here on Gardiners Bay in 1874).

Out on the bay, even in summer, a few solitary loons and gun-shot sea ducks left behind by the northward migrations would be scattered among the gulls and terns that nested on Cartwright and on Gardiners Point. Among the white birds dip-ping on the fish were the roseate terns that hunted out over the tides from their nesting place in the old gun emplacements on Gull Island. One day, bluefishing in the Race, I saw a big ice-colored glaucous gull that had wandered down out of the Arctic.

In midsummer, the snapper blues would invade the channel, attracting summer children with long bamboo poles and red bobbers who fished in small excited flocks from the Commercial Dock. The snappers reminded me of Cap'n Posey, an old bar-nacle of local legend, who was popularly supposed to say at this soft, misty time of year, "Some foine day, bub! Yis, yis, bubby! Goin' out, goin' citch m'silf a miss o' snop-uhs!" Not until many years later did Bill Lester tell me that Cap'n Posey was his father,

Nathan Lester. "In the old days, now, all the Lesters was fishermen, and farmers, too, but I guess the Amagansett bunch was the only ones that never stopped—kind of the offsprings of the family, don't you know. And they called us the Posey Boys or Posey Lesters because Father used to wear a rose in his lapel goin' to church. So they called him Cap'n Posey, and all around here near the old homestead, they named that Poseyville."

I loved the quiet of the summer bay, the blue water and the hot sand shores with their acrid horsefoot smell and windrows of stout quarterdecks and light gold jingle shell that in other days was gathered up for oyster cultch; the gulls plucking scallops from the shallows, swooping upward, and dropping them on the old erratic boulders carried down out of the north by the great glaciers that formed the high moraines of "fish-shaped Pommanocc"; the ospreys lugging glinting fish across the sky, the bright lobster buoys and white sails, the yelp and crying of the nesting gulls, the screech of terns; the dull red shadow in the sea made by myriad gills of flat oily menhaden that turned that red purplish, so the bunker captains said, when the school was thick; the phosphorus from the plankton in the night water that thickened in the boat's wake as it entered the warmer water of the harbor; the rising of the bow wave as the shallows neared, in warning to the boatman (baymen say that the boat has a natural pull toward the deep of the channel). On every shore were the long silhouettes of pounds, or fish traps, with their weed-hung mesh, looped up on the stakes for drying in the August dog days, on every stake a tattered shag perched spreading its ancient wings to dry.

In August of 1956 I was approached by Lewis Lester, who had been picked as the new captain of a rig owned by Reggie Bassett and was putting together a new crew. "Got most of 'em, I guess," Lewis said, "but I'm still looking for a good, experienced man."

I shook my head; my days as a commercial fisherman were over. My marriage had disintegrated, my old fishing partners were scattering, and my friend Jackson, driving drunk, had destroyed himself and a young woman passenger when he lost control on the Springs–Fireplace Road. I had lost all heart for charter fishing, which meant that I could not afford to keep the *Merlin*, and I soon sold to Jimmy Reutershan a beautiful piece of woods high on Stony Hill, in Amagansett, where I had once planned to build a house.

It was time to move on, but Lewis's words sent me on my way feeling much better. I would never be a Bonacker, not if I lived here for a century, but apparently I was accepted as a fisherman. The three years spent with the commercial men were among the most rewarding of my life, and those hard seasons on the water had not been wasted.

THE FIRST KILL

GAVIN MAXWELL, *in this excerpt
from* Harpoon Venture, *tells the
incredible account of his first harpoon
kill of the monstrous basking shark
off the Isle of Soay, Scotland, where he
began a commercial shark fishery after
World War II.*

EVERY MORNING, THEN, I motored into Mallaig, and on calm days it had become a habit to stop at the top of the hill above the harbour and search the sea with field glasses. West, one looked down over fourteen miles of sea to Eigg and Rhum; when it was calm the sea would look flat and white, and every black dot upon it was suspect. It was hot that summer, and the atmospheric shimmer of the air would play tricks with one's eyes, distorting a floating fish box, a shag, or a cormorant, to the rounded triangle of a shark's dorsal fin. I remember many loudly acclaimed sharks that took wing and flapped heavily away across the sea.

On this morning I searched the nearer water first and lingered for some time over a motionless object perhaps a mile out before I identified it as a tin can. I raised the glasses higher, and into their field came a great concourse of resting shearwaters spread over the water like a carpet hundreds of yards square. They breed on Eigg, where the clifftop is honeycombed with their burrows, and these gigantic flocks rest motionless upon the water or skim past the boat at tremendous speed, an endless train of long narrow wings, keen and graceful as scimitars.

From the centre of the flock a patch of birds began to rise, running for a few steps upon the surface with wings held stiffly outstretched. This spread like a ripple from the centre outward, until the whole flock was on the wing, wheeling to reunite; and where the movement had started, a black object began to rise above the surface. It rose quickly, and in a few seconds it was unmistakable, glistening wet with quick flashes of light as the sun caught it. I watched while the tail fin appeared, moving from side to side with that strange ponderous leisure, and then I became aware that there were other black objects away beyond it. Turning the glasses on to them, I saw that the sea was dotted with fins for perhaps a mile beyond the one that had disturbed the shearwaters. I could count eighteen, and the farthest was very tiny, so that there were probably more beyond the range of the field glasses.

I got the car started and tore down into Mallaig, where I found that Bruce had already heard from the ring-net boats of a big shoal of sharks lying about six miles out and two miles south of Point of Sleat.

There was a lot of preparation to be done, as we had just moved the Oerlikon gun from the *Dove* to the *Gannet*, partly because the *Dove* was always either out of action or engaged in carrying factory materials, and partly because we hoped that the low bows of the *Gannet* might help to overcome the deflection of the harpoon which had caused our persistent failures. The gun platform of the *Dove* was ten feet above the sea, while the *Gannet*'s was only three, allowing a shot at point-blank range. But the recoil of the gun firing a heavy harpoon would have split the *Gannet*'s bows, and a great deal of reinforcement had been necessary below deck. This work was barely finished, and it was midday before we were ready to sail with the gun securely mounted near the starboard gunwale, and two double-barb harpoons that had just arrived from Birmingham.

Beside Bruce, Tex, and a deckhand called John Cameron, we had with us the son of the house where I was staying, Jackie Shaw Stewart, and an Eton friend of his, who had a camera along.

The sky had become overcast by the time we sailed, a thin layer of cloud through which the sun diffused over a hushed white sky and sea, so calm that even the floatpods of drifting weed showed hundreds of yards away. There were nothing like the number of sharks at the surface that there had been in the morning. By standing up in the *Gannet*'s bows I could make out the fins at about two miles—there seemed to be only three sharks, and none of them steady at the surface, though the three were never all submerged at the same time.

We decided to take the first shot that offered and headed straight for them; when we were still a mile away I saw a great grey shadow as big as the boat pass diagonally below us, and knew that we were on the fringe of the submerged shoal, but no more came to the surface.

We were hardly more than a hundred yards from the fins when for the first time all went down together. I was standing at the gun, trying to accommodate my shoulder to its unrelenting awkwardness, and taking practice sights along the barrel. We had removed the iron protection plate, but even without it the gun was as clumsy to handle as the fifteen-foot iron pipes on the hand harpoons had been. I heard the engine slip into neutral, and the *Gannet* stole very gently forward towards the rippled surface where the sharks had gone down.

Then, and up to the very last shark I killed years later, this waiting for a shark to resurface, straining one's eyes for the faintest ripple or gliding bulk below the water, set my heart hammering savagely against my ribs, as though it were a sort of overture, a roll of drums leading up to the climax—the gun's roar and the flying rope and the tail towering out of the water in a drench of white spray. This was the first time that it really happened.

The gun was mounted where we had become accustomed to stand with hand harpoons—well forward on the extreme edge of the starboard bow, so that one must approach the fish from astern and to port of him. At first thought it would seem more sensible for the gun to be on the extreme point of the boat's nose, giving a much wider field of fire, but to use this field of fire the gunner would have to step off the boat and into the sea to keep behind the gun when it turned. But when a shark does not swim on a steady course it is often impossible to make certain of a stern approach—one must take any shot when it comes within range, and that is what happened on this first occasion.

A fin reappeared fifty yards away on the same course, going slowly and straight away from us. The *Gannet* jerked forward as she went into gear and headed for the shark at half throttle; then I heard Bruce's voice to the man at the engine, "Dead slow," then, "Take her out," and we were drifting up to the shark on a perfect approach.

But at about ten yards the fish turned abruptly left, at right angles to his former course, so that our bows would have passed behind his tail, or at best rammed it. I yelled "Hard aport" to Bruce, but did not feel certain that the *Gannet* had enough way on her to answer the tiller. She seemed to come round very slowly, but the shark was moving slowly too, and his whole length was suddenly there, right across the *Gannet*'s bows, so that she would have rammed him amidships. I had slewed the gun round until it was pointing as much forward as its traverse allowed, and I pulled the trigger cord as soon as the dorsal fin came into the gun's field of vision. The Etonian succeeded in taking a photograph a fraction of a second after the impact; it shows the very tip of the tail fin beginning its first swing towards the boat's side as the shark tries to dive.

The fish had been swimming very high; there were only a few inches of water over his back when I fired, and I felt quite certain that the harpoon was in him. The tail behaved as usual, hiding everything with a storm of spray; then, when it had subsided, I saw the shark a fathom or two down in clear water, swimming fast on an opposite course. I could see the end of the harpoon shaft sticking a foot or so out of his side—below the point I had aimed for—and a dark plume of blood trailing from it in the water, like smoke from a chimney. Tex saw it too, and gave his war cry for the first time, a war cry that I came to associate with every kill, and which in a later season I remember hearing across half a mile of sea, following the boom of his gun in the summer dusk: "He feels it! He feels it!"

The shark took fifty fathoms of rope in a rush before he slowed up enough for us to be able to take a turn on the drum of the little hand winch. We let him tow us sluggishly for two hours before we began to haul up.

For nearly another two hours the five of us hauled on that rope with all our strength, dragging it in almost inch by inch. Everything worked perfectly. When we began the tug-of-war the rope was leading down from the bow fair-lead at about seventy degrees, and for the first few minutes the shark tried quick changes of direction, the rope leading sometimes ahead, sometimes to port or starboard, then down under the boat. But after ten minutes the rope was vertical, as rigid as a telegraph pole, and he was three hundred feet below us in the green dusk of the sea, being dragged inexorably upward.

We had pieces of coloured cloth tied into the rope at ten, twenty, and thirty fathoms; when, after an hour and a half, the ten-fathom mark came up over the fair-lead and came edging down the dripping foredeck to the winch, I left the hold and went up the *Gannet's* bows. I lay flat on my face on the deck and strained my eyes to follow the rope down into the dim water. I could see perhaps twenty feet before it became lost in darkness; the three feet of it between the surface and the *Gannet's* fair-lead felt as hard as wood, and if one pulled sideways upon it it would vibrate fractionally, but would not give half an inch. It was some minutes before I could see anything but the tensed rope leading down into obscurity; then, at the extreme limit of vision, I saw something that looked like a gigantic punkah swinging rhythmically to and fro.

I had already seen several sharks at close quarters; I had seen those giant tails sweeping clear of the water to slam down upon the sea or the boat; there was no logical reason for this tail to come as a surprise, but it did. Foot by foot it came higher into the clearer water and defined itself, six foot wide at least and swinging over an arc of several yards as the shark tried to swim vertically downward. Every now and again he would foul the rope as it swung past, holding the tail itself vertical for a moment, then he would break free with a shuddering wrench into his pattern of impotent effort.

I could see part of the body beyond the tail now; the body of a dragon, six feet through and showing a glimmering white belly as he twisted and lunged. At the far end of the belly there seemed to be two gigantic flippers—I was unprepared for the size of these pectoral fins, which had been minimized in the drawings I had seen.

As soon as his tail came clear of the surface the power of that punkah action became apparent; at each lunge it exploded a fountain of water from the sea. Several times it struck the *Gannet*'s stem, leaving gobs of black slime as it struggled free. We were busy with ropes now, and after several near misses succeeded in dropping a noose over the long upper half of the tail fin as it jammed momentarily against the bows. The next lunge carried the tail below the surface, and for a moment it looked as though the rope would be flung free, but as the tail rose again towards the boat we saw the other half of it slip through, and the whole fin was in the noose. We almost knocked each other overboard in our hurry to pull it tight, but we saw it close firmly on the narrow isthmus of body below the fin, and the shark was ours.

He behaved then as I do not remember any other shark behaving afterwards. The fight seemed momentarily to go out of him; he stopped trying to bore downward, and the whole length of him came up close under the surface alongside the *Gannet* like a great downed elephant, rolling belly upwards before he righted himself. As he did so I saw a giant parasite detach itself from his back and wriggle quickly away into the darkness—an eel-like creature that seemed six feet long. Someone made a grab for it with the boat hook, but he was a second too late, and this monster specimen of *Petromyzon marinus*, the sea lamprey found on all basking sharks, but whose length is not known to exceed a yard, went unrecorded. We all agreed upon its length, nor, in the many that we saw later, did we find ourselves apt to overestimate their length at first sight.

The shark rolled and twisted as he lay alongside, and on one of these rolls the harpoon came uppermost. For a moment I think we all forgot that we had him securely by the tail—we only saw that the harpoon was practically out of him, turned sideways and holding by one barb just beneath the skin. I know I shouted and grabbed the rope to try to pull the barb in deeper before I remembered that the harpoon phase was over now. Our luck was holding, as it was to hold for the next twenty-four hours, no matter by how narrow a margin.

It was late afternoon before we had made the shark's tail fast to the stern of the *Gannet*. He was still alive, and with the boat hove to he still tried convulsively to bore downward. When we put the engine ahead his nose broke the surface twenty-five feet astern of the boat; we opened the throttle wide and began to move forward at a rate of perhaps half a knot, with a tremendous commotion of water astern. It was like trying to tow a house. We did not know then that we were trying to tow him in an almost impossible position, in which his distended gills were held open by the backward rush of water and formed a brake as effective as a large sea anchor. Later we learned to tow sharks tied fore and aft alongside the boat, nose foremost and with the jaws roped closed to give the minimum water resistance.

There was no other boat in sight, and our powers of invention temporarily failed. We had caught a shark and we were going to get him home; we just kept plodding away at less than a mile an hour over that oily white calm. Most of the shark's tail was inboard, and we fingered it curiously, examining the strange black slime and the great keel ridge of muscle that began at each side of its root and ran back to power the thin afterpart of the body.

After an hour's towing Mallaig seemed little nearer, and Sleat Point little farther astern of us. Five miles away we could see the white smoke of the evening train coming up to Mallaig; it ballooned out and hung motionless in the air as the engine passed through the short tunnel. Some small boats were beginning to put out for the evening mackerel fishing at Point of Sleat, and as the first of these passed half a mile to northward of us it turned and made south, a man standing up in the bows. With the field glasses I made out that it was Ian Macintyre, the marine engineer who had made most of our hand harpoons.

Within hailing distance his voice came from between cupped hands, "So you got one at last!"

"Yes, but not with your trash, Ian."

"Just for that I think I'll away and fish mackerel and leave you to it. Is he a big one?"

"Too big for us—it's all wake and no way. Are you on?"

He was on, and with his boat tied alongside the *Gannet* and both our engines full ahead we began to move at three or four knots. Until now we had believed the fallacy that this would kill the shark, that the back pressure of water through his gills would make him unable to breathe. It was a surprise to see that after several miles he was still very much alive.

It was near dusk when we reached Mallaig. It was the tourist season; Mallaig was performing its brief seasonal function of Gateway to the Hebrides, and the train had disgorged its cargo of holiday-makers, would-be mountaineers in huge climbing boots and swathes of rope, brightly tartaned Highlanders from Glasgow and the industrial cities, earnest hikers with gigantic rucksacks and skinny legs, and sad-looking elderly couples who seem to visit the Hebrides annually to lament the climate. Word had reached Mallaig that the *Gannet* was bringing in a shark, and the attention our project had received from the daily press had thronged the piers. As we passed the big stone pier where the island steamers berth, and headed on for the inside of the fish pier where the herring catches are landed and bid for, I remember that parts of the crowd began to run back to intercept us before we reached our berth beside the *Dove*. There were something like fifteen hundred people crowded on that short pier by the time we churned laboriously round the end of it.

With some difficulty we transferred the shark's rope from the *Gannet* to one of the uprights of the pier. First we made the rope fast to it, then took the knot from the *Gannet*'s hand winch. This almost cost Bruce his right arm, as the shark took up that extra six feet of line suddenly allowed to him. The rope slammed taut with a noise like the plucked strings of a double bass, catching the boat's gunwale a hundredth of a second after Bruce had snatched his arm away.

Tied there, the shark was evidently very much alive; again with slow rhythmic lunges he tried to bore down to the bottom. His tail was about a foot below water now, and from its hidden sweeps great ripples spread outward over the still harbour and slapped small disintegrated waves among the supports of the pier. From above we could see perhaps the first ten feet of him; beyond that there were distant glimmers of white where his skin had been torn in the long struggle.

We had intended to lift him onto the decks of the *Dove* with her steam capstan. I think we had very little idea of the weight with which we were dealing, which was certainly several tons. It took about an hour to get up steam on the *Dove*'s boiler. The rope was transferred again, this time to the *Dove*'s capstan, and the shark had something like three or four fathoms of rope between him and the boat. He used it at once, turning outward to the deep water of the harbour, and making the *Dove* strain at her mooring ropes. We started the vast and antiquated capstan, and he was dragged back foot by foot until his tail was once more below the *Dove*'s stem. After a great deal of difficulty we managed to pass a rope round the forepart of his body, attached this, too, to the winch, and heaved him up until he was lying horizontally at the surface alongside the *Dove*. In this position we meant to drag him up the boat's side until he would roll over the gunwale onto the deck. Time and again we raised him until most of his body was clear of the water, but each time the winch failed as it began to take the full strain unhelped by the water's support, the rope drum beginning to whir and slip as the limit of the steam's power was reached. There was a great sag in his body between the fore and after ropes that were lifting him; his head and tail would come up almost to the *Dove*'s gunwale, but there were tons of unlifted weight where his belly still sagged down into the water.

It was dark when we gave up the attempt. The disappointed crowds had already begun to disperse, but they reassembled when they learned that the skipper of a boom ship, lying at the big pier, had agreed to try to lift the shark. Two of these ships, which are equipped with huge cranes, were in Mallaig to lift the submarine boom (to prevent the passage of enemy submarine through the narrows of Skye) at Kylerea; and their massive derricks stood out against the night sky like the silhouette of a London dock. It was difficult to manoeuvre the *Dove* alongside them, because with the drag of the shark we could not get her to answer the wheel in that confined space. It was a long time before we got her satisfactorily placed; the crowds grew denser, so that, from the *Dove*'s deck, the whole pier seemed serrated by a forest of heads.

At last we were ready to transfer the shark's rope to the giant crane above us. The second boom ship turned her searchlights upon the swirl in the black water at the *Dove*'s bows, where the rope led rigidly to the still-struggling tail. The stage was set.

Inch by inch the crane began to winch in. Even before the shark's tail broke the surface of the water the sense of strain was terrific. It gleamed and came clear, nearly seven feet wide, black and slithery, all movement stopped by that vertical lift from the water, but deeper and heavier ripples began to surge outwards as twenty feet below the surface the body of the shark still lunged fiercely from side to side.

The narrow neck just below the tail seemed infinitely prolonged; then, very slowly, the girth of the body began to rise. Size always appears greater in the vertical than the horizontal, and by the time fifteen feet of the shark were clear of the water and the girth was still increasing, he appeared literally monstrous, a creature of saga or fantasy, a dragon being hauled from its lair. The darkness, the shifting yellow reflections of the harbour lights, and the white glare of the searchlights combined to give a stage effect of mystery and magnification. There was an excited gabble from the packed crowds on the pier, gasps and exclamations, and a group of women near the edge panicked and forced their way back into the press behind them.

"Oh, wha' a crayture!"

"Ye wouldna' believe it!"

189

"It canna be a fish!"

The cogs ground on, the ropes creaked and juddered; each sound was one of infinite tension and effort, like sobbing breaths from lungs strained beyond endurance, and the elephantine black silhouette grew to a towering monument.

Then, with twenty feet of him standing clear of the water, there was a slight snapping sound, as a man makes when he steps upon a rotten stick. The crane stopped at a quick order, and for a second there was utter silience—followed by a tremendous crack and a sickening, tearing sound as the great carcass plunged back into the water. For a moment the severed tail hung suspended in midair; then that, too, fell with a mighty smack into the oily black water of the harbour.

After these six years I can still hear the noise from the watching crowds, feel again the almost unbearable disappointment of that moment, that last unbelievable frustration of Tantalus.

I did not think the shark was dead; even tailless he would probably wriggle or drift with the tide into deeper water outside the harbour. I felt quite certain that we should not see him again, and not even the tail remained to prove that we had at last caught a shark and brought him to harbour.

I slept aboard the *Dove* and was out at five-thirty in the morning. For nearly an hour we cruised about round the place which the boom ships had left during the night, but we could see nothing in the now limpid water. We were tying the *Gannet* up again when an outgoing lobster boat hailed us.

"Major! He's here—I can see him!"

The man was bending over the side of his boat, peering down into the water about a hundred yards out from the end of the stone pier. I felt a tremendous leap of the heart, but I was not feeling strong enough to face a second disappointment, and I tried to be sceptical.

"Are you sure?"

"Aye—I can see the ugly head of him. Come out here and look for yourselves."

It was the shark right enough, lying in about four fathoms of clear water, his mouth half open and glinting pallidly. I had a Polaroid filter for my camera lens, to cut out reflection upon the water's surface, and by screwing this into my eye as a monocle I could see him plainly. I didn't doubt for a second that we could recover him; we had a shark, after all.

Bruce and Shand, the owner of the lobster boat, took charge, lowering an ordinary line and fish hook to grip inside the open jaw. They were fast into him after not much more than ten minutes, and the great carcass, lightened by the formation of gases in the belly, came looming up in the water until it was once more alongside the *Gannet*. We passed a rope through the gills and out at the mouth, and a quarter of an hour later the *Gannet* and the dead shark were berthed by the *Dove*. It was only seven o'clock in the morning.

We were not going to try to lift him again. I went and called on Henderson the boatbuilder and got his permission to beach the shark on the boatyard's slip. When I got back to the *Dove*, Bruce and Shand had disappeared. Tex put his head up from the fo'c'sle.

"He wasn't content—they're away to look for the tail this time, so the shark'll be all complete when Mallaig wakes up. Come below for a cup of tea—they'll be hours yet."

But it was only twenty minutes before Shand's boat was alongside us again, with the huge tail shining like patent leather across the bows, and our dragon was complete when Mallaig woke.

ASKING FOR IT

WILLIAM McCLOSKEY, *formerly a staff
member of the Johns Hopkins University
Applied Physics Laboratory, recounts
his rocky start as a commercial
fisherman in Alaska at age forty-five.
A retired scientist with advanced
degrees, he can land only cannery jobs—
until his big break, launching a second
life and a career at sea.*

NOVEMBER 1976

Y OU'RE UNLOADED," says the canneryman. The snow on his parka melts quickly in the heat of the boat's galley. It is three in the morning. The poker and drinks and guitar playing began at eight last night, after the boat arrived from a week on the Bering Sea with a hold full of crab.

"Ve go," says Leiv, the skipper, and, to a lady friend bunked with one of the bachelors: "Get your ass on the dock."

Minutes later the crew has fitted the hatch cover back into the deck, battened gear, and cast off lines from the ice-slick pier. To starboard the domes of Unalaska's little Russian Orthodox church slip by, dark against the blue glow of the snow-covered mountains. Leiv turns the *American Beauty* at a right angle to the church and heads toward the mouth of the bay, past Dutch Harbor. A snow squall hazes the lights on the steaming processor ships scattered alongshore, finally obliterating them. The close white mountains are dim and shardlike. Leaving their lee, the boat plunges head on into the seas of a forty-knot northwester. Within an hour of the final poker chip on the galley table, we have left all traces of even the tenuous Aleutian civilization. Protected only by the deck beneath our feet, we're on our own.

It is a long 150 miles to the grounds where the crab pots lie. The boat pitches, thuds into troughs, takes crashing tons of water over the pilothouse. The crew stands watches in turn, and sleeps. I lie in my bunk, seasick from too much drink (I thought we'd spend the night calmly in port), listening to a monotonous groaning creak overhead. In the fore-peak locker just beyond, cans fall from the shelves and tumble back and forth with each roll just an inch from my face.

A new night begins when Leiv homes in with loran to locate the first string of pots. He shouts and slows the engines. Everyone pulls on oilskins and silently goes into it. Hail splatters like glass in our faces, black waves swell higher than our heads, the wind roars and whines, and sea foams across the deck.

The deck lights pick up the two pink marker buoys of the first pot, dipping in the troughs. Frank throws a hook and grapples the buoys aboard. He bends the pot line through the hydraulic crab block and starts to coil it as Dale operates the controls to reel it in. Frank's hands fly like pistons, dropping three hundred feet of line by his boots in even rings. I bait, chopping frozen herring and fish heads. My knees dig into the wooden tub for support. Up comes the heavy, square, swaying seven-foot steel-and-mesh pot. Terry and Steve grab the sides as it bangs against the rail, and guide it crashing into place on the launcher rack.

The pot—essentially a big box trap—holds dozens of six- to eight-pound purple king crabs that crawl sluggishly against each other. The spikes on their shells will tear our hands without heavy rubber gloves. The door of the pot opens like a hamper: a picker pot. We lean in to pull crabs out, hand over hand, sorting on the run, flinging back females and undersized, splashing obvious keepers into the circulating water that fills the hold, piling doubtfuls to be measured. (Minimum size for this Bering Sea opening is six and a half inches across the carapace. The farthest spike point on the carapace does it.) In the rush we still take care not to smash or dismember the creatures, since busted crabs die and benefit no one.

I unhook the perforated bait can that has been soaking for days and dump the rotted remains of old herring over the side.

Hundreds of seabirds screech and dive to retrieve the pieces while I retch from the whiff. Always pushing it, we rebait, mend a tear in the pot's web, secure the lid, stack the line to uncoil properly, and at a shout from Leiv lift the pot, followed by line and buoys, back into the sea.

It takes seventeen hours to work one hundred pots: six an hour. In just a few years, by the 1980s, hydraulic pot lifters will have speeded up and be able to coil automatically, and hard drivers like Leiv Loklingholm will expect to work twice as many pots per hour. Yet, only two decades ago, the technology for this fishery was still so experimental that the lifter, the big square pots, and the very design of the boat under our feet were all in the future. Stability had been the major concern: Boats that could buck rough water with a net on deck capsized routinely under a load of heavy pots that raised the center of gravity. And wooden boats proved inadequate because the crabs needed to be kept alive in steel tanks of circulating seawater.

The steel 108-foot *American Beauty*, engineered by Marco Marine Construction in Seattle, has a raised fo'c'sle and other adjustments to elevate its freeboard, and a centered fish hold—all to keep the vessel trim, even with pots aboard, when the bow plunges into heavy seas.

Suddenly, a big wave sweeps over the side and drenches us, hitting with such force that we grab for support. Frigid water trickles down my neck through the raingear and fills one of my boots. Leiv thrusts his bearded face from the pilothouse and assesses anxiously, then roars a Norwegian *har har* against the wind. "Hey, dot'll vake you bastards, eh?" We yell casual obscenities and throw things at the quickly closed wheelhouse door. His apology will show in honed alertness so it won't happen again. He'll mind even more tensely—every second, every hour—the relation between rolling sea, careening steel pots, and fragile deck.

Some fishermen have nine or ten lives, some barely one, no matter their caution. One chilly January day another year I arrived late in Kodiak and bunked with a friendly crew who had delivered their catch, then moored for the night. We were joined by the men of another crabber whose skipper planned to put to sea in a few hours. His crew included two brothers, Jim and Clint, shaggy-haired, quiet young guys shipping out together. They had fished enough years to be experienced but were still, somebody joked, just ol' country boys. They grinned, but didn't contradict.

Next afternoon at sea the country brothers were working together on deck. The boat had already run a string of crab pots. A wave no worse than many others washed over the rail. "Clint! . . ." Jim called quietly. Clint looked up in time to see his brother disappear over the side in a blur of orange raingear. No one saw more of the cause than this. As the boat circled back wildly, with the men throwing life rings from the deck, they saw Jim's bearded face in the orange hood bob up twice among the waves. And that was it.

The crabber made it back to the Kodiak pier at 2:00 A.M. In the dark and cold I watched the surviving brother stumble off carrying duffel bags for two. Nobody spoke. A part-owner of the boat took the youth home, to wait for the early Anchorage flight and connection to the lower states. The Kodiak police withheld names in reporting the accident so Clint could make it home first to tell their parents. The crabber, with its stunned skipper and remaining crew, was a top-of-the-line boat, with more safety equipment than any law required. It hadn't helped.

Aboard Bering Sea crabbers, the square pots (six and a half to eight feet square by three feet high), at 650 to 800 pounds empty, are monsters, and with sea life added their weight rises quickly beyond a ton. When the deck rolls and pitches, the pot becomes a wrecking ball with sharp edges as it clears the rail and swings aboard. A hand or leg in the way can be smashed. Maverick seas have swept pots overboard with a man leaning inside to mend or bait, taking him to his death as if hitched to an anchor.

When the pots begin coming aboard *American Beauty* with only a crab or two, Leiv decides it is time to chase the migrating creatures elsewhere. He gives the word to start stacking. As each pot comes aboard we empty it but, instead of returning it to the water, stuff the coils of line and marker buoys inside, then horse the heavy pots across deck to tie them frame to frame from the rails. Soon, little maneuvering room remains. We work backed against a wall of shifting steel frames, booming a second and third layer of pots on top of the first, cautiously handling the dangerous weight.

Terry, assigned to secure the top stack, scampers up and down like a monkey, tie ropes slung over his shoulder, boot toes slipping on the frames, fingers clutching web. Later, I will try this on another boat, and I will make the mistake of crouching atop an unsecured pot as I tie it to the others. A sea hits and the pot lurches. As the others cry warnings, I scramble off the swaying structure that likely would have taken me with it, into water rough and cold enough to keep whatever it received. One crab skipper I know hires nobody over twenty-two, because young reflexes are so important.

Open-sea crabbing in Alaska is dangerous in other ways. The fishery occurs when gales and ice descend, because king crabs fill their shells fullest in fall and early winter, and tanner crab fullness starts in January. In late winter, boats in the Bering Sea battle icebergs as well as the weather. During my first week on a crabber, in November with the worst weather to come, a man on one boat lost a finger, a man on another lost the bridge of his nose when a heavy hook flew out of control, and seas smashed the windows of two pilothouses. A vacancy had been created when two converging hydraulic bars crushed a man's thigh. A few months later, another crab boat I'd ridden briefly from Dutch Harbor to Akutan took a trick sea near the Pribilofs, capsized, and sank within five minutes—incredibly with no loss of life thanks to survival suits and nearby boats.

Sometimes the sun shines on the Bering, glittering on whitecaps. At other times, within minutes of the sun, fogs roll in and stick to the waters. Occasionally the sea turns glassy calm, but it is always cold. Gusts up to ninety knots cut through oilskins and thermals, chilling the sweat inside. Regardless of care in the wheelhouse, waves sometimes roll straight over like a mule kick. The workday lasts up to twenty hours, steadily, for a week or so until the hold fills enough to deliver. Working thirty or forty hours straight is not uncommon under a driving skipper with an experienced crew: Pay is based on a share of the catch, the catch might not always be there, and the season is limited.

When the boat cruises between strings, steered by a coffee-strung skipper who gives himself no rest (these boats cost over a million dollars, shared often with a partner, but with plenty of mortgage to pay), we peel oilskins to our boots, flop on an inside deck, and sleep instantly. When the engine slows at the approach of a new string we rise automatically—near agony if not done fast—and stumble back on deck, bones aching until the work lubricates them again. Meals become sporadic, taken as snacks stuffed in passing until Frank, the man designated to cook (everyone has an ancillary job), can find time away from deck. And thirst! We consume gallons of "bug juice," flavored water. Life turns primitive, a simple push against fatigue and against the pain of muscles pushed strenuously, over and over. It is exhausting merely to stay balanced on the heaving deck. Terry keeps going by clocking his share of each keeper: "That's a quarter . . . a buck . . . two bucks . . ." Some fishermen at the worst of it bite their lips and cry, but they continue to work. You have to be there to understand.

Terry is the bright presence aboard the *American Beauty*. He has a natural bounce however much the deck pitches. Inches shorter than the others and a bit rounded, he looks unsuited for the work but handles loads as heavy as anyone's. Even under fatigue he spouts a quip or joke. Terry regards me, the novice, protectively. If I slack or err he offers a hand. We banter above the noises of ocean and machinery. This crew is young and un-superstitious enough that my tendency to whistle while I work bothers nobody, while I find it a comfort. (I check carefully first, man by man. This is no casual matter aboard a fishing boat.) After one day of storm and rotten bait, I'm seasick despite all the fresh air and facefuls of clean salt water. At table I stare at Frank's Norwegian fish balls without eating. Terry pauses from wolfing his food. "The Baltimore warbler is silent tonight," he says gently.

A steam-letting with Terry can turn explosive. Once, a rotten sea blob comes up in the pot. Terry slings it at Frank, a generally quiet Norwegian, who flings it back full force. Within seconds a wild game of catch erupts. When the original sea ball disintegrates, Terry leaps to the storage deck, cuts loose a spare inflated buoy, and throws it down. Only when the buoy shreds does the game end. Another time, during about the fifteenth hour of steady work, we're returning stacked pots to the water from both sides of the boat. Terry grabs one of the seven-hundred-pound monsters and, pushing with the roll of the boat, hefts it across deck single-handedly to the starboard rail. Not to be outdone, Frank shoves the next pot by himself. The others join. I run back and forth pulling out the heavy coils and baiting as everyone competes to have pots ready to heave overboard the instant Leiv calls the command. When it is over we're all panting, sweating, grinning, and reinvigorated.

On another typical night around 1:00 A.M., as hail slashes in streaks across the deck lights, I brace by the rail to hook a pot, balancing on ice underfoot. Beyond the boat, white patches of foam and gulls move rhythmically in a darkness that is otherwise a void. Mountainous swells tower above the little deck. Suddenly I am pressing my knees into the steel side for solid protection. "Well, stupid, you got yourself into this," I mutter. But if a deus ex machina were to swoop from above as in a Greek drama to take me back to warm, safe comfort, I'd refuse. Then the pot surfaces, leaving no further time to be awed by vulnerability.

How indeed did I get into this? It started boldly, though not with the facing of primal forces. In the 1950s, I served on a Coast Guard ship in Alaska, plying coasts of wondrous scenic wildness. The imprint was indelible, and in the 1970s, with two children raised and a career duly pursued, Alaska and seafaring remained in my system. Atavism, self-indulgence, whatever, at the mid-forty mark I craved my dreams and had the luck of an understanding wife and employer.

In 1975, I found my way back to Kodiak briefly while researching an article for *The New York Times Magazine* on foreigners fishing American waters. With an extra day to kill, I asked my way aboard a fishing boat netting salmon. We pulled up fish. I felt them in the net, and slapping around my legs. Freighters, military ships, passenger liners, sailboats—all had figured in my previous seafaring, and they all offered experiences with the sea, but they had dealt only with the surface. The fishing boat interacted with life in the unseen depths, a different dimension altogether. I couldn't forget it.

There was also the passage of progress to consider. Small-scale fishermen with their own boats might soon be a thing of the past, like the vanishing family farmer or the iceman who once delivered pearly, dripping blocks on his back to my grandmother's icebox. Plenty of woeful opinion supported this. If I wanted to see, I'd better look before fishermen became a memory.

In Kodiak, the main town of a hundred-mile island off the central Alaskan mainland facing the open Pacific Ocean, where I had pranced as a young Coast Guard officer knowing everything, I found myself walking boat to boat with hearty facade, asking crewmen half my age if they needed an extra hand. Nobody was unkind, but nobody said come aboard. I followed the expedient course of many greenhorns and hired onto a cannery line for money to keep going. And the best way to persuade some fishing skipper to hire me, I reasoned, was on scene in oilskins, when boats delivered, showing I could work.

The Kodiak salmon season had not yet begun, although seiners were gearing up. But other boats were trawling for shrimp and bringing in big loads. (A few seasons later, the shrimp would simply disappear, as would the king crab—a story for later in the book.) At the canneries, men waist-deep in shrimp shoveled them into hoppers, to start the creatures' course from livestock to food. I fancied myself behind a shovel deep in some hold, ultimately seabound after calling up merrily, "Hey, guys, need a crewman?"

Instead, the foreman assigned me to a conveyor belt deep inside a big, gloomy building. Surrounded by odors of disinfectant, I stood picking small white candlefish and wisps of seaweed from among the passing tons of pink shrimp. My partner, a sullen, pimpled teenager, lacked even a hello. The grating we stood on, as water rushed beneath our boots, had devilish protrusions that interfered with comfortable stance. The shift each day lasted twelve to fourteen hours. Half-hour lunch break, fifteen-minute coffee breaks, no time to rush the near-mile to the docks for another go at the salmon seiners in the harbor.

Candlefish picking was closer to the real world than the romance of a fishing boat, the truth of life's work at the bottom rung, the lot of millions. My eyes followed the foreman each time he rushed past. When finally I grabbed his attention I tried to make it sound offhand and amusing: "Hey, going crazy here! I'm good with a shovel." He stopped for the seconds it took to absorb the information over the hiss of water and clang of machinery. "You've got a very important job. Keep at it." And he was off. My last chance for hours.

Suddenly one day the foreman grabbed my arm and hustled me to a new location. Instead of descending to a boat hold, we clanged up metal stairs to the steamy ceiling. With the heat and concentrated odors of cooking shrimp it felt like the inside of the cooker itself. Within minutes I had on long rubber gloves (which leaked), and a Japanese was instructing me in the distribution of shrimp that sluiced by the thousands from huge shining vats into a battery of peeler machines.

At least I could move in a twenty-foot arena. And my fellow peelermen, all Asian, would nod back and take time to show me the tricks of the machinery. My trough had a trap door to each peeler, and these metal plates required frequent adjustment for an even flow. Sometimes the trough clogged, calling for swift measures. After the candlefish, here was action and intellectual involvement. Soon I became king of the trough, orchestrating the trap doors, playing games to see how long I could withhold shrimps from one chute without emptying it, how much I could stuff another without clogging it.

The candlefish shift had started at 5:30 A.M., confirmed on my time card. At about 7 P.M. I glanced from my new height to see the sullen teenager and his newest assistant hose the belt, pick out bits of seaweed, and punch out. Theirs was an initial step in the cannery process, while the product of my new post still poured from the cookers.

Two hours later the cookers stopped steaming. I hosed and scrubbed with the others, pushing more vigorously than they. Time still to walk the docks and perhaps find guys aboard their boats. Viewed from above, the peelers were clean. I waved and started to leave. The others laughed and beckoned me back. When they lifted the baffles, a jungle of antennas, eyes, and slivers lay matted in every crevice. They took a coffee break first. We punched out around midnight after hosing, picking, scrubbing, hosing, dislodging, and disinfecting. The boats in the harbor, as I walked past, lay dark, their masts black against a sky with remaining vestiges of northern latitude light.

I was not destitute in Kodiak. During the quick visit the previous year I had met Tom Casey, head of the local Fishermen's Marketing Association. Casey, a bear of a man with a foghorn bellow and a knack for writing narrative poetry, had befriended me to the point of offering me a room. Nor, now, was I lonely. My son Wynn, age fifteen, had followed, finding it inconceivable that I should have all the adventure. We bunked with generous Tom. Wynn worked at a different cannery, his own man. (We said nothing about the husky kid's age.) In Tom's living room where he slept, Wynn roused enough to mumble as I tiptoed in to general snores, and we exchanged whispered notes of our day. "Mom and Karin phoned, said hi and be careful. And Da: Happy Father's Day."

The salmon season was about to start. A hill of seine nets and corks rose on the decks at the town floats. Each net, when passed through the suspended power block, spread with the grandeur of a sail as the men inspected and mended. The boats themselves were saucy, scuffed, businesslike, the essence of contact with the sea. The more I watched, the more I yearned to be aboard.

Next morning at coffee break I forewent free cookies to patrol the cannery dock, staring at shrimp boats that came to deliver. Crewmen aboard had little interest in chatting with an obvious cannery hand, betrayed by lightweight oilskins (laundered, disinfected, and reissued daily) of a kind that would have ripped under heavy deck use. Beyond the canneries toward town, two seiners glided from the harbor and pointed north, the route around the island toward Cape Igvak, on the first salmon run. The fleet was leaving.

At lunch break I ran the unpaved road to the town docks, gulping bits of sandwich. The full harbor last night now had empty slips like missing teeth. The air was charged with whoops and high-keyed shouts. Two weeks before, shoulders and carts had carried boxes down the ramps containing nets, machine parts, paint, canned food. Now the boxes held fresh groceries and frozen meats, signs of imminent departure. Engines turned, puffing blue smoke astern. On decks, crewmen once willing to chat barely nodded as they hustled. The boat rails separated us like a wall, as if the men had already put to sea.

On one boat a skipper who had been remotely sympathetic, arousing my hopes, called: "Wanna throw me those lines?" I unmoored his boat. It backed smoothly from the slip, its graceful hull suddenly a thing of heart-stopping beauty. I watched it glide toward the breakwater as the men on deck tied down. The sinuously stacked corks of its seine caught a gleam of sun through the clouds. At the breakwater the boat responded to the sea and began a gentle rock. A minute later it pitched. Mast and booms swooped. To those fortunates aboard, the boat came alive.

I raced back to the cannery, the sandwich a lump in my stomach. The foreman—usually scarce given his far-ranging duties—passed and frowned as I punched in late. The yellow oilskins of my fellow peelermen in the loft already moved in patches through the steam. I geared up, sweating from the run, hastened to my post pulling on soggy gloves, and with a tight smile relieved the man who had kindly filled my place and his own. The heat of cooked shrimp stuck in my throat like brass. I worked madly without games, and reviewed the realities.

I phoned Tom Casey at his harbor office. During one of his meetings with seiner skippers as head of marketing association, I had stood up to introduce myself and ask for a berth, winging it about my ability to cook, to learn, to do anything. (Polite, sympathetic indifference—I was, after all, forty-five and green.) One skipper had at least smiled. Tom identified him later as a highliner, respected throughout the fleet. In harbor I had seen many boats and would have signed aboard the scummiest, but the fifty-eight-foot *Polar Star* of the man who smiled looked particularly groomed and able. "Tom! Do you think Thorvold Olsen would take me along just for the ride? I'll pay for my food."

"Thor's probably left, Bill. He doesn't wait around. No, I can see the boat. Want me to call his house?"

"Please!"

I waited as the minutes of the coffee break ticked away. When someone tried to use the phone I begged him off. Coffee break over. In the distance down the road (where twenty-six years ago I had strolled critically among fishing boats as a Coast Guard officer on a sturdy ship) I could see masts moving toward open water.

The phone rang. "Okay," said Tom. "Thor'll take you. He leaves in an hour. I'll come get you to pack. Be outside."

I raced through the cannery to find the foreman, now scarce again. "Look, this isn't my way, but I'm quitting. Sorry. Thanks. Okay?"

"Don't come back."

An hour later, giddy with good fortune—having sent Wynn a message to stay with Tom and hang tough—I stood on the deck of the *Polar Star* holding boots and a thrown-together seabag, backed against the cabin to be out of the way as the four crewmen made final stowage. The rocks of the breakwater glided past and the scrubbed decks began to roll. Fittings on the tightly battened boom clicked with the motion. The roofs of cannery row became mere buildings like all the others of Kodiak nestled on flats and hills beneath the green slope of Pillar Mountain.

Between protective islands the open Pacific Ocean swelled in. Spray shot back from the bow. The stern rose and slammed into water. "You going to be seasick?" asked one of the men, Corky, pleasantly.

"Nope," I grinned, feeling queasy. I had gulped a pill. It helped.

The *Polar Star* passed wooded coastline, beyond which rose peaks still snowed in June. Eagles flew. A sea lion's whiskered snout poked from the water, then flipped away. In a corridor between islands the water curled in whirlpools. Corky, who had turned chatty, volunteered that this was Whale Pass, to be navigated with caution and best at slack tide. In the wheelhouse where everyone settled, Thor Olsen unrolled a chart, plunked a quarter beside it, and beckoned me over with his slight smile. "A quarter if you can find our position." (I did.)

By light next morning we had crossed forty-mile Shelikof Strait, which separates Kodiak Island from the jagged snowy peaks of the mainland south of Anchorage. The high granite Bird Bluffs of Cape Igvak rose above us, white from guano, cawing with birds. Two dozen other seiners maneuvered in the same area, waiting. Thor took position and held it, scanning as did everyone for signs of sockeyes. There was life beneath the choppy water. Glint of silver and a splash. "Jumper to starboard three o'clock," muttered someone, adding to me: "Don't point, Bill, let other boats find their own." Thor eased us toward the splash.

When Fish and Game announced by radio that the season had opened, Thor snapped "Go!" and the skiff clanged away. We towed, then hauled back in a series of steps. Everyone knew his part. I stood aside, watching. How had I ever expected someone to hire me green? At last the boom raised a netful of big silver fish. Their muscular thrashing thumped the deck before they tumbled into the hold.

By the second or third set I had identified some little piece of work to do—a strap or a line stowed or provided—without intruding into the general rush. By week's end I had been accepted with good humor into the process, coiling purse line, stacking web, lining up with the others to pull large catches over the rail, pitching the stiffened fish from the hold at delivery time to a tender. Even the dead salmon, each a slippery six-pound handful grabbed from sloshing, bloody gurry, felt good.

Thor ran it all, from the wheelhouse or with a leap to deck during haul, barely raising his voice. (Other skippers, I was to learn, become shouters and screamers in the heat of a set.) Appropriately, his men called him "Boss." He was the boat's presence, quietly easygoing but driven, all business, confident, the master of every gear and part aboard his boat (most installed by himself.) I had chosen wisely.

By summer's end I was crewing with a share aboard another, smaller boat. Indeed by then Wynn had joined me on the water and we crewed together. I had settled in enough to be a short-tempered cook (doing this in addition to deck work), loud and salty when the boat lurched and pancake batter spilled over my stove's two burners.

My son and I returned to Kodiak and the boats the next year, and the next. By then the glow had faded for Wynn, thanks to a seiner skipper from hell and another slightly less so, plus a stint trawling in the Bering Sea with a Korean joint venture that barely made expenses. He decided fishing would be a part of his résumé, not his life, and now satisfies his sea urges making sophisticated deepwater mixed-gas dives on sunken wrecks. I, though, had swallowed the bait, taking even longer leaves from the office in Baltimore to be a fisherman.

I'm back in Alaskan crabbing water in early winter, aboard a different boat with different crewmates, glad to be here, but not that certain at the moment. The boat thuds to the clack of tight-stowed dishes as we hit a sea. Outside, water bubbles over the deck, and white scud flecks and smokes on the crests rising beyond the rail. It is the rail I watch from the warmth of the galley, or rather the gleam on the rail visible through a back window while bracing my mug on the table. Although painted no more than two months before, part of the rail has been abraded back to gray metal by the scrape of gear, while brown rust nudges through a nick in the paint. In the seconds between seas, wind ripples the wet surfaces of metal and rust, and even blows patches dry enough to lose their sheen. Suddenly the gleam stays glassy.

Fifteen minutes later, brown rust and gray metal have turned milky under an unwavering gleam. The heavy wire stays have begun to thicken. Tight-lashed ropes that always retain a small amount of sway now jerk rigid until a thud of the boat dislodges ice like broken glass. Our big crab pots are stacked astern three high to the height of a man and a half. With each roll their steel frames shift as always a fraction against the lashings, no more than a cough. The webbing looks clear, a lacework of mesh beyond which moves the sight of pointed seas.

I climb to the wheelhouse. Cautiously: "Might be icing."

"Tell me." Jack, the skipper, crouches over the wheel with his head thrust forward like a turtle, his beard nearly touching the window. Cloudy mountains of water roll beyond. The wiper labors. Each stroke pushes a thin sheet of ice.

Another boat is thrashing a quarter-mile to starboard. She crests high enough to seem on air, then troughs to her mast-top. Both boats simply jog to keep the best heading possible through the storm. The nearest haven at Dutch Harbor lies a hundred miles away. Dutch, a raw spot that people usually wish to leave, seems now the heart of warmth.

Is it my imagination, or have we started to roll more slowly? I know the crab yarns, how boats stacked with pots become top-heavy with ice and capsize all hands. Alaska crabbing is a fishery young enough—developed after World War II—that this was the lore of trial and error before the advent of wide-beam boats like ours, built specifically for the work. But capsizing still happens.

The others remain calmly asleep in their bunks, a reassurance. Hours before, while we emptied pots and stacked them on deck to try a new location, three straps in a row snapped in the surging water and Jack shouted down to halt fishing. We had been working at least a dozen hours after four hours' sleep. The others secured gear, peeled boots and oilskins, and went straight to their bunks. With danger Jack would have kept them awake, I told myself. Yet, although I have the watch, he chose to keep the helm as the wind increased, waves rolled higher, and the temperatures dropped.

Jack turns to look through the back wheelhouse window, but ice has nubbled it opaque. "Down in the galley, check the pots outside," he says. "Don't go on deck."

On the way I touch the thick orange bag with my initials on it, stuffed in an open closet along with the other survival suits. Mine is on the bottom. Should I tug it out and push it on top for quicker grabbing? No, nothing's wrong, I tell myself, and hurry on deck.

The web lacework of the pots has thickened. I can now barely see the waves through it. The steel frames have turned white. So have the rail and the ropes I had been watching. When Jack hears the news he blasts the horn used to wake all hands for deck. The others appear from below within seconds, pulling coveralls over their thermal underwear.

"Maybe have to dump the goddamn pots," says Jack. "First get out and break ice around them." To me, the least experienced: "Stay off the pots. Tie yourself in somewhere."

Nobody speaks. My hands tremble as I pull on layered clothes, trying to balance protection from cold against bulk. Anybody who slips overboard in this can expect no retrieval. My boots, rolled back by the stove to dry, remain damp from taking seas hours before. They pull on slowly. Suited against weather, gloved hand clutching a mallet, I follow the others to deck wondering if I'm going to die.

Action diminishes fear. Wherever I slam the mallet, ice clatters down or flies to sea in the wind. My eyes water, the hairs in my nose frost, and soon fingers and toes feel as breakable as the ice. I hear rather than take the time to see the others chop at the wall of ice covering the pots. Death becomes incidental to the importance of banging layers of white frozen water.

And then, unseen forces take control. The wind eases and shifts to lose its sting. Great swells of water continue to roll, but surfaces banged free of ice stay free. At last Jack shouts us back inside.

We tumble against each other back into the galley and dog the back door tight. Tim and Moss laugh mindlessly, unable to stop. Ralph, quiet in a corner, appears to be in prayer. We can't stop shivering. Despite the galley heat, ice feels lodged in my marrow. Jack, haggard, cries jokes to us from the wheelhouse.

The storm passes. The crew rotates thirty-minute watches, allowing Jack to catch some rest. After each watch I barely crawl into my bag before falling asleep again. Four hours later Jack appears back in the wheelhouse, red-eyed and silent, the last of cold bitter coffee in his mug. He examines our position, cruises for half an hour, then sounds the horn. "Move it. Goddamn pots on the deck don't catch crabs." Nobody objects.

SWORDFISH

PAUL MOLYNEAUX, *deckhand on the* Irene & Alton, *harpooning swordfish off the Georges Bank, is the only one aboard who has not yet spotted a fish.*

N THE DARKNESS, two hundred miles offshore, long ocean swells gently rock the *Irene & Alton* as she drifts with the current. The silhouette of her sixty-foot mast sweeps across the night sky.

In the fo'c'sle a cone of aluminum foil wrapped around a light bulb focuses its beam on a man reading at the galley table. Three sleepers in their bunks breathe in rhythm with the creaking hull and the lap of waves against wood. Two inches of cedar separate them from the sea. Dolphins swim by and their shrill whistles carry through the planks. The only discordant sound is the tearing of pages from a book:

Moby-Dick. I had come to the chapter where Melville admonishes captains and ship owners not to send young dreamers into the mast, for their ships will sail past shoals of whales and never sight a one. " 'Why thou monkey,' said a harpooneer to one of these lads. 'We've been cruising now hard upon three years and thou hast not raised a whale yet.' " How simple it would be for Bernard to open up this book and be awakened to the fact that I am that monkey.

I drop the pages into the stove, and watch them curl into black balls, feel the warmth. Up the ladder the dog-house doors open into the night, and the empty deck lit only by the masthead and running lights; still the storm petrels crash-land on us all night. I go up and toss a stranded bird overboard. Scanning the darkness for lights, I see nothing but stars and a black edge where they disappear. All seems well, and I slip back down into the warm fo'c'sle to my book.

Out of the quiet, the engine roars to life. "What the . . . ?"

She slams into gear and the boat surges ahead. I leap up the ladder and hop aft to the wheelhouse.

"What's going on, Bernard?"

"Supertanker."

"I was just up here. I didn't see anything."

"When they're coming right at you, you can't see the lights."

"How did you know?"

"I heard the engines." Bernard waves me up. "Have a look here."

I watch the phosphorescent bar of the radar make its circuit around the screen. A massive blip flashes inside the one-mile marker ring off our starboard quarter. Outside, the dark silhouette passes astern of us, running and masthead lights now clearly visible.

Bernard stays at the wheel and runs for an hour back toward our cruising grounds. I am back in my bunk when he shuts the engine down. We drift again, over the one-hundred fathom edge of Georges Bank.

Ten thousand years ago the glaciers scoured New England and left the wealth of the region deposited out here, covered by the sea. The Labrador current brings cold arctic water sweeping around Nova Scotia, where it mixes with tropical eddies spun off from the Gulf Stream, causing seasonal upwellings that boil with nutrients, the foundation of the marine food chain. We drift through the turmoil. In alternating wafts of cold and warm air we can smell icebergs and coconuts.

At dawn the smells in the fo'c'sle overpower everything: bacon, diesel fumes, and tobacco smoke; the farts of four unwashed men just waking. Georg the cook reaches his long arm up into my bunk and squeezes my leg. "Breakfast. You wanna go get Bernard?"

On deck I light a cigarette. Bernard stands in the door of the wheelhouse, bathed in an orange glow as the first tangent of sunlight slices across the water. I stay by the doghouse, the sheltered entry to the fo'c'sle, and take a look around, watch the light turn to gold. Bernard disappears. A moment later the engine fires up and I feel a familiar jolt as he slips her into gear. We steam into the light breeze, back toward the edge.

I swing up next to Bernard. "Morning."

"Well, good morning, Mr. Paul."

"Breakfast is ready."

"Good. Keep her going west by north a quarter west."

I watch him waddle up the slanted deck and disappear below. In the wheelhouse the chill of the night still lingers.

Below us somewhere in the depths are swordfish, warm water travelers who cross into the cold water to feed on the abundance of boreal forage fish: squid, herring, and sandlance. They have charged slashing through the schools of herring, turned back and swallowed up the dozens of injured fish. Now they must warm themselves in the sun to jump-start their metabolisms and digest their feed.

Out here near the edge where Ice Age rivers cut deep canyons in the Continental Shelf—Oceanographer, Hydrographer, Corsair—the big fish, two hundred pounds and up, rise toward the light. We want to meet them, to drive our sharp bronze darts through the fabric of the fish's tough skin and into its gut cavity. There the dart will turn like a toggle, firmly anchoring the fish to one hundred fathoms of ⅜-inch line. Halfway along the line we hook a small float, and at the end a large orange polyurethane ball, still anachronistically known as a keg, and a radar reflector, or "highflyer." Sometimes the striker will drive the dart straight through the fish, buttonholing it. A fish struck like that will never pull free.

Brad, the mate, comes on deck and lights a smoke, then saunters aft. Out of the corner of my eye I see him with his back to me, knees braced against the lee rail as he pisses over the side.

Bernard comes across the deck, and steps up into the wheel-house. He checks my course and the loran. I hear the chart table drop open behind me.

After a few moments, "Steer north by west."

I ease the spokes around, until the needle begins to drift and then counter back. Bernard watches me steady the new course.

"All right, you can go get your breakfast."

As I reach the doghouse, Brad cuts past and dives into the fo'c'sle ahead of me.

"The *Ocean Clipper* got a fish," he says to Spic.

"This early?"

"I just heard Bernard talking to Dickey Stinson."

Brad begins suiting up to climb aloft. He pulls insulated coveralls over his jeans and sweatshirt, puts on oilskin pants over that, grabs his hat, sunglasses, and cigarettes, and heads up the mast. Spic cranes his neck up to look out the doghouse. "What's Bernard doing?"

"Nothin'."

He lights a one-hit pipe and takes a long drag, holding the smoke in tight, before he relaxes. "You sure you don't want some."

"Nah."

"Might help ya spot a fish, Cap."

I shake my head. He springs up the ladder and follows Brad aloft. "It's only seven o'clock."

"You can't predict these fish," says Georg. "Sit down and eat. The *Ocean Clipper* keeps a man in the mast whenever it's light enough to see."

It's an unheard-of hour to head up into the swaying rigging, exposed to the chill air and constant breeze. Reluctantly I climb the tarred ratlines. Up the aluminum topmast, around the radio box, I keep looking up, conscious of every move.

"Where the hell you been anyway?" Brad looks away at the

water, not wanting an answer as I climb past and up onto my little perch at the top of the mast. By the time I reach it the roll of the boat is accentuated to the point that I am flying in thirty-foot arcs through the air as I hop over the aluminum ring and into my seat. Alone, I roll within a half-sphere of ocean and sky, supposedly looking for swordfish to kill. Below me the boys chatter and laugh.

I watch the sea, mesmerized by the swirling blues and greens of the Northeast Peak, the edge where two worlds collide. "The edges are where you find the fish," Georg tells me. Though he did the cooking, and spent more time on deck than any of us, he also spotted the most fish. "You can't stick'm if you don't see'm."

I try to scan the ocean Georg's way, let my mind empty and see the whole picture. "You're looking for two crescent fins or a purple torpedo," he says. Everyone else has raised a few fish, but I am still waiting. My sunglasses fog up; I clean them with a tissue, rubbing the lenses between numb fingers.

In the wheelhouse Bernard watches the temperature gauge. Most fish bask in water between 61 and 63 degrees. Below us, the pulpit, a twenty-foot aluminum gangplank, protrudes from the bow; the harpoon lashed alongside it. Bernard comes out and unties the long shaft. He repositions it across the safety rail, which runs around the end of the pulpit, and lashes it there, ready. And so *Irene* cruises, with her harpoon held out foremost, as if she carried it across the palm of her hand, offering it to a fish.

This year we are handicapped by the new Hague line, which has cut us off from our best grounds. Where we once worked side-by-side with our Canadian brethren, the world court has separated us. We hear their chatter on the radio; they have the fish to themselves now.

Dickey Stinson, captain of *Ocean Clipper*, first went swordfishing with his grandfather out of Block Island when he was eight years old. His grandfather came from Maine and helped get the fishery going in the late 1800s. Stinson knows swordfish. He believes there are two groups of fish, the southern group that used to show up around Long Island, and is now virtually wiped out, and the northern group that shows up later in the summer on the northeast peak. Bernard only started swordfishing in 1979, so he talks to Dickey, and reads about the biology of the fish, and the history of the fishery.

"They used to harpoon the fish from a schooner and then sent a man over in a dory to gather up the kegs," Georg tells me as we sit in the mast. "That made it easier for a boat under sail. In the old days they used to go from fish to fish, there were so many." According to Georg, the season used to start as early as June off Long Island. "But since the longliners have been fishing down south every year there's fewer and fewer fish," he says. "They're working the spawning grounds off Florida, killing the pups."

"I know. I seen it in a fish market. I said to the guy, 'That's a damn small swordfish,' and he says, 'That's a big one.' "

A streak of white and red screams out of the sky, shattering our conversation. Fred Brooks buzzes the little Piper around the boat a couple of times.

"Morning, boys," he says over the VHF.

We wonder about his night ashore.

Brad grabs the mike out of the radio box. "Did you bring cigarettes?"

"I'll drop'm on the next pass."

The plane comes in low, a garbage bag drops out from under the wing, and splashes in front of the boat. Bernard, listening to the radio in the wheelhouse, comes out and gaffs the bag. On deck he opens it, shakes out a wet newspaper, and tosses the cigarettes in front of the doghouse. Fred heads out to fly his lazy circles around our perimeter.

"Now maybe we'll see some action," says Spic.

From the mast, Brad steers us over to look at a pair of sperm whales.

Days of no fish come often enough in swordfishing. We had seen a week of them already this trip, but with calm seas, good water temperatures, and the plane on hand, they particularly frustrate us. A few false alarms cut the tension in the mast. "Swordfish!" I holler.

"That's a shark," says Georg.

"So you want to be a flatlander but you don't know how to wear sandals, eh, b'y?" Brad mocks me with a parody of the National Sea commercial, done in a Newfie accent.

"Swor . . . !"

"Where?"

"It's gone."

"Got one over here, Bernard. Two o'clock, thirty boat lengths."

Fred has a fish.

Brad hauls down on the throttle and steering ropes, making a hard turn to starboard.

"Eleven o'clock, twenty-five boat lengths, she's pretty deep."

I drop down the ratlines onto the deck and take my station along the starboard gunwale just forward of the mast shrouds. Twenty feet out on the end of the pulpit, Bernard stands with his harpoon resting on the short rail that keeps him from going over when he throws.

"Twelve o'clock, six boat lengths. She's deep," Fred's voice comes from a speaker on the forestay behind Bernard.

We bear down. From where I stand I can see nothing until the last moment. Bernard swings his harpoon around, poised to throw, one hand on the very end. With two fingers capping the butt of the eighteen-foot-long shaft, his other arm stretches out as far as he can reach toward the point. He rests that forward hand, and the weight of the harpoon, on the rail. Two loops of line hang down from the harpoon and swing with the roll of the boat: One ties the shaft to the boat, the other runs from the dart, fitted on the end of the shaft, back through a series of clips along the pulpit to a milk crate holding one hundred fathoms of line.

"Twelve o'clock, three boat lengths."

By now Brad has visual contact, and he lines Bernard up on the fish. "One boat length."

Bernard sees the fish. His whole body turns toward it as the harpoon comes up and he lets fly. He drives the dart deep into the fish just behind the sleek dorsal fin. As the line snaps out of its clips toward me, I throw the fifteen-pound weight I have ready. The big fish dives toward it and the line sings out over the side. I throw half the coils over and in the resulting slack moment snap on a small poly ball.

Fred's voice comes over the radio again: "I can see three fish right now, Bernard. Ten o'clock, three boat lengths." I toss the rest of the coils overboard, followed by a large poly ball and a highflyer.

"Swordfish! Four o'clock!" Georg has one.

Out of the corner of my eye I see Spic land on deck. I run a new dart, trailing its line along the length of the pulpit, out to where Bernard stands, straightening his iron. Quickly I hook up another weight and check that the lines are running clear. Spic brings more poly balls and highflyers forward. Bernard poises to throw again. He hits the fish hard before the iron leaves his hand and I can see the shock move up through his arm. The fish breaks the surface, spraying blood. I toss the weight and heave the coils overboard.

"The big fish chase the weight straight to bottom," Georg had told me. "We hauled one back once and its mouth and gills were full of mud. If they get out beyond the one-hundred-fathom edge you can kiss your gear good-bye. They'll take the whole works down."

The fish keep coming. Fred spots them from the plane, Brad and Georg from the mast. Spic and I race around on deck, passing Bernard fresh darts and rigging up the lines. Bernard stays cool, seeming to move in slow motion next to us.

"I don't know what we're going to do about kegs if this keeps goin'," says Spic.

I pass him a line and he ties it to an old highflyer with a chewed-up Styrofoam float on it.

Bernard strikes another fish and I throw the weight. Spic tosses the poly balls and highflyer over while I carry another dart out to Bernard. The VHF speaker is quiet. Aloft, Brad and Georg are silent.

"Look at that." Spic points aft. The sea behind the boat is littered with bright orange balls and highflyers. Fourteen fish in less than an hour. We finish the melee with three rigs to spare.

In the aftermath, as I stow gear, I hear people talking about fuel, and Nova Scotia. Brad comes down out of the mast.

"What's going on?"

"Fred's low on fuel. He's talking about going to Nova Scotia."

"How much closer is it?"

"He could trim about fifty miles off, but the wind's swingin' round to eastward. Counterclockwise, too. You know what they say when the wind backs around counterclockwise."

In the end Fred chooses the tail wind for home.

The breeze picks up; choppy seas make the high flyers hard

to spot as we start to haul the fish in. Only Georg stays in the mast, keeping an eye on our gear and continuing to look for fish.

Bernard gaffs the first high flyer and passes me the line. I begin hauling it in, taking long pulls and gathering in the slack.

"Go ahead and use the hauler."

I bend the line into the groove of a hydraulic hauler set against the starboard rail, and open the valve.

"Easy, we don't want to lose him."

The line flakes in loops into a milk crate.

"There it is."

I bring the fish thrashing alongside, Spic slings a heavy rope around its tail, and hooks it to the jilson. Bernard takes a few turns around the winch head and hoists the giant up out of the water. It swings above us and in over the rail. As soon as the fish lands, I grab the sword and cut it off with a saw. Spic drives an ax into its throat and blood spurts across the deck. I saw down across the back of the fish's head while Spic chops off the fins and tail. Together we roll the big fish belly up and I begin to open it. Spic goes for another fish Brad and Bernard have hoisted aboard. With a sharp knife I make a careful cut around the anal vent, so as not to nick the intestines and have that mess to clean up. As soon as I cut enough of a slit from the vent toward the throat I reach in under the knife to hold the lining of the guts out of the way, and carefully open the belly.

"Open his stomach up and see what he had for dinner," says Bernard, watching me from the winch head. I cut open the guts and long thin fish spill onto the deck, exuding a tangy smell of bile.

"What are these?"

"Sandlance."

In the pile of guts I see the heart, still beating. I pick it up and hold it in my hand, feel its ebbing pulse, the life of the fish.

"If you want to be a swordfisherman, you've gotta eat the heart of the beast," says Brad, watching me.

I hand it to him and he takes it down forward.

The roll of the boat continues to increase throughout the late afternoon. The fish on deck have to be slid aft and jammed between the rail and the wheelhouse. Brad opens the hatch and drops into the hold. One by one we drop the carcasses below, and by evening Brad has entombed them all in ice.

With the decks cleared we hunt down the last two highflyers in the darkness, pounding into a head sea, the staysail snapping loudly back and forth.

After an hour the boat slows and the deck lights come on. Bernard glides out of the wheelhouse, scoops up the gaff, reaches out with it into the darkness, and snags a highflyer. Spic lifts the rig out of the water. Bernard hauls on the line. I get behind him and together we lean back hauling on the dripping line, gathering in the slack, and hauling back again, until the fish comes into view. Spic lassoes the tail and I hook onto it. The fish comes out of the water heavy, its smooth skin scraped from the bottom. Spic and I dress it quickly and hoist it into the hold. Brad jumps down, shoves some ice into its belly, kicks a little more around it, and that's it. We fit the hatch covers. Brad goes aft to talk to Bernard. He comes forward again with a heavy tarp, and Spic and I lash it over the hatch.

"Bernard wants to get the parachute ready."

That's our weather report. Bernard has brought a new parachute to use as a drogue if we lay to in heavy seas.

We continue searching for the last highflyer marking a big fish out there somewhere, dead, dragging blindly along bottom. I think of a man in his dory, with the fish lashed alongside, an oar up, waiting for us to come find him, the growing black seas lifting him without malice in the dark.

Not long after we go below, Georg comes down into the fo'c'sle.

"Braddy, Bernard wants to set the parachute, and set up a lifeline."

"What ails him, that fucking parachute ain't going to hold this boat."

Brad and Spic go on deck and we hear them thumping over our heads as they set out the drogue and make it fast to the bit.

Georg sits down to eat. "I heard the Canadian forecast," he says "They're calling for fifty-to-sixty-knot winds with higher gusts."

"Surf's up, Moondog."

The boat swings around and comes tight on the drogue, the rolling stops, and we ride over the waves smooth and steady. The parachute acts as a shock absorber.

Spic's watch starts at ten; the rest of us turn in. "Somebody put the aluminum foil on the light."

In the darkened fo'c'sle we lay listening to the wind picking up in the rigging. Brad comes below and Spic goes up the ladder to stand watch.

I wake up a little while later to the sound of voices. Someone strips the aluminum foil off the light. The boat rolls violently and I wedge myself into the bunk to keep from sliding out. *Irene* lays down hard to port on every roll and never comes all the way back. Bernard has the engine running and is bringing the bow up into the waves.

I crawl out of my bunk.

"The parachute broke."

"No shit."

"I told him that piece of shit wouldn't hold us. For Christ's sake, Bernard."

"What time is it?"

"Almost midnight," says Spic. "I was about to wake you up."

"Is there hot water?"

"No, the stove's off."

"Is the Lister on?"

"No."

"Shit."

"Forget your fuckin' coffee. Come on, let's get the parachute in."

On deck Spic and Brad start to haul in the hawser as Bernard jogs forward. I coil the line into a box lashed along the starboard rail. Cold spray blows over the rail, and slaps the pillow warmth from my face.

The parachute comes aboard in silky shreds, literally blown to pieces from the strain of the boat. We stow the remains back down in the engine room and go below, rolling side to in the mounting seas.

The Lister starts. I make my coffee in the electric kettle, but spill most of it trying to make my way aft. In the wheelhouse Bernard hunches over the chart table, planning to run somewhere. Spic stands at the wheel trying to keep the bow into the seas, occasionally getting blindsided and rolled.

"Okay, Spic."

"She's all yours," he says, and slides out the lee door as I step into the wheelhouse.

I check the radar. Blips and storm scatter flash all over the screen, but no lights show around us. Outside the rails of the boat, uniform darkness surrounds us. The sea and sky, rain and wave form one black roiling mass.

Bernard reaches up and adjusts the throttle. He takes the wheel and puts us on a west southwest course, with waves rolling up our port quarter, some hitting us a little closer to broadside.

"West southwest," he says, stepping away from the wheel. "If you see a big one coming turn away from it."

I glance at the chart. We're heading for Cape Cod and it looks like a tight squeeze. In order to get around the Nantucket shoals, Bernard quarters the waves rolling in out of the east as close as he dares.

"If I see a big one?" I can't see shit. I can only feel a big sea lift us from behind and turn us sickeningly as if it will roll us, our great high mast now acting as a lever to heel us even farther over and hold us there indefinitely. Heeled over like that in a cross sea, the green water pours across the deck, driving the lee rail out of sight. The boat spends more time under water than out. Bernard sleeps; *Irene* will find her way.

I see Brad come up out of the doghouse. He stands there with a cigarette hanging out of his mouth, watching for his chance. In a lull he dances down the deck to the lee rail alongside the wheelhouse and starts to piss over the side.

A big one picks us up. I can feel the boat speed up as the wave gets hold of her and drives us into a sea that crests the bow and sweeps the deck with a three-foot wall of water. I hold the wheel until it passes and then look out the door for Brad. Gone. I turn to holler, "Ber . . ." but stop short. In the open port-hole at the back of the wheelhouse, above Bernard's bunk, eight white fingers show.

Brad lets go and comes around next to me.

"I thought you were gone."

"Nah." He looks at the compass. "Where you going?"

"Who knows."

Brad waits his chance again and runs forward, vanishing into the dimly lit fo'c'sle.

I stand alone at the helm, glancing at the clock and out across the deck. Whips of wind-blown spray stream out of the black, through the meager light on deck, and back into the rich darkness I catch glimpses of nocturnal waves.

Another big one starts to lift us. I spin the wheel down hard to starboard, but the stern rises and twists sickeningly broadside again, burying the starboard rail, the great mast heeling us down.

I hear Bernard shift in his bunk behind me as the big sea loses its grip and rolls past.

"It's almost your watch, Bernard, do you want me to get you anything?"

It is our custom for the man who stands watch before Bernard to bring him a soda or coffee. Tonight I only want to get forward into my snug bunk and let the storm rage on. Bernard gets up and checks things.

"You could get us a better place to be," he says as he takes the wheel.

"So where we going?"

"Same way we been going, only farther."

"Looks like we're headed around the Cape."

"Well, maybe that's a good idea, better than staying here."

I jam myself in the lee door and light a cigarette, feeling the occasional warm blasts of tropical air waft over us. Cherishing the rarefied moment, I am reluctant to leave. Bernard stands at the wheel and squints out past the bow, in concentration. Above him hangs a little plaque that says, "You can learn a lot by watching."

"So did you grow up in Owl's Head?" I ask as a wave lifts us and Bernard rolls the wheel hard down to leeward.

"No, I grew up on Matinicus."

"Were you born out there?"

"No. I was born on Vinalhaven." He pauses, looks down at the rocking compass, then adds, "On the Fourth of July, but I never heard a sound." Holding the frame of the door I cough, and laugh. "I can't remember much about the time I was born," he continues, "but a couple of years later I realized I was on the island."

A wave slams into the side of the boat and whips spray across the windows. Water dripping down the glass reflects the red binnacle light.

"Your mother must've been there when you were born."

"Well, I think so, but I can't remember. It might've been her, could've been somebody else. I don't know."

I laugh, wondering why he still lets me come fishing with him when I have not seen a fish in three years. The boat lays over hard to starboard, and I grab the doorjamb quickly to keep from falling. Bernard glances toward me.

"Did you go fishing with Alton?" I ask.

"No, I fished with my grandfather, Dalton," he says as *Irene* pulls herself back up.

"Did he build his own boat?"

"Most everyone did."

Waves continue to pound us. We can hear the wind-driven spray hit the staysail like buckshot, but we hang on, dry and safe in the dimly lit wheelhouse.

"Was it a dory?"

"No, my great-grandfather Horace was the last to go dory fishing. There were three boats started taking dories to the Grand Banks out of Belfast. Horace got on with them and stayed with them for years. Grandfather had an open boat with a rounded hull."

"Like they use on the south coast of Newfoundland."

"Something like that. I went lobstering with him in it. It had an old Knox make and brake engine. The way that engine worked, whenever he came to a trap he had to shut it off. I used to go along. 'Engineer,' he called me. I'd start the engine for him. When he sold his lobsters he'd usually get some change, and I'd get the change. Some days I worked for a nickel, other days, ninety cents."

I flick my cigarette out into the black. The red spark vanishes in the turmoil.

Bernard carries on with stories. His watch ends, but I take the wheel rather than leave him.

"The man on deck doesn't think the same as the man in the wheelhouse," Bernard says of his own transition. "When I went on deck with father, in the fifties, I thought about how I could do my work better and faster so I could go turn in. Then when I got into the wheelhouse I had to think about making a trip. I realized that in order to put a trip together, I had to learn to think like a fish. I'd imagine the bottom and try to figure what it looked like and how the fish would move on it. I'd be so caught up in that, the days would run together. I didn't count days, I counted fuel and grub, and water. Sometimes we'd have to melt ice for water."

I say nothing, standing at the wheel, listening to Bernard's stories. Foaming green water rolls in over the bow, washing the length of the boat. I imagine a boat of my own—something very much like *Irene*, but maybe a little bigger.

In the last moments of darkness, we stop talking. I roll the spokes back and forth, holding our course. No seas have washed the deck in the last half hour.

At dawn Bernard takes the wheel and turns back northeast into the rising sun. To the west we see the thin line of Nantucket on the horizon. In the fo'c'sle Georg cooks the swordfish heart for breakfast and Brad and I sit down to eat it.

"What d'you think?"

"Kinda tough."

"It's good for you," says Spic. "It's the best meat there is."

We steam all day back to our cruising grounds. But the fish have crossed into Canadian waters, and we can no longer follow.

In four more days we see only one fish. I spot it only two

boat lengths off the port bow. Basking, it makes a gentle flip with its tail, no mistake. Like in a dream the word sticks in my throat, finally:

"Swordfish!"

Brad turns the boat, as I drop past him to throw the weight. Bernard hustles out into the pulpit and harpoons it.

"Bernard says not to cut the sword, and save the head," says Spic, after we get the fish aboard. "I think he's gonna get it mounted."

I stand looking at the sharp sword, the smooth gray-blue body, and the big saucerlike eye, staring distracted up into the rigging. This is the fish that makes me a fisherman. "Thank you," I say, before driving an ax into its throat and watching its blood flood the deck.

On our twelfth day out, a heavy fog rolls in. The radar and the loran both fail.

Bernard steers for home by dead reckoning, running his course and adjusting it to compensate for the set of the wind and drift of the tide.

It is night when we make the buoy off Matinicus. Bernard plots a course for White Head on the mainland.

Brad calls us on deck.

"Bernard wants everyone in the bow."

"What are we doing?"

"Listen for the horn."

Bernard slows the engine and we hear the horn dead ahead, a little to port. Brad points. Bernard closes with the land until we can see the dim light through the fog.

The fog is so dense we can barely see from one end of the boat to the other but Bernard turns for the home stretch. He is running courses and speeds. In order to make each buoy as we head up Mussel Shoals channel, he has to run a three-quarter throttle.

We plow ahead through the fog, knowing any deviation will drive us onto the rocks on either side of the narrow channel. We make each buoy right on the money. After a tense hour, Bernard cuts the engine back, and we crawl ahead. Brad mans a spotlight. We see nothing but its beam cutting through the haze. Finally, almost amazingly, our dory, tied to the mooring ball, looms into sight.

In August of 1985, the *Irene & Alton* completed the last trip made by any Maine boat strictly to harpoon swordfish. My first fish was her last.

CATCH
AND RELEASE

DEBRA NIELSEN *recounts her struggle*
for survival in the sinking of
The Wayward Wind *in the Bering*
Sea, and her struggle afterward to
reconcile the losses.

THE VIVIDNESS OF the flowers floating on the dark gray water rivet the eye like bright balloons in a cloudless sky. Sprays of delicate baby's breath, burgundy roses, and purple iris entwine a pale blue ribbon that reads, "Beloved Son." A breeze brushes over the wreath, trembling its petals.

A large woman stands dockside. Beside her is a wheelchair, next to which a man peers into a videocamera. Occasionally he utters an explanatory narrative, or makes a quiet observation.

As the woman fumbles with her camera, her ragged breathing mingles with the cries of circling sea gulls.

"I can do this," she says.

I can't.

I don't want to be here. I don't want to be standing here on this dirty dock, splattered by sea-gull droppings and smudged by creosote, staring at a ten-year-old tribute, floating on a monochromatic sea. I'd rather be anywhere else. I'd definitely rather be fishing. Maybe casting a net over sparkling salmon or reefing a halibut from the fathomless deep. I'd rather be feeling the hope of the hook, the anticipation of the baited pot, or unloading a deckload of dreams.

Instead, I am here . . . an honor-bound captive of two flatlanders with a need to float their flowers.

One week ago, the woman called to tell me they were coming. She didn't say she could barely walk. She didn't say the man would be with her. She didn't say that she smoked nonstop . . . or that she was dying. Years ago, I met her briefly when we went to Wisconsin to see his folks.

"This is Connie, my younger brother's wife. She can clear out a barroom all by herself."

She seemed nice enough, but I had a different criteria for friendship, and I wasn't in the market for Barroom Betty.

As a matter of fact, the entire factory mentality of Kenosha, Wisconsin, left me cold. Pickled eggs? Retirement? Not for me. I had my eye on an entirely different horizon.

Now, she tells me she has a rare neurological disorder, something called reflex sympathetic dystrophy. Originally, she says, it was associated with farm women. It seems that occasionally, while canning produce, a heavy jar would accidentally drop sharply onto a woman's foot. The signal sent from the foot to the brain would somehow arc due to the distance of the extremity. Apparently, this uncompleted circuit reacts similarily to a live wire, continually sending a message of pain to a mystified brain, and, consequently, plays havoc with the nervous system.

"The doctors didn't want me to come," she says, "but I told them I'm going. 'I'm going to Kodiak, Alaska,' I said. And I told Ma, 'I'll buy you that memorial wreath you want and float it for your red-headed Billy.'" She shakes her head.

"Ten years . . . I just hope it brings her some peace. If it brings her some peace, it's worth every step I have to take."

The wreath is drifting into the dock. I bend to give it a gentle nudge toward the center of the stall.

I think about shocks to the nervous system. Arcs of pain ricocheting about, endlessly seeking solace from a recoiling brain. Do the aftershocks ever cease? Or are these unquelled sparks of harm snuffed out only by death? As I straighten, the woman draws me into her arms.

"I'm so sorry to cause you more pain," she says. "I wouldn't cause you pain for anything, and I know I am and it hurts me. It hurts my heart to do it. You don't know how it hurts me."

Her face is contorted with emotion. I nod into the smother of her shoulder and she tightens her embrace.

As soon as I can, I pull away, cross the dock, and face the open ocean.

It is January, the sky clenching snow, the iron sea below—no wind, only the push of our passage through the icy stillness. The harbor has begun to freeze, and our props churn through a blended margarita of iced pewter, chilled mercury, and bits of silver. The ocean steams where it touches the frozen air and ice fog smudges the horizon.

We wear thick neoprene gloves and heavy raingear as we secure the deck for travel. Each movement realized through resistance, like working under water. Lines are stowed below; left on deck, they would freeze to useless lumps of ice. Even as we coil, they begin to stiffen.

I take the lines and go below, shedding my raingear and gloves before descending into a well-lit laboratory-clean engine room. It did not always look like this. We spent five years of nonstop effort and a small fortune on her refitting. After stowing the lines, I check the gauges on the main. The stack temperature on the port exhaust is running a couple of degrees high, but everything else reads normal. I wipe a seep of oil from the forward head of the auxiliary and wait. It does not reappear. After securing the toolbox to the bulkhead, I wipe a ¾-wrench with an oily rag and hang it in its silhouette against the hull. The wrenches make metallic music to the rhythm of the engines. I stow a wooden box of hydraulic fittings in the forward compartment before ascending once more to the galley.

Thick white mugs hang from evenly spaced hooks above the sink. There is enough space between each mug to keep them from colliding in heavy seas, but all of them are chipped. One has black electrical tape wrapped tightly around its handle. I grab our mugs, fill them with fresh coffee, then balance them the three steps up to the bridge. Red receives the smooth porcelain heat into his hand.

The skipper, Red, has spent over twenty years on the water, most of it on the bridge. His jaw is square, his eyes the color of the winter sea, and his hair a banner to his temperament. He can run a boat with a bit of spit, a paper clip, and a few choice words. Red's praise is as rich as his rage, the copper fire of his hair surging equally hot through his veins. In his rough, capable hands, equipment comes to life. In his sure, calloused hands, I do also. . . .

For fourteen years, we've powered through the seasons, netting herring in the spring, chasing salmon in the summer, harvesting halibut whenever we could, and risking everything in pursuit of lucrative crab during the worst of winters. This season, we have a first-class boat and a great crew. Confidence is running high.

Outside Ugak Island we set three strings of pots at different depths just to get a feel for the movement of the crab, then run till we get a little protection from the island. We anchor up to get some rest. I awaken as Red crawls out of our bunk and fumbles for his clothes.

"Go ahead and sleep for fifteen minutes more," he says to me, walking out and closing the door. The engines rumble and the anchor winch growls as it seizes the chain. There is a high-pitched whine as the hydraulics tug at the firmly entrenched anchor, then a clanking rush as the anchor lets go. We head out to check our pots.

Rising from the bunk, I pull on dry clothes and go to the galley to start breakfast. If we eat before we hit open water, it won't be as rough, so I hustle to prepare scrambled eggs, fried potatoes, bacon, and toast. Coffee is already making and the breakfast smells draw the guys to the galley. Red eats in the wheelhouse, adjusting the jogstick or checking position between bites.

"Mornin' dear," Mike says, grabbing a mug and filling it with steaming black coffee. Mike, his brother "Little Dave," Jay, and Jim are the other crew members aboard. In the summer, Mike and I run salmon seiners, Jim has a charter boat business, and Little Dave works a beach seine operation. Jay, also a seasoned mariner and longtime friend, rounds out the crew. The guys suck down their food, inhale their coffee, and don foul-weather gear within ten minutes.

"Great grub!" Mike calls cheerfully from the companionway.

"Yeah, like you Hoovers tasted it!" I scoot everything into the sink and am out on deck before the first long swell of open ocean lifts the hull.

Now it's "boat time." Every move at triple speed. No mistakes. No hesitations. There's an adrenal quality to it, an indefinable satisfaction in its execution. You learn to tie a bowline with your eyes closed so you can do it in the dark. You learn to leap, in just about any sea conditions, from boat to skiff and back again, both vessels under power, careening wakes adding interest to the calculation, split-second timing the only alternative. Greenhorns discover firsthand that for every action there is an equal and opposite reaction. Speed and precision often come at a painful price.

Looking out over the water, I can just make out the bobbing pink of the first string of gear. Red idles up to the first buoy and Mike throws the hook, snags the trailer buoy, and lays slack over the top of the hauler. Dave coils. Rapidly the line snakes upward till the coil stands knee-high. At twenty-five fathom shots, we slow the hauler slightly for knots, flip the line, and keep coiling.

"Bridle!" I yell as the pot begins to emerge. I hook it and the whine of the deck crane accompanies it over the side. Several long-legged snow crab cling to its webbed sides—spider monkeys of the sea.

I unhook the door and we pull the crab out carefully, measure their carapace, then toss them into the tank. All but three are keepers. Meanwhile, Red is jogging to another pot. Mike throws the hook.

Overall, the catch around Ugak is disappointing. Red decides to head toward Sitkalidak, at the south end of Kodiak Island.

Once more we are underway, steel hull creasing a silver sea, the sky darkening to soot as it begins to snow. We are tanked down, pumping fresh seawater on our crab to keep them constantly aerated. Water pushes out from under the main hatch, sloshes over the dock, then finds the sea through scupper holes cut in the base of the railings. All other deck hatches must be securely bolted down to prevent flooding. The pots are stacked on the stern, securely tied, lines and buoys inside.

In the Gulf of Alaska, storms brew up with little warning. Lines are triple-checked, rigging cinched until hydraulics squeal, and eyes are always moving. You look for slack or fray or leak . . . you listen to the cadence of the engines, the auxiliary's high whine, the deep throb of the main. You watch and you listen, for any sign that something's not quite "right." Seasoned fishermen call it "running a little scared."

Up in the wheelhouse, I put on *Elvis Presley's Greatest Hits* just to rag the guys about being older than me. Once in a while, Red gyrates his hips or pantomimes slicking back his hair.

"I'm going to be violently ill if you don't quit that," I say. Apparently, any attention is encouragement because he starts singing off-key, wailing along with the music.

"Love me tender, love me true . . ." He's really getting into it now and I cover my ears as he closes in all dreamy-eyed: "Never let me go-o-o-o."

"Somebody save me!" I yell. Nobody looks up. "You guys don't even care if I get drooled on!" I push Red toward Little Dave. "Sing to him," I say. Little Dave's eyes brighten with amusement as Red leans in his direction.

"Don't come one step closer," Dave warns.

Outside, the snowflakes have fattened to heavy cartwheels. They do handsprings against the portholes before the wind blows them past. Beyond the momentary vision of the snowflakes, we can see nothing. Inside, the wheelhouse is also dark. It makes it easier to see the luminous radar screen, read the sonar, scan the numerous neon gauges, and watch the plotter guide us south. Radio chatter punctuated by static interrupts the silences. The wheelhouse is a cocoon, womblike in the vastness of night.

"We'd best get some rest, Angel," Red says to me, untangling his long legs from the chair where he's been draped. "I'll wake Jim." As the watch switches, I go below to the engine room for a quick inspection. Everything looks fine.

Back in the galley, I get a couple of bowls of ice cream and join Red in the stateroom. We eat, stretched out on the bunk, pillows behind our heads, cold sweetness on our tongues.

When our bowls are empty, we reach out for each other, then fall asleep, lulled by the hum of the engines and the rise and fall of the hull pushing through the waves.

"Get up!" Jay yells, slamming his fist against our door as he runs past. "The back deck's under!" He shouts it over his shoulder as we tear open the door and run out. From there it is dark mayhem . . . survival suits pulled and donned, Maydays sent and repeated, Red in the engine room, water to his waist, starting emergency pumps, me urging him up and out, fear in my voice.

"Do you need any help?" So many other times, he has needed my help. "No, Angel. Get your suit on. Get mine ready." He yells it to me as the emergency pump kicks in.

With my survival suit on, I can barely function. The suit is big for me. The mitts are cumbersome as lobster claws, the hood stops my ears. I make my way back to the engine room hatch. Red is still working frantically, trying to save the boat.

Everyone else is outside, standing on the bow. The deck is slanting sternward at a forty-five-degree angle and I know we won't bring it back. Red knows it too and makes his way to the ladder to grab his suit from me, already soaked and shivering. He goes out on the back deck after ordering me to get to the bow. I make my way, shakily, clinging to the walls as the boat lurches forward into the swell and settles deeper astern. Water is halfway up the back deck now, and I cannot see Red.

I pull myself out the wheelhouse door. The wind is cold on my face, the men silent as statues.

This frozen moment, I realize the degree of danger in every cell of my body, and my mind searches frantically for insulation from the yawning fissure opening at my feet. Adrenaline floods my blood. . . . I feel like I am running, leaping just ahead of feral jaws . . . or hanging miles above a void—the crack of the branch I cling to the only sound in the stillness of the sheerest terror one can own.

My voice is snatched into the wind as I find a small handhold in sanity's cliff. "Does anyone have a line?" I shout. No one answers. *"Does anyone have a line?"* The men stir but do not respond. "We need a line to stay together!" I yell again.

"There ain' no time, girl," Mike says.

"The lines are right here—we're standing on them!" I shout back, feeling tremendous relief as I remember the extra coils of crab line we stored on the port side of the vessel toward the bow, and then dismay as I recall that it is sinking line. We'll just have to hang on to it. Mike is galvanized into action and quickly locates a shot of line in the darkness, unties it, and threads it among us.

"Does anyone have the EPIRB?" I ask. No one does. By now, the boat is sliding seaward, the bow trapping air, and I have to hang on with all my might to direct my motion back into the boat. The floor slants downward and only my arms keep me in place. Inside, the wheelhouse is dark and still. The neon gauges of the electronics are like eyes, open in the blackness. The radio spits our name again and again into the stillness . . . *"The Wayward Wind,* calling *The Wayward Wind. . . ."*

I lift the EPIRB carefully from its receptacle and hang on tightly to it as I make my way back outside. It is a twelve-inch-tall cylinder about six inches in diameter. It is capable of signaling our position via satellite to the Coast Guard personnel in Kodiak who will be trying to find us. I muscle my way out, the EPIRB tucked under one arm, so that I can use both hands. My feet are practically useless, and I press into the wall to get to the door handle. I grasp it in one hand as the floor suddenly disappears completely from beneath me. Clinging to the door, clutching the EPIRB tight to my body, I swing for a moment, regain footing, then pull myself outside.

Red is on the bow. His suit is on, but the hood is not up. His bright hair is tangled and wet with sweat, his eyes tender and quiet.

"Are you zipped up, Angel?" he asks.

"I'm fine," I say. He goes to the stern to check, maybe to see. . . . I do not see him after that.

The wind and waves are increasing, or maybe it only seems that way as we get closer to them. I am concerned that I will lose the unwieldly EPIRB as I enter the water, so I try to hand it to the person next to me. He does not respond. I tuck the EPIRB tightly under one arm. Now, the water is midway up the house, the back deck several feet under. One by one, we slip silently into the sea. The man beside me is suddenly gone and the sea rises up to meet me. I attempt to propel myself outward, hoping to get as far as possible from the pull of the ship's hull. The line is wrapped once around my right arm. Both my hands are clamped tightly onto the EPIRB.

I am immediately dragged beneath the water and thrust deeply into a wave. It bursts against the hull and my face scrapes steel. Plastered against the curve of the hull, the sea slides me toward the surface. My chest, then my knees bounce off the boat. I push backward with my feet. I push hard. The distance gained allows a wave just enough room to curl around me and throw me once more into the hull. This time, I am upside down, and my head hits hard. I am desperately trying to protect the EPIRB from impact; twisting, I manage to get my feet against the hull once more, and kick off with all my strength. At some point, I am floating free.

The swell of the ocean seems calm after the surging rush of the sinking boat. A trailer buoy is bobbing beside me. I grab it and slide it under my neck, elevating my head. Someone bumps into me.

"Hang on to me!" I shout, "I have the EPIRB!" He drifts by without response.

Now, I am all alone. I can see nothing but darkness. After a time, the black ocean looks slightly darker than the blackness of the sky. More time passes, and I can distinguish the breaking brightness of waves. Large white snowflakes define the sky. Sea gulls appear like apparitions of light. They look like luminous angels until they extend their feet. None land.

As I float, buoyed by the massive sea beneath me, looking upward at an inverted bowl of sky, a mighty calm pervades me.

For the first time in my life, I understand my place in the universe. I understand fully the privilege of life—I absorb the precious fragility of that privilege. I feel a part of everything . . . selfless as seaweed, rimed by salt and slime, storm-tossed or becalmed at the whim and will of the waves. A bright blob of orange on a blackened expanse of ocean . . . Poseidon's small plaything, a momentary diversion from designing beaches or escorting migratory whales. I do not feel fear. I feel everything else.

From time to time I call out for Red. I want to tell him that I'm okay, that I'm not afraid, that I have no regrets. I'd like to thank him for the experiences we shared, the way he taught me to absorb the layers of our combined humanity, to enjoy the manifestations of our abilities and to savor the saturation of our days. Together, we became so much more than the sum of our parts that now, facing obscurity, I am undaunted.

A strong wind parts the clouds high above me, revealing small shimmers of light. I've often watched sea otters float like this, toes scuffing the sky, bright eyes reflecting the stars. They have more hairs per square inch than any other mammal. Silken armor to guard them from the piercing cold. My back is numb where it touches the sea.

Only the waves and the occasional cry of a gull can be heard. The blackness is a shroud.

"Red!" I cry out again, "Red!" Someone yells out in the darkness off to my right.

"Over here! I'm over here!" I strain my ears. Probably only a gull.

It is uncertain how long I float before something bumps into me in the water and I am pulled close to a large rubber body.

"Hang on to me!" I yell, "I've got the EPIRB!" He holds me, but I cannot make out what he is saying. He's trying to tell me who he is. Jim or Jay.

"I'm Jay!" he yells again. It is such an overwhelming comfort not to be alone.

I rest for longer than I should.

The cold has begun to weaken me and when I rouse myself I maul the EPIRB with awkward mitts. All night I have been trying to activate it. The recessed toggle switch is about half an inch high and approximately the diameter of a chopstick. I know where it is located, but with little feeling in my extremities, the mitts seem slightly more dextrous than boxing gloves. Each wave rumbling toward us interrupts my efforts as I am flung about or tumbled under. Each struggle to right myself, reposition the EPIRB, and commence once more the frustrating search for the elusive switch takes its toll. Each fight to the surface weakens me as the freezing water seeps into my suit. After the waves break us apart, it takes fatiguing effort to find each other. Somehow, we keep managing to find each other.

Now the waves are growing larger. A big one tells us it is coming by the pull at our bodies and the resulting crescendo of its tumbling waters. Our recovery takes longer as the waves get rougher. At some point, I realize I am becoming hypothermic and try to tie the lanyard of the EPIRB around Jay's leg.

"What are you doing?" His voice carries above the waves. I am too tired to reply, and my attempts are unsuccessful anyway.

I want to close my eyes. It has been hours since the boat went down, and I can feel my body losing purpose. Only the outside chance that I might be able to influence our survival keeps my efforts alive. As my systems begin to shut down, my brain narrows its focus. I keep trying to direct my mitts over the puzzling surface of the canister.

I feel stuck with the frustration of the uncooperative EPIRB. If not for it, I could just go to sleep. Now, I'm angry as I fumble with the damn thing. I yank and puff and push and jerk at it and suddenly, I snag something and a tiny red light comes on in the darkness. It blinks off, then on. I yell out in amazement and relief.

"It's on!" The EPIRB is on!

"Try turning it off, then back on again, just to make sure!" he yells during a lull in the wind and waves.

I reject this idea without reply, holding the EPIRB carefully, almost warmed by the blinking red light and the hope surging through me.

"It's on!" I yell back.

Now that my goal has finally been achieved, I remember the line wound around me. I had completely forgotten it in the shock of entry, in the stunning unfolding of events, and in my intense focus on the EPIRB.

"Help me pull in the line, we need to tell the others!"

We began pulling on the line. It is a Herculean effort to reef it through the waves. It takes a very long time. Finally, we get to the end of the line.

I hold it—empty—in my hand as we float in the darkness.

Some time later, I hear the sound of engines. A plane is over-head. Homing in on our signal, the C-130 makes several passes before a rescue helicopter arrives on scene. Now there are blades whipping the snowy blackness above us, then piercing light and deafening noise. A steel-framed basket is lowered. Pulled by the chopper, it jerks and pitches erratically, buries itself in a wave, then yanks free and is gone. The next time it comes close, Jay tries to stop it and heave me in. The basket hurtles past.

This time, I am ready. I swim hard when I see it lowered, wait for it to settle in the belly of a wave, then grab on to the metal web and curl myself into a tight ball. I am pulled sideways, dragged deep beneath the waves and nearly drowned before the lift begins. Suddenly, the sea no longer holds me. There is a moment when I become sky.

Kneeling beside the dock, I memorize the curls and peaks, the variation of hue, the balance of color of the memorial wreath.

The man and woman have begun their journey up the dock. She insists on walking, and he pushes the empty wheelchair behind her, shaking his head at her stubbornness. I admire her courage. She does not succumb to pain. She makes it wait its turn when she has living to do.

"I'll be there in a moment," I call after them.

I stare at the dull gray water. It reflects nothing; it absorbs everything.

I think about pain.

For too many years, I've carried their deaths in my thoughts, the weight of their dreams on my heart. For over a decade, I've polished their memories, fondled their faces, and smoothed back their hair. Leaning as close as I can to the memorial wreath, I touch my fingers to my lips and place a farewell kiss upon the waters. Closing my eyes, I stay for a bit, then stand and start to walk back up the dock.

Ahead of me, the woman rests against the man. They talk for a moment, but I do not hear what they are saying. I fall in step behind them, walking slower than I have ever walked on the busy conduit of a dock. We push our way forward as if the air itself were a cushion of resistance. She pauses as the ramp begins its steep incline. The tide has fallen and the ramp may as well be a mountain. Inexplicably, she begins to sing as she places one wobbly foot on the ramp.

"There were ten in the bed and the little one said, 'Roll over! Roll over!' " She takes a step, "They all rolled over and one fell out. . . ."

The man and I exchange concerned glances.

"There were nine in the bed and the little one said. . . ."

The man shrugs his shoulders and joins in: "Roll over, roll over! So they all rolled over and one fell out . . ."

I realize I am gritting my teeth. They sing louder as the incline steepens. Other people pass us on the ramp. They give wide berth to the crippled woman stoutly singing as she struggles with her pain—"They all rolled over and one fell out, there were four in the bed . . ."

I feel slightly foolish as they avert their eyes. A couple of guys I know are starting down the ramp when I finally let go.

"Roll over," I sing. "Roll over!" A sense of joy washes over me at the release and I sing out loudly. Connie hears me with her entire being and shoves herself upward with renewed purpose. We look at each other. "They all rolled over and one fell out, there were two in the bed and the little one said. . . ."

She takes a final step to the top of the ramp. She is soaked by rain and sweat. She is shaking with fatigue and pain, but her eyes are bright with triumph and her face looks almost beautiful.

OUT WEST: NOTES FROM THE BERING SEA

TOBY SULLIVAN *has fished for twenty-five years in Alaska. Here he writes of what should be his last winter crab season: the peril, the sweet moves in the "industrial ballet" of crabbing, another friend lost on a boat.*

C OMING IN FROM the north on certain rare and exceptionally clear winter nights, the stars in midocean would shine in colors that were ordinarily washed out by the moisture in the atmosphere, as if every molecule of dust and water vapor had been sucked away. The stars would be visible right down to the horizon, and if the sea was very calm (I saw this maybe twice), the seam of horizon between sky and ocean would disappear entirely and the night sky would form a perfect sphere around the boat. With no other visual reference points all sense of motion stopped, and you had to look back at the wake or down to where the hull met the water to see that you were still moving. It was an amazing sensation, like being in outer space, and the skipper got us all up to look at it the first time I saw it. But it only lasted a few minutes before a leftover swell from somewhere started bending the water's surface like a fun-house mirror and ruined the effect, and we were left to argue sleepily whether it had been worth crawling out of our bunks for it.

It was an eighteen-hour run from the Pribilofs to Dutch Harbor to deliver our crab, a run we usually slept through except for wheel watches. Alone in the wheelhouse at night, trying to stay awake, with the green radar sweep going round and round in a way that could mesmerize you even when you were awake and alert in daylight, the mountains of Unalaska Island would start to rise out of the south, an indistinct mass between the black ocean and the sky. Once, around three in the morning, when I was so tired and so afraid of falling asleep I had all the windows open to the cold air, Makushin Volcano started rising up off the dark horizon, a pale white shape, at first almost invisible in the distance. In a weird semihallucin-ation brought on by the lack of sleep it seemed as if we were in a spacecraft orbiting above the night side of a planet, and the mountain was the top of a weather system down on the surface of that planet, a massive vortex of a hundred-year storm silently moving across the place where we would be landing in a few hours, above it and all around the stars shining in a black void. And ever afterward on other trips, even when we were much closer and I could see the rhythmic white line of surf at the bottom of the cliffs at Akun Head as we turned into the outer harbor, and the serrated ridges of snow above the beach shone blue in the predawn starlight, the illusion stayed with me, so that coming into Dutch Harbor at night always had that sense of approaching, as if from a vast empty distance, a station on a remote asteroid, a lost outpost in deep space.

The clusters of sodium vapor lights from all the boats and processing plants up in the inner harbor would become suddenly visible as you turned in around Priest Rock, and the snow on the mountains that surrounded it would glow pink above them, and all the lights would block out the stars, even on a clear night. In January 1991, before the pollock "A" season opened, a mas-sive array of hardware was assembled in Dutch Harbor, one of the world's great fishing fleets, designed to kill 200 million metric tons of fish in three weeks and 100 million pounds of crabs in three months. Those were the "guideline harvest levels," the quotas, and that winter there were twenty-four factory trawlers and two hundred other crab boats and shore-based trawlers waiting there for their seasons to open on the fifteenth of January.

The factory trawlers were in a league of their own, 250-foot ships with crews of 150 on each one, $100 million apiece, freshly painted and beautiful in the way things designed to a single purpose can transcend themselves, like a well-chromed Harley or a square-rigged clipper ship. "These boats are serious tools for serious fishermen," an engineer off one of them told me one night in the Unisea Inn, the fact of the fleet's $15-billion debt load to banks in Oslo going unmentioned. How mortgaged they were, how terrifyingly slim the chances were that they could all catch enough fish to show a profit for their corporate owners after they were paid for, was understood viscerally in Dutch Harbor, and fishermen who owned and operated their own boats called the factory ships the dinosaur fleet, doomed to economic extinction. But they were beautiful to look at, and the other boats in the Bering Sea, the crab boats and shore-based trawlers mostly around a hundred feet long, impressive in any other harbor in America, seemed small and inconsequential tied up next to them. You'd see crab fishermen who hated factory trawlers on principle standing on the dock staring in abject envy at Hynautic winch systems bigger than the wheelhouses of their own boats and at the long curved hulls rising thirty feet up out of the greasy harbor water, and then later on you'd meet them with a beer in one hand and a shot of tequila in the other up at the Elbow Room talking with a sense of awe about "the hardware aspect" of the factory fleet, as in "I can't handle what they're doing to the resource, but from a hardware aspect, they are definitely cool."

The presence of all the boats and the infrastructure that supported them onshore in Dutch Harbor showed what people could do when they set their minds to it, when there was money to be made, to design all those boats and plants and ship them all out there to the end of the earth to "harvest" something. Coming in at night, the tawdriness of the place was not apparent, the broken Dumpsters and piles of discarded equipment, the stacks of rusting crab pots and the raw scraped hillsides, all that was invisible. Instead you saw hundreds of sodium lights from all the boats, together with the strobes out at the airport lighting the sides of the mountains and the massive hulls and the masts and cranes and processing plants and corrugated modular housing. Steam rose in huge clouds from the plants and mixed with snow blowing through all the rigging, the steel gantries and ducting, and it all looked so utilitarian, so intricate, so deliberately designed and so delicately beautiful, that seeing it from the deck of an approaching boat, coming in from the Bering Sea, the whole thing was like one massive holistic structure. It had that same sense of unintended artistry as the factory ships themselves, only on a larger scale, an extrapolation from them of purpose and aesthetic. And set up there inside the bay with the wilderness of mountains surrounding it, sheltering it, the town was like a huge steel hive hanging up inside a cleft in a rock, consumed with its own purpose.

The season began in January and by the end of February we were tired, exhausted beyond physical fatigue, and it showed on our faces in a way that reminded me of those photographs of soldiers after a battle, mud-covered men standing in a trench in France in 1917, or those haunting Larry Burrows shots of Marines walking out of the Citadel in Hue in 1968, that same thousand-yard stare, that same pure, unfocused dream state with the sunken eyes, an old look with a new name, the Aleutian stare. We'd sit at the galley table between running strings of gear, so numb with the pleasure of just sitting down it was too much effort to pull our rain pants all the way off over our boots, and we would just drop the shoulder straps and peel them down around our ankles and collapse onto the bench around the galley table. Sometimes we wouldn't even get that far and would just lie on the galley floor in a puddle at the foot of the wheelhouse stairs, curled up against each other like wet dogs, the water from the ice melting off our raingear and running back and forth across the galley as the boat rolled. I would watch the rivulets going back and forth, counting the rolls in a hypnotic repetition until the skipper called down the five-minute warning and we had to go back out on deck, or until somebody let their cigarette burn down into their fingers and started swearing and jerked us back awake.

Some time after midnight we'd pull the last pot in the last string, take our raingear off, and go inside and eat bowls of cereal before we crawled into our bunks. Curling up in your sleeping bag in those last moments of consciousness felt so good after a day on deck that guys used to make jokes about it, about crab fishing being like beating on your head with a rock—it felt so good when you stopped—or about which would you rather have, a blow job or a nap. And once, when we were talking about this and I wondered out loud if there was a way to get to that incredible soft warmth of those last conscious moments without having to push crab pots around for two weeks with no sleep, if maybe there was a shortcut to feeling that good, the engineer I was drinking with stared off through the wall behind the bar and said "heroin," with the kind of quiet authority that made me wonder where he'd been before he landed in the Bering Sea.

Everybody hurt a little most of the time, from muscle strain and bruises there was no time to let heal, from the tendinitis in the wrists that everybody had, or from more serious injuries that the ethos of being a bulletproof fisherman made guys try to ignore and try to work through. Sometimes guys would get hit by a swinging pot or smacked in the shins with a deck tote full of crab and everybody else would wince just seeing it and the guy would never say a word. A guy on the *Mariner* broke his leg out past Kiska and splinted it himself with a couple of tanner boards and then kept working, filling bait jars for the rest of the trip. He never asked to go to town and the skipper didn't volunteer to cut the trip short, and by the time they got in the bones had started to knit the wrong way and the doctor had to rebreak the leg and reset it. One whole trip, ten days, I watched the skipper's brother-in-law, a fiberglass-boat builder who was there for the adventure, he didn't even need the money, eating with his fork clutched between the heels of both hands because the tendinitis in his wrists was so bad he couldn't close his thumbs to his fingers. Whenever it did not seem possible to feel worse than I did, when facing another hundred-pot day with four hours of sleep made me inclined to feel sorry for myself, I only had to look across at Warren at breakfast to know there was someone worse off than me.

There were never enough hours to pull all the pots we should have, and as we got into the end of February there was always too much weather. The storms rotating up from the ocean east of Japan followed closer on each other's tails until we watched the forecast curl out of the fax machine and knew the deal with a glance before the ink was dry, all those isobar lines jammed up against each other around a low-pressure system like a clock spring wound tight. "A genuinely fucked-up gradient this morning, gentlemen" the skipper would say, and we could look out the window and gauge how hard the gulls had to fly against the wind to stay even with the wheelhouse, or we could read the fax, it was the same thing, and it was the same thing every day for weeks. We'd do ten-day trips, fill the boat, deliver in Akutan or Dutch and come right back out with fresh bait and a little sleep and do it again. That the weather would be bad was accepted, even taken for granted, and when a nice day came we treated it as gift and stood on deck admiring the view of a clear horizon like it was a day off from real work.

After a while the repetition of pulling thousands of pots transformed the three-minute operation into an automatic response for most crews, a skill, and sometimes even a kind of Zen thing, where the pots swung in and we pulled out the crab, rebaited it and reset it without thinking. Sometimes you went for hours without talking, focused down into the world so intensely that you broke through into a kind of hyper-reality, where you could hand off bait jars or hooks to the man moving behind you without looking, knowing his hand would meet yours by some unconscious sense, like hearing the engine noise change slightly as he moved between you and the engine exhaust stack, or seeing his shadow out of the corner of your eye, cast by the deck lights into the momentary cloud of glowing mist created as a wave disintegrated into a million pieces against the side of the boat. In some way that we all recognized when it was happening, the work could become a vehicle for a certain exhilaration, a feeling that we were perfectly in tune with the ocean and the wind and with ourselves. We'd smile out from under our raingear hoods at each other when somebody made the sweet move, stepped just the right way in the industrial ballet of landing two thousand pounds of crab on a rolling deck, giggle when the guy at the rail would throw the hook perfectly to snag the buoy setup alongside the boat for the hundredth time in a row, knowing before he even threw the hook a gust of wind would push the hook over the buoy line. And being able to work like that, intensely and perfectly, with an almost spiritual grace when the wind was up and everybody was hungry and tired and daylight was hours away, had an addictive intensity that could never be duplicated on land and grabbed all of us for a while, and made some stay longer than they should have.

Sometimes you got the strongest feeling of being a participant in a lost world beyond common knowledge, of being alive in part of God's original plan, somehow still in working order, forgotten and overlooked by everybody but us, rediscoverers of the last vestiges of Paradise on the vast empty steppes of the Bering Sea. Once we came in on a brilliant sunny day in February, the air so cold and the ocean so flat it had frozen in a thin sheet extending five miles out from Akun Head. Thousands of birds were standing out there on it, watching us cut past them at ten knots, looking like they did that every day, walked around on the ocean with their bellies dry, with the blue sky reflecting off the perfect mirrored surface of the ice beneath their feet. And I thought of that last scene in *Bladerunner* we all loved, the scene where Rutger Hauer, the android, is dying, and he tells Harrison Ford, the soulless human, "I've seen things you people wouldn't believe, attack ships burning off the shoulder of Orion, seen sea beams glitter in the darkness of the Tannhauser Gates, and all those moments will be lost in time like tears in rain." We knew he was talking about us.

We all believed in signs and magic numbers and things we could almost see, elements of the nonrational world we knew surrounded us on the ocean. There were certain foods we ate religiously, for luck, and others we avoided. We had favorite sweaters and talismanic gloves, worn-out hats and pictures of Jesus and letters from our girlfriends tucked into the molding above our bunks. All these personal pieces of anchored reality to keep from sliding away over the side when the last great wave came over the rail, the one that had come all the way from Kamchatka looking personally for you, or almost as bad, falling down into that void inside your own head where you just gave in and collapsed beneath the work or the wind or the great impersonality of the sea, knowing in an essential way that you'd passed your own limitations, and arrived at that final place where you begged without a shred of dignity to be taken back to land. Lying in my bunk in the middle of the night I used to wonder if all the years of being there, living and working out there, were no sure guarantee that it wouldn't all suddenly become too much, that instead those winter years were being counted slowly toward a certain turning moment in an unspecified future where experience and the long view would count for nothing and the next day would be the one where I went up in the wheelhouse and told the skipper to take me to town.

The first winter I fished out west we had a skipper named Gary, and instead of some icon he could hold in his hand or a picture he could look at stuck between the radar and the bottom sounder, he had tapes of some radio station in Seattle from '66 or '67. Wilson Pickett, Herman's Hermits and Aretha, all that Top 40 golden pop, complete with deejay chatter and Clearasil commercials. It was like listening to live radio, with special requests from call-ins: "Hi, you're on the air, what do you want to hear?" and the weather from another age ". . . continued clear through Tuesday with highs in the low seventies." We would listen to that through the loudhailer out on deck and cruise on it; any kind of music sounded good while we pulled gear, but it went way beyond that for Gary.

Working on deck, we had that physical mountain of work to climb every day, and the pain and exhaustion that went with that, but the skippers out there had the strain of running a boat, making money for us, themselves, and the owners, and keeping everyone inside the rail on a winter ocean. Somehow none of that ever really got to Gary, though, because somewhere inside, no matter what was happening on deck, it was ". . . sunny this afternoon, clear this evening, clear again tomorrow." On days when he couldn't find the gear and the wind was coming up, when it looked like he'd already spent too many years out there already and maybe it would be better to just turn around and head for Akutan and call it for good, he'd tune into "Dock of the Bay" and bliss back while Otis smoothed it out. All the rough edge to our world became merely temporary, a passing low-pressure system he could afford to ride out, high without drugs, or at least maintaining, secure in his own private landscape. In some secret room in his emotional being, where that was desirable, or even necessary, he'd be cruising home with the top down, reliving his nineteenth summer.

One day near the end of that winter we came up into the wheelhouse after running gear since some time early the day before, too far gone to remember exactly when anymore, running on reserve will and trying to focus down out of that stare that seemed almost normal now. He was sitting there in his swivel chair, the motion of the boat rocking him back and forth while he watched for the next string of buoys a couple miles up ahead, listening to "Little Red Riding Hood" jumping out of the tape deck, and it was like walking into a time vault, just punch in the coordinates and wait for it to come on. We stood there, salt water dripping from our hair down the sides of our faces, stoned out on exhaustion, listening to that old, old music, that leering sexual tension strung like barbed wire through the melody, looking out ahead for the buoys, watching the wind move across the gray water.

Sometimes things went badly, and there was nothing to do but hope it would end soon, before somebody got hurt, or if the hurt came it didn't happen to you. When it was blowing eighty and there were ten more pots in the string, you'd start wishing a hydraulic line would break so you could quit without giving up. One February afternoon a wave came over the wheelhouse and blew the pot out of the launcher rack, washed it all the way to the stern rail and swept the deck clear of everything else, and we could feel it coming before we saw it by the way the bow of the boat dropped off the lip of the crest, the exact feeling you get at the top of a roller-coaster hill just before you drop down the track, that same long pause before gravity takes over. Standing behind the house waiting for the buzzer signal to launch the pot, we had felt the boat start to fall into the trough, and we dodged beneath the little overhang in back of the galley porthole, gripping a stanchion post, waiting for the impact. The seas were running somewhere over thirty feet and when we got to the bottom of the trough and hit the face of the next wave there was the initial slam against the bow and then a weird delay as the boat buried itself, and then water started coming over the top of the wheelhouse. We stood there by the hydraulic controls, sheltered under a three-foot overhang of the wheelhouse deck, watching the water come down in a translucent green mass we could not see through, like standing in a cave behind a waterfall, the water filling the deck in a matter of seconds, burying the boat to the rails. The boat stopped making headway and lay dead in the water and we huddled under the overhang, water up to our chests, and looked out at the open sea where the deck had been. The water surged around and pulled our feet out from under us and as we hung onto each other and the stanchion. All I kept trying to remember was whether we had shut the watertight galley door when we came out. The exhaust stack prevented our seeing around to that side of the deck, and for a long minute we watched the level of the deck to see if it would rise up out of the water, which meant the door was shut, or stay under, which meant the door was open and the boat was sinking. The galley porthole we were scrunched up against was too fogged up to see whether there was water in the house, but after a long moment the deck rails came back up, like the rails on the conning tower of a surfacing submarine, and the deck cleared off, the water pouring over the rails and taking the plastic crab totes with it, and then draining out the scuppers. We were still huddled up holding the stanchion post, shivering with cold and adrenaline, when Gary's voice came down on the loudhailer next to our heads, "Uh . . . is anybody out there?" and the three of us started laughing hysterically, and he kept asking what was so funny in a voice that kept breaking up because the wires into the speaker were shorting out, and that was perfect really, him not really being able to hear us or see us under the overhang, and made us laugh even louder while we secured the block and the bait tub for the long ride to Akutan. Because we knew before he said anything that the trip was over, that we had pushed the weather by even being out there and trying to work in it, and that we shouldn't have needed a wave to tell us that. That the deck had cleared and the boat had risen back up was a fact that might just as easily not have been, and we knew that in a world of choices and chances we were being given another one, one we didn't really deserve.

We knew we were going in before he said it, and he knew we knew. And later he was a little embarrassed to show us the broken jog steering handle he'd been holding when we hit the wave and ripped off the console as he went down out of his chair. All the way in I lay in my bunk not sleeping, partly because it was too rough to sleep, and I had to keep putting my hands above me to keep my face from hitting the bottom of the bunk over mine. And partly too, maybe the real thing that kept me awake was thinking about the galley door being shut, and how that was an accident, not a sign of prudent thinking, and about the random way things happened out there and how despite any skill you might have on deck or how much you thought you knew about the sea, you never knew enough, and there was always going to be a universe of things that could happen that you would never see coming.

There were a zillion things that could go wrong; fires, the boat rolling over from too many pots on deck, pots shifting and crushing people, guys getting whacked by swinging crab pots, but those kinds of things happened all the time and were so common and easy to list they were mundanely predictable. It was the oddball things that made you wonder, like the guy who was walking between the hydraulic pot launcher and the stack of pots on deck at the very instant someone started the auxiliary engine that had the hydraulics inadvertently engaged so they came on as soon as the engine revved up. The lever on deck that operated the pot launcher had been bumped by someone into the "up" position hours before and the hydraulics came on just as this guy was between the pots and the stack and it came up, a six-foot rack made out of three-inch steel pipe, hinged at the rail, and crushed him into the rebar of the pots and killed him. What were the odds of being alone on deck in that one spot with all the necessary hydraulic levers turned the wrong way at the very moment someone in the engine room started an engine?

One morning toward the end of February 1991, years after that first winter in the Bering Sea, I sat in the wheelhouse of a boat with a friend of mine named Brad Hall who was running the boat we were on, listening to the *All Alaskan,* a floating processor up at St. Paul Island, calling their boats on radio schedule. The plant superintendent went through his list of the boats fishing for him, talking briefly to the skippers, and when he was done he called the *Barbarossa* again several times because they hadn't come back the first go-round, but there was still nothing there except the white noise of dead air. The night before, the *Barbarossa* had left St. Paul, one of the two Pribilof Islands, and headed out to the grounds after loading on a full stack of crab pots on deck. The man running the *Barbarossa,* a friend of ours named George Brandenburg, had arranged to talk with a couple other boats he was working with when he got out on the grounds early in the morning, but he never called, and their own calls to the *Barbarossa* went unanswered. By the time the *Barbarossa* missed the morning cannery schedule at eight o'clock most of the opilio crab fleet fishing around the Pribilofs knew the *Barbarossa* had left St. Paul at midnight and hadn't been heard from since. Ordinarily there might have been a good enough reason for not making contact with his fishing partners that morning, but when he didn't come back to the *All Alaskan* either, Brad and I looked across the wheelhouse at each other for a second and then we each just stared out the side windows at a beautiful day, cold, some whitecaps, but good working weather. We went to work after that and pulled pots all day, and between strings I went up in the wheelhouse and got the latest word on the *Barbarossa*, which was no word at all until around two o'clock when we heard the Coast Guard had a C-130 on scene twenty miles southwest of St. Paul. Later on we heard they had seen some debris, but we all knew the pack ice was moving south pretty fast under a northerly wind and would cover the area over by morning, and people were hustling to get their gear out of the area before the ice carried the buoys away. After dinner that night we heard that someone on another boat had heard a panicky voice calling "Mayday! Mayday! We're going over!" around 2:00 A.M., but no call sign or position was given and the call was not repeated.

Two days before, I had gone up to the Elbow Room in Unalaska, the village across the bridge from Dutch Harbor, and run into George standing at the bar. We had lived together a long time before, in a house on Hemlock Street in Kodiak with Brad and assorted other people and dogs. We all were just starting out then, and we were always going in and out on boats, and we were never there all at the same time. The local whorehouse was across the street and at night we would sit around watching the cabs pull up, laughing at the fascination exhibited by our girlfriends with the goings-on across the street. Once I woke up on the couch to see George standing in the doorway shooting a 30.06 down the street at a pack of dogs that kept tearing up our garbage cans. He walked out and came back with the carcass of one of the unlucky ones and draped it across the rail of the front porch as a warning to the survivors, and when the police came by they decided the shooting was justified and left after a jolly ten minutes talking with George.

Eventually he married the girlfriend who lived there with

him, though it didn't last, and we all moved on with our lives. After the divorce he spent about ten years working his way into the wheelhouse, working out west in the Bering Sea most of the time, and then he met a woman, fell in love and married her. When I saw him that night at the Elbow Room I hadn't seen him in a long time and he told me he was the happiest he'd ever been. George Junior's first birthday was in a couple days and George was going to miss it, but he only had one opilio trip left before he was flying out; he'd had it with the boat and the owners. We stayed late at the bar and when we came out it was snowing and a crowd stood in the street waiting for a cab to come. George started messing in a good-natured way with a couple of giant Norwegians who had been embracing in a long-lost drunken buddy way and George started calling them faggots, but with a smile on his face. They were too drunk to see he wasn't serious, and they started shouting Norwegian obscenities and it took a bunch of us to calm them down, and all I could think was I was getting too old for this life. The cab finally came, a club wagon, and we all piled in and drove off into the falling snow, the flakes swirling into the windshield the same hypnotic way they did against the wheelhouse windows at sea. When I got out of the cab to go down to my boat I shook George's hand and waved and they drove off toward the spit, George and the two Norwegians screaming hilariously at each other, the Filipino driver hunched over his wheel, looking terrified.

In the morning we moved over to the fuel dock and tied up to the *Barbarossa*. George was up at the store and his crew was standing around, waiting to untie and leave as soon as George showed up. It was a beautiful day, the sun shining, the mountains around the harbor brilliant white with the new snow. We fueled up before he got back and then headed out and were on the grounds the next morning. The morning after that was

George Junior's first birthday, and I remember thinking about that while the C-130s flew their pattern search above the horizon north of us, looking for the *Barbarossa*.

One night a couple years later up in the Pribilofs a king eider duck came out of the night and stayed for more than an hour about six feet from the wheelhouse window, where I was trying to stay awake on watch. He stared in at me with his great golden eyes while a snowstorm blew the snow at us in a flat stream, the particles flying in under the crab lights like stars falling in our faces. There was a detailed pattern of tiny red and yellow and black feathers across his head and around his eyes, and the effect in the middle of the night in the blowing snow was like the masks I had once seen in a museum case in Anchorage, Aleut magic masks that the wearers believed changed them into the animals and birds that live in the Bering Sea. And as we looked at each other through the glass with the snow flying past, I started wondering if with my exhaustion and the trippy way the snow was moving and the odd fact of the bird himself just flying there next to the window for such a long time, maybe the usual frames of reference were being proved mere assumptions, and that another kind of reality was out there looking in, and that I should know this bird. I told all this to the guys in the morning, we were always telling each other our dreams, and they were only too ready to believe whatever it was I wanted to read into it because it was the kind of story with just enough ambiguity to make it seem credible, or at least not incredible, but eventually I came to the conclusion he was just a bird after all, looking for his own reference point in the storm, and after he flew off into the darkness I never saw him again.

At some point it became obvious that I could keep going on, another trip, another season, another species; or I could stand on shore and let the tide recede down and away from around my boots and call it finished. When was enough enough and one more winter at sea too much? How much more was there to squeeze out of being cold and wet and tired? If there was a thing to learn, some elemental truth from watching the essentialness of the sea, from living in it and seeing the land as a smudge on the horizon or a green line on a radar screen, I'd either learned it by then or I never would.

I thought of how the relatives of dead fishermen show up in Kodiak for the funerals, led around by the deceased's friends to the main sites of this little town, the boat harbor, the view from the top of Pillar Mountain, The Fisherman's Memorial with the brass plaques for the names of the lost, and the wide empty area for tragedies of seasons yet to come, like empty acres beside a cemetery. The wind is always blowing, because it is always winter when these things happen, the inescapable view everywhere of the blue ocean that took them, the whiteness of the snowy mountains rising out of the bay, the clouds tearing across the sky faster than anything in Wisconsin or New York or wherever they are from. They stare at the sheer presence of everything, the unobstructed power of the place, a world in such motion that when the angle of the sun is right you can almost see the rock bending from the tectonic forces beneath us, see the progress of the spruce trees recolonizing the capes after the scouring of the last ice sheets, and they see Kodiak the way we all once saw it who came here from somewhere else, a brand-new place in the world, still rising from the sea.

CASHING OUT
ON THE BERING SEA

MARTHA SUTRO *leaves her high school
classroom to work as a deckhand on
an Alaskan crabber in one of the most
intensive and dangerous fisheries
in the world.*

MY BUNK, DOWN BELOW, was my only real refuge on the F/V *Obsession*, but it was there that I brought, face-to-face before me, the most emphatic creations of danger. In one dream, I'm sorting crab and I can't keep up. I grab a shell. I yank its legs from a tangled mass, and toss it to a tank. A ton—a literal ton—of unsorted creatures, raised like a heap of slag, clicks and sloshes and dissembles around me. Dislodged crabs, unsorted, back away by the dozens across shining deck boards. I reach for another crab, yank on it, toss it in a tank. I'm waist-high in sea muck, pot bridles, tangled lines: I'm stuck in a sewing machine that won't turn off. A wave breaks, shifting the matter of the deck into a dark and vital soup. Crabs and octopi surge up my legs. Lost fish slip away overboard. A halibut, long as I am, rips and flaps from the slag, slides from my gloves. A wave slaps the back of my hood. Seawater fills my breath. I can't keep up, can't see, can't sort fast enough.

Fear came in vivid swatches. Only yards from the boat's engine through a few wooden panels, that bunk was my only zone of privacy for several thousand miles around. Letters, crumpled editions of *The Kodiak Daily Mirror*, a ratty sleeping bag, yesterday's socks, and a sole clean sweatshirt all stuffed the edges. It was room, bed, and personal cave—all at once. I slept on top of my hardcover copy of *To the Lighthouse* and I didn't even know it.

Dream: a codfish's eyes rise into mine. A crab ticks up the edge of some close rim, the pot door, the lip of my bunk, a tangle of blankets. He stares at me, climbs like a primitive. I turn, sit up, try to sit up, try to unseal my eyes. I push my legs around and out of the bunk so they dangle, familiar, over the edge. An engine grinds on. I open my eyes—no light. The wooden bunk lip takes the place of safety, presses against the backs of my knees. We're driving somewhere, still.

Bob had the bunk above me. He was the oldest guy on board, the gentlest, most self-effacing, most enduring member of the crew. He'd been working on and off on the *Obsession* for over twenty years. Forlorn, accepted, he could drink so much in Dutch he pickled his withered body, chain-smoked through his days, slept as if barely alive. I never knew, when I stammered awake from nightmares of crab crawling through the sleeping bag, or lurched out of the darkness because a voice was booming "We're on the gear!" whether Bob was up in the wheelhouse on watch, up having a smoke outside, or right up above me in the bunk, asleep. He had a drunken wife in Anchorage, sometimes saw his two children. Their school photos were tacked above his bunk. He fished to keep them going. Bob Boyle. He slipped in and out of the stateroom like a weary old cat, smoked behind the windbreak just outside the pilothouse, bones and skin, faded fishing shirt, the same black jeans.

If you were a mother, this might have concerned you: your daughter was disappearing between anonymous waves, out of the reach of any reliable signal short of a Coast Guard contact, on a sea so distant the maps nearly rendered it polar. I did not know the extent of my mother's fear when I went crab fishing, but I do know that it was shapeless. There was no order no structure for her fear, and structureless fear is the worst kind. Hers came in the form of the underground: the bottom of a well, the bottom of a coal mine.

I went to work on a one-hundred-foot crab boat with five men my mother had never known nor imagined she'd want to know. In 1992, *Forbes* magazine ranked crab fishing second only to coal mining in danger. *Forbes* measured "danger" in the industry's number of work-related deaths per year. My mother ripped the article out of *Forbes* and taped it to her refrigerator in Virginia.

Two years before I went to fish, I'd met the captain of the *Obsession*, Ted Goss, when we'd both signed on to a guided climbing expedition in the Alaska Range. When we left Talkeetna, at the end of that trip, Ted, as if offhandedly offering me a weekend getaway, said to me, "If you ever want to crab fish on the Bering Sea, just give me a call." Ted had the worn, sturdy texture of a farmer, nothing like the men I had ever known. The pulse of his life was just as unrecognizable to me: It was determined by plane schedules, fishing openings, Fish and Game quotas, the weather. I promised myself a trip to the Bering Sea.

In the two years that elapsed before I went, I saw Ted twice, once on the West Coast, where he lived, and once on the East, where I taught teenagers at a tiny school in northern Vermont. When he visited for a weekend one spring, he brought a pile of Kodiak newspapers and a cooler full of crab. When he left, he sent letters that read like lists. Sometimes he sent only lists: quotas, loran readings, measurements for pot bridles, pot doors, webbing, pots. Sometimes I couldn't read the handwriting, but what I could read was the constellation of different pressures, smells, timetables, people.

There was nothing formal about my arrangement to go work for Ted—no contract, no promises, no real schedule, short of my duty to show up in Dutch Harbor at the beginning of February, ready to work. Part of Ted's appeal was his hard-working, successful, laissez-faire approach. I bought right into it. We made our plans roughly, in a couple of quick and casual phone calls. When my mother asked about Ted, I defended him unequivocally to her, without even really knowing him.

A month before I left home to fish I received a package from Ted. Inside, there was no letter, only texts: a worn copy of a book, precipitously titled *Working on the Edge*, its cover shot a wash of orange bodies blurred against a veil of green water. There were also a few random nautical charts: *Shumagin Islands to Sarak Islands. Alaska Peninsula and Aleutian Islands to Seguam Pass.* Last to fall out of the envelope was one video case, unmarked, with a tape inside.

The night the package arrived I sat on the floor of the living room at my parents' house in Virginia and stuck the video in the TV set. The frame of the image on the screen floated out to a nebulous, pancaked mass, an ice pack. White and white and white against a terminally gray sky, against slivers of a terminally shaley sea, rising and sinking with a sanguine, prehistoric reliability that forgave the witness of a camcorder. The frame panned from the stern-mounted wheelhouse of the vessel, where the camera was filming, up toward the bow of the boat, showing the deck in between, a space low, rectangular, and enclosed, like the sunken stage of a theater. Ice shagged the railings. Rusty crab pots, hoses, boxes, coils of line, equipment I couldn't recognize sat usefully but quietly in the frame, like farm equipment looks when it rests, dirt-encased, in between shifts. The shot drifted back to the ice pack. A disembodied voice outside the picture made a simple, muffled comment: "Pretty tight pack." Nobody, nothing answered. Just the nervous static of a nylon sleeve in the wind, and a granular moan, shifting and rising. Not a lot of speech in this world, I thought, but a thousand kinds of cold. No work, either, when the hull of the boat is hugged by a shoreless game board of pack ice. The image on the screen floated back to the deck, up to the bow, and the coarse wind surged, wavered, resurged. Boat to sea. Sea to boat. That's all there was.

I was sitting cross-legged on the carpet. My mother watched silently behind me in a chair, watching as if sure something astonishing would appear on screen. When nothing happened and the tape went to gray, I turned the set off.

Out of the long silence, she spoke, "Why in the world would you want to go to a place like that?"

The grandfather clock in the hall struck and rested. Outside, a mild winter breeze pushed rain across the sycamore trunks and I thought of the laced fingers of ice on the stanchions of the *Obsession*. Winter here; winter there. No contract, no promises, no schedule. Just show up in Dutch, ready to work.

"I want to see the Bering Sea in winter." I couldn't begin to fabricate anything close to a real answer for her. I had a pilgrim's importance, which felt complete only when it was charged with the possibility of this scale of transformation. Good-bye to the secure and well-laid paths, the careful civilized corridors that had molded me. They no longer suited my questions. Crabbing was an idea that only my will could realize. Still, it was just that, merely an idea—immune to details of threat or danger.

On an end-of-January day I stood at the Richmond airport, a wool sweater itching my neck, my duffel of sweatshirts, thick socks, gloves, and notebook packed and already on the airplane. Just as I'd anticipated, the dim sense of ambivalence I'd had for about a week was steadily sharpening into a crisp panic. After this, the basis for motivation was just a hunch. Mother saw this, whether she knew it or not. "I'm certain I should, of course, without hesitation or decision, cancel this plan," I started to hear myself say. Absolutely.

Not five months earlier my same mother had been putting me on the plane for Kathmandu, where I'd determined a solo journey through the Himalayas was to originate. What I'd said, at that departure, was, "See you in three months," acting out a well-kindled carefreeness. In between treks into the mountains of Nepal, I'd called home every day, sometimes twice. Mother knew the power of these hunches.

She was standing in flats and a blue overcoat, a dutiful confidence written into her eyes. She looked me over, top to bottom, even wishing, I knew, she'd scrubbed the hiking boots I was wearing. I was twenty-seven, but she, in her strained belief in me, was trying to lend a physical support, as if I, her only daughter in a family of boys, were twelve again and it was camp on the other end of this flight. I waited for a minute, hoping she could detect my sense of rising vertigo. The passengers were gone, the desk attendant called for the stragglers. Mother hugged me hard around the neck: "Call us when you get there."

Her shoulders pressed against mine and my instinct, a quick and fortuitous signal, reached me with the closest intensity. Suddenly, I felt saved by it. I was meant to stay there in the soft southern winter. Perhaps get a job at a sandwich shop. I spoke. "Ma, maybe I'll stay. Maybe this is just a dumb idea. Maybe I should just not go."

She hugged me again, not so tight. Was she caught off guard? Willing to believe me? Had she even heard me speak? "You've gotten yourself into this." Her eyes looked directly at mine. In my impression of the moment I cannot remember a time when I felt her as connected to me as then. "You have to see what it's for, where it's taking you."

I felt like a motor inside me had stopped. I could say nothing, of course. I turned from her, the panic replaced by a vibrating emptiness that rendered me just a body that walked down the long throat of the airplane entryway, knowing she watched. Many kinds of fear, many kinds of boldness came out of the succeeding months, but nothing that crystallized, that cumulative, nothing, in action, that automatic.

. . .

Flying across the continent, past its edge and out toward its hooked and fragile tip, I realized that for the sum total of twenty days of my life I'd known Ted in person, he was not even as clear a figure in my mind as the water I'd known and the water I was expecting. I imagined the Bering Sea as snow-filled, deathly, corrugated in black. Capricious, elastic, familiar, seas and dreams of seas sank and stretched in my mind, a torrent of verb forms. The saltiest water I'd known was the Chesapeake's, an almost deciduous sort of liquid, that soft and safe, that resilient. On a capsizing Sailfish, the sail meets the wave with a little sea foam. There's a jump, an easy collapse backward over the hull, a miniature bravery in righting it again, the boom at an anxious shudder and drip, the sail flickering like tin.

Fog and clouds matte the iron-streaked Gulf of Alaska and the Bering Sea all winter, and indeed, for most of the year. On a plane, looking down, nothing appears, nothing, until a grind of wheels dislodging from the belly starts. Just then, barren, barren islands—the lonely hummocks of the Aleutians—rising white and wind-scoured, not a single tree. A Russian Orthodox church, its tips as brown against snow as burnt onions, cast the gloom of a forgotten country on the margin of the bay. This was Dutch Harbor. From above, container ships, crab boats, freighters, draggers, and a tugboat all appeared as toys. Big pickup trucks, supply trucks, and vans routed through potholed, muddy roads that ran between jetties, brown hills, and the messy shoreline of boats. At that first sight of it, the clouds slung so low, the ocean outside the harbor swelling, iron-backed, tracked by cords of foam, I let my head fall back against the seat rest and looked down from only a corner of my eye. A loose knot shifted in my stomach. I had never been on a winter sea.

On the second day there I found a pay phone in the entryway of Stormy's pizza place in Unalaska, the village across the island from Dutch Harbor. "This is the end of the earth," I told my mother. She could only respond with questions about the weather, the people I'd met, questions about the flight. She really wished she could say nothing. She'd already started a kind of endurance race, a daily, weekly, terror-management seminar, forcing excruciating detachment, unable to restrain intense bewilderment.

Outside the cracked glass of the phone booth the wind was ramping in off the water. A rusty pickup truck, its bed loaded with a hundred coils of line, splashed through flakes blowing exactly sideways. Someone else was waiting for the phone. I hung up, zipped up my jacket, and took off across driveways and parking lots, making my way down to a black beach where waves were crashing, a beach rimmed by clapboard houses, junked cars, and totem poles. Every so often, a big wintry dog looked my way through eyes mostly covered over in blown fur.

I got my fishing gear at Carl's General Store, in Unalaska. One each: a blue wool cap, a pair of brown steel-toed fishing boots, orange bibbed overalls, and an orange hooded slicker—the raingear made by a Norwegian company called Grundens. Several each: rubber fishing gloves, some orange, some black, and polypropylene liner gloves to go inside the rubber. Also one jacket, called a Stormy Seas jacket, to wear all the time, even under the slicker, that reminded me of a baseball jacket, except this one zipped up in front, so high its collar covered most of my face. It was warm, lined in pile, and, between the pile and the shell, was fitted with an inflatable cushion. Inside the left chest pocket was a CO_2 cartridge and a ripcord. "If you end up in the water out there when we're working," Ted said to me as

I left for Carl's, "that'll help you stay afloat 'til we can come around and get you." There was firmness, even affection in his voice, and simultaneously, a kind of aloofness. He was working, after all, dressed in navy coveralls, hands coated in grease, down in the engine room of the *Obsession*, getting us ready to "get out of town," as they said in Dutch.

I was the only new member of the crew that winter and I went alone, with Ted's suggestions, to buy the gear. I spent three hundred dollars on it and walked back to the boat, carrying it in a plastic shopping bag. Our diesel tanks and water tanks full, our cupboards stocked with groceries, our bait freezer packed to the ceiling, and our deck loaded with sixty pots ready for fishing, we drove out of Dutch the next morning at 3 A.M., motoring past other draggers and fishers silently clustered in packs and lit by the sodium lights on their rigging. Ahead of us, Priest Rock marked the entrance to the harbor. The sea, farther out, was as black and still as ink in a well. The scrubby, cold peninsulas of the harbor passed behind us. I stood up in the wheelhouse, looking out, sensing a giving way, an ungrasping. "Should be a good night out there for driving around," Ted said, the bright lights of the controls setting off his face, his hands on the toggle that steered us. I walked across the wheelhouse and looked at the loran: 54.28.78 N, 166.39.06 W.

How was it I had come to that moment, driving out to the middle of the Bering Sea with five men I barely knew? "Martha's fishing with us," was the introduction Ted had given me. No one questioned him, or me. Bob, the old time crew member, accepted my addition with a kind of sad friendliness. Bill, Steve, and Mark, all, like me, in their twenties, formed a kind of brotherhood, taking over a cramped stateroom and sharing a style of working, a lingo, and a silent admiration for Ted. I knew they would test me on deck. Their brotherhood was in no hurry to accept an East Coast English teacher who'd never even been on a fishing boat, much less a crab boat.

After two days of driving, we reached the fishing grounds, a plank of water that looked no different to me than any other part of this ocean. It was thirty degrees out on deck, and the bow of the *Obsession* was charging through swells cresting in a flinty chop. Spray, caught by a thirty-five-knot wind, slapped on the rigging and pots we were carrying. Stacked three-deep as they were, they rose with a shimmering brown architecture, forty-feet off the surface of the ocean.

The whaleback rig of the *Obsession*, with its stern-mounted wheelhouse and bow-mounted forepeak, made for a vessel that initially seemed awkward in my eyes, but out at sea I could appreciate its layout immediately. From the wheelhouse windows, the entire theater of the deck, the crane, and the ocean surrounding ahead was visible. Atop the forepeak, eighty feet bow-ward from those windows, was a smaller, open deck where, when we sometimes—nervously—fished in waters covered in an ice pack, we stood with binoculars trying to sight our buoys out in the jigsaw of water and ice. Bundled in warm gear, Mark and I would climb the ladder to that forward deck, and, once we had the buoys in our glasses, we would turn and look back at the wheelhouse windows, where Ted was driving, and point in the direction of the red buoys.

The Bering Sea extends a lonely and storm-fraught sixteen hundred miles westward from the coast of Alaska to Russia; the Continental Shelf forms its floor for the first four hundred of those westward-reaching miles. This shelf is home to the greatest stores of king crab on the planet. Bering Sea weather—gloomy, monotonous, sometimes monstrous—is all a fisherman must endure, because the water, rarely greater than six hundred feet deep on the shelf, makes crab fishing relatively manageable. To the thick yellow bridle of each pot we've attached three 200-foot lengths, called shots, of line tied together. At rest on the seafloor, the line will string to a pair of buoys, called a setup, which floats on the surface of the sea. Eight to fifteen pots, set in a line on the ocean floor, form a string that the skipper sets where he's historically found crab or where he hopes to find some.

Up in the wheelhouse, a computerized plotter records the location of these strings. As we set the pots overboard so they could attract crab for a day or two or sometimes more, Ted entered their location, tracked by loran coordinates, into the plotter up in the wheelhouse. Miraculously, we could spend two days crossing a seascape as undefined as a liquid desert, and—if northern Bering Sea wind hadn't pushed the ice pack dramatically southward, covering and snarling the pots—suddenly arrive exactly at one end of a line of buoys tacked on the surface of the misty and inconsequential sea. The electronic plotter became the dictate of time, record, and action. If you were down in the galley slapping peanut butter on English muffins, or changing sweatshirts, or watching a video on the scratchy television, you climbed up the stairs to the wheelhouse to look over Ted's head at the number on the plotter. With twenty nautical miles to go to the beginning of the next set, you had time for more peanut butter. With two and a half, however, you'd better pull up your straps and stuff a candy bar in your pocket, so you were on deck and ready when the *Obsession* pulled alongside the first pair of buoys.

On the first day of my crabbing career, however, I understood this system only roughly. Part seasick, part petrified, partly in denial, I sat on the floor of the wheelhouse and pulled on my Grundens. I tugged the boots on over thick socks, and the bibs on over long underwear, sweatpants, and the Stormy Seas jacket. The rollers ahead of the boat bore wind-sheathed crests of foam that broke as if combustible across the bow and the side rigging. Out the long line of windows, I could see the iron frames of the pots so thick with spray that it formed a frozen coating, barely glinting in the distant winter sun. This morning we were going to bait the pots we had on deck and set them in this stretch of ocean. Bob and the brotherhood, well sealed in their own gear and saying nothing to acknowledge my tangle, clambered around and past me, out the side doors of the wheelhouse and forward across the stacked pots to the bow. I couldn't get the straps of the bibs adjusted and Ted had to tie them in back, saying calmly and not quite convincingly. "Don't worry, you'll be fine out there. Just listen to Bob and you'll be fine." I snapped up my jacket, swearing to myself that I wouldn't be late or last or even slow.

The physical objective was clear: get across the stacked pots and up to the bow of the boat where the boys stood, somewhat protected, between the stacked pots and the small forward portion of the vessel, where a room, called the forepeak, is tucked underneath the raised forward deck. Getting there involved a couple of tricks, tricks I'd mastered easily when the boat was tied up in Dutch Harbor, when the pots on deck seemed like nothing more than an extravagant jungle gym. Out on the open sea, on that first day of fishing, the jungle gym lurched hysterically and unpredictably. If I missed a step there was no pier to swim to, no neighboring hull to reach for. Even getting from the wheelhouse to the first step on the bars of the pots involved a maneuver outside the boat's railing, where, when I looked down between my new brown boots, I could see our churning wake thirty feet below. Human beings didn't last but about ten minutes in that water, even if they were floating in Stormy Seas jackets.

I swung out over the water and stepped up onto the pots, feeling the new armor of my bright rubber work clothes securely, almost heavily around me. Once I made it away from the edge of the boat, and chose a line up the center of the stack, I crossed from wheelhouse to bow, stepping on the pot bars as if they were railroad ties, slowly but evenly, knowing the boys were ahead of me, somewhere down on the deck, feeling Ted's eyes on me from the wheelhouse. No falls, no crawling on my ass, all the way forward. I had no idea what I was supposed to do when I got there, except follow and obey the other orange shapes. I did know that my ignorance made me afraid. And that I had other fears: not being strong enough; not being calm, bold, or effective enough in Ted's eyes—or in my own.

That first day of work I spent at a kneel. Under the shelter deck, a kind of porch roof covering a forward corner of the deck, the metal bait box, bolted down, was a place I could work with in only one way, by kneeling. I sat back on my heels so I could use my lap. The red-lidded jars with holes in them were just small enough to fit in my rubber-gloved hand, but not nearly tacky enough. I jammed them against the side of the bait box, against my slippery thighs, between my knees and the box— anything to hold them while I stuffed bits of herring in them and then screwed on the lid and then screwed the jar onto a wire hook that fastened at the top like a giant safety pin. With a few wedges of codfish also dangling from the hook, those rank, ugly ornaments, called bait setups, weighed about twenty pounds each.

I plugged those bait jars as full as possible with the slimy fish bits. When the bait box emptied, I rose, gray and pink flecks of herring covering my orange front sides, herring somehow stuck in my hair, and tipped unsteadily across a bucking deck for several feet to the bait freezer. I dislodged a fifty-pound box of frozen herring, tore its cardboard and plastic wrapping off, and thrust the icy chunk into a chopper, where a blade, operating with a deafening clatter, made an icy mush ready for the bait jars.

The proverbial shelter deck was the salon of this dignified process, but really, it was not elaborate shelter. Spray, sometimes even spray from a portside wave coming over the portside shelter deck, spat persistently on my hood. The sound of wind in my ears, a sound I would come to recognize permanently, was one that didn't find shelter anywhere, ever, on the boat. From the kneel I worked in all day and into the dark hours, I shifted between weather systems: the one on the empty slate horizon, which I looked continually toward as if expecting an appearance; the one on deck, four men I hardly knew and could barely distinguish from one another, at their tasks with the pots and crabs; and the one in my stomach, a cemented, persistent grind.

My first day, my second day, my third, my first night, my second, my whole first fishing trip, two weeks long, was not about work, it was about surviving. It was about negotiating mistakes, learning how to step forward or back on a steep and icy deck, how to stand and even work in direct blasts from the wind, how to stay out of the way of the work that wasn't mine. Steve and the boys had each other to keep up with, and they pushed me out of the way to get where they needed to go, thrust work at me, snatched work away, and yelled at me as much as they could. I didn't have this job from walking the docks of Kodiak or Dutch like they did; I had it from a connection, from Ted's curiosity in me, from luck. I was there for the money, but not like they were, since I'd ended up somehow with the privileged option of adventure, not the requirement of it. Mixing a little resentment for me with a dim, unsuspecting allegiance to me, they kept me at a distance. Some skippers maintain that it's never good to have a woman aboard a fishing boat, especially a crabber. Ted didn't think that, but I knew already that it was tricky to sleep with the guy who was driving the boat, and work on deck with the guys who weren't.

I was what they call a half-share in the fishing wage world, and Steve, full share like everyone else, was the fiery deck boss. Knowing that I should never, ever correct a single phrase of his speech was my only sustaining intelligence on deck. Silence was not a comfortable state for me, but I moved, knelt, stuffed, stood, and obeyed, mostly with perfect silence. Red-headed, red-bearded, with an agility that sprang and popped when the deck was busy, Steve narrated: his impressions of the weight of each incoming pot, his impressions of the wind, his guess at how long we'd work that shift. He called out to me to speed the hell up on the bait. He yelled, hard and quick, at me whenever I came within ten feet of a launching pot or the lines and buoys spewing overboard after it: "Stay the fuck away from the fuckin' lines!" "Hurry up with the fuckin' tote!" "I said hurry up!" Some moments, I could do it. Fuckin' crab. Fuckin' pots. Fuckin' wind. Fuckin' deck boss.

Crabs, whenever possible, Steve compared to humans at a vigorous, elaborate sex act. When the pot surfaced, its webbing strained by the load, Steve calibrated the degree of heat in the bait those crab were feeding on, "like hung-a-ry men on the hottest puss-y." The wave hitting over our heads was freezing, mixed with snow, enough to kill any of us, really, whether we were wearing rubber outfits or not. Steve would say he wanted some warm pussy. Warm pussy would make that frigid, stunned feeling disappear.

Bill, smart, lazy, dangerously subdued around Steve, was the hydraulic crane operator. He had a wintry, inverted spirit that seemed to place him in the faraway—even if that's where he found himself. He moved slowly, almost sufferingly around the boat. The crane operator has the joy of avoiding racing deck work; he also has a boredom that verges on peril, sitting still for hours in freezing spray, I never knew what Bill, running the crane from a deep, almost Tolstoyan motivation was thinking. When he spoke out against Steve, he guaranteed a lashing in return, but a lashing with a futile, nearly impotent ring to it.

"So how much warm pussy you been feeling these days?" Bill asked, at a pause in the work. He had a wad of Copenhagen in his mouth. He mumbled.

"What did you say, man?" Steve almost spat, wanting, more than anything, to rupture Bill's passivity.

Bob stood by the rail with a helpless-looking cigarette in his mouth. I collected bait set-ups and set them in a ready tote.

"You fuck," said Steve. "You've never even had any piece of pussy. You fuck."

I wanted to speak, to be less than a bystander, something, but the wind surged, my voice was too deep in my hood, and, by the tenets of the crab fishing world, Steve, hard-fisted and top brother on this deck, really had nothing to lose, even if every claim and narration he made felt like a provocation directed at the rest of us on deck.

When we weren't working, we were waiting to work. While we waited, we drove around the ocean. While we drove, we slept, read, rotated through watch schedules, ate microwaved pizzas, watched *When Harry Met Sally* over and over. The boat was its own private world. If seas were calm enough, we'd take showers. If big swells were running, I'd feel green if I stayed upstairs in Ted's stateroom, and I'd retreat to the bunk down below, in the little room I shared with Bob. When seas were really rough, even Ted couldn't stand that rolling up in his bunk. I would stumble out of the black air of the stateroom into the fluorescent light of the galley, and see him sleeping stretched out, a sudden, thick form in a sweatshirt and jeans on a bench beside the galley table.

Radical seas and winds had their own clear face, especially in the long nights. After a twelve-hour or twenty-hour or even sometimes longer run of work, we scrambled for the food we needed in the galley, set a watch rotation, and went straight for sleep, many times so exhausted we skipped cleaning up. Once awakened for a watch shift, and once then awake for the two or three or four hours it entailed, I could put together the fragmented pulse of the boat. Sodium lights high on the rigging of the *Obsession* lit the equipment and the deck or stacks of pots out beyond the wheelhouse windows. In a high wind, with rain, snow, or spray flying out of the impenetrable night ocean, the space shone like an eerie clearing in a storm. Murres, so homeless and urgent that far from land, flipped wildly through the chasm of our light.

Minuscule, heroic, the task of moving matter from this great fluid seemed apparent to me in those hours. Like a small and rugged noun, we seemed the very gravity that the dissonant sea required. We offered foundation, buoyancy. Sand, iron, sun, crab—they were objects in space with no stake in movement, time, or even readiness. A boat on a blank sea. A crab pot tipped swiftly off the boat and still visible, just for a moment, before coils of speed and space took it, a red buoy its only suggestion. Nouns, so many, such a quantity, became the matters of importance on a fishing boat. How many pots? How many strings of pots? How many pot bridles? How many feet in these particular shots in this particular string? How many knots, as in knots on the pot ties? How many knots, as in boat speed? As in wind speed? How many nautical miles? How many gallons of diesel? Water? Oil? How cold? How fast? How high? How many? With the tanks full of crab, the bow iced up, the crew and the captain in their bunks asleep, we possessed every potential, every capacity for energy. In the storage yards of Dutch Harbor, nouns and nouns of pots, each 7×7×3 feet, or 8×8×3 feet, stood rusted, stacked, and waiting for the integrity of some movement. Webbed iron, boat- or land-bound, towering, imminent, replicated, looks as placid and entropic as piers sticking out across the pond of a park. We were a conduit, a completion, dissembling towers, abiding by a seafloor we could locate, smell, contact, and never see.

I pictured my mother leaning against the dishwasher in my parents' kitchen, a March sun breaking across boxwood bushes out the window, the *Forbes* magazine article straight ahead in her gaze. The notes of a Chopin étude filtered from the background. I was at a phone booth at the fuel dock in Unalaska. We'd delivered 8,500 pounds of crab from a ten-day trip, sold at $1.92 a pound, and we were trying to get out of town in an hour. How cold was it? she wondered. How do the clothes work? I avoided saying anything about the inflatable Stormy Seas jacket. How was Ted? She put some stake in my knowing him, as if the fact of him, through her personal equation, connected me to a recognizable safety. She didn't know him, and never could have known him. For the seven years I came to know him myself, she met him only once, for an afternoon lunch on a silty California day, five years after I'd gone fishing the first time. By saying that she never could have known him, I mean that even I, as her daughter, could not have brought her together with him. There were so few forces involved in even my knowing Ted. There was no context, no face on it that we could recognize. We strained to know something, whatever we could, of each other, yet had nothing but our wills working in our favor.

Crab fishing is not a sport. The objective is merely to shift, with speed and accuracy, the pinchered creatures from space to space. The fisherman's job is to find the crab, coax them off the seafloor, into a webbed box, and then, once on deck, out again by turning the pots nearly upside down and shaking the odd, clattering mass onto a metal sorting table or into knee-high plastic totes. Bob and I were always the ones to plunge into the frenzied activity of sorting. The rejects, anything female, anything illegal because it was too small, anything of an out-of-season species, we threw into a plastic tote, which we dragged across the deck and dumped overboard through a chute under the rail of the boat at midship. The keepers we stuffed into another tote, which we dragged to the middle of the deck, where a lid to a hole in the tank, manhole-sized, was pushed aside. We poured, pushed, and stuffed the crab into that tank. Pumped-in seawater kept them alive until we delivered them to the canneries of Dutch Harbor or the Pribilof Islands of St. George and St. Paul.

A boat that is fishing well, pulling the gear and resetting it right away because it's "on the crab," is a fantastic orchestra of human and mechanical energy. It's full of the geometry of heavy gear, the movement of massive loads of crab, and a precision of timing that doesn't leave a second to think or even to look around and consider it. A full pot of crab makes a sound like a shattering when it tumbles on the metal table; the dark surface of water in the tank snaps when a crab hits it; pots and lines and human efforts move at the pace of the wind and waves that the *Obsession* dug through. At certain sharp moments I did feel a part of a game.

Mark Trilling was an All-Star third baseman in Oregon before he dropped out of college and started fishing. Bob might have been the resident grandma of the crew, the only person on deck I really trusted, but Mark was the one I aspired to work along- side. He ripped into me a couple of times for standing too close to a stack of lines attached to a pot just dumped in the water, lines feeding overboard in a blur, but he didn't spend much extra effort baiting me, like Steve did. Mark's job on deck was to throw a grappling hook attached to a delicate white line out to the buoy setup when we drove up beside it. Even when the boat was bucking into abrupt waves, Mark had a loose stance. He also had a smooth, low way of talking to himself, as if he were standing on the bow of a drift boat on a calm river: "Come 'ere, come on 'ere, come on it 'atcha. . . ." He sounded like he was talking to a small, invisible bird he was trying to bring to a nest. Ted, up in the wheelhouse, idled the engine. The boat slowed and ground downward in the water. Mark waited until we were as close as we would get, about thirty-five feet, to the buoy, swung the hook and line like a lasso, and then let it go.

To miss it was to fail. To miss it was to blunder. To miss it was to incite the harassment of Steve and Bill, neither man any more skilled at throwing the hook than Mark. Both of Mark's arms would shoot up and the white line followed the hook out across the water like a ribbon, even if the buoys rose overhead on a swell. Mark paused a moment to let the hook sink, jerked back on it, and then, hands a blur, he hauled in the hook and the line attached to the buoys. Once they were at his feet, he fixed the line into a crevice in a hydraulic block that dangled right above the rail of the boat. Steve hit the switch. Line began coiling blindingly through the block and then into the mechanical coiler, where it built into a circular pile. A few yards down the rail, Bob and I stood poised on either side of the pot launch, waiting to see what broke the surface in the pot.

That afternoon we're on the crab. The pots, 450 pounds when empty, were breaking the surface bulging, crab legs poking through the webbing, almost a thousand pounds full. Leverage and balance are the keys to landing a pot on a heavy launch. Each pot landed with a thick clap, metal to metal. As soon as we could unhook the rubber door ties and flip back the door, we cleaned the crab out in a mad blur, wildly chucking the refuse overboard, rebaiting the pots, and dropping them back in right away. The boat engine idled when we pulled the pots, surged while we sorted, slowed again as we neared the next buoys and Mark gathered the hook for his toss. Bill, in a lethargic stealth, ran the crane from a stool near the forepeak. Steve and Mark handled the coiler and the heavy shots of line. I was on the bait chore and, with Bob, the sorting. While the boat barreled forward from string to string, we huddled under the shelter deck, stuffing down Milky Way bars and Cokes. Was this an eight-hour shift? A gray storm moved in. Gulls drifted and called above the frenzied deck. Everything moved in succession, almost a temperance; as it extended, it eased; as it passed meditation, it reached sympathy: Dump the keepers in the tank hole. Jog back to the crane well corner under the shelter deck. Lean on old coils of rope and watch Mark look for "the bag" across dark water until our sodium lights caught it, toppling in a crest, gleaming red. Was it a ten-hour shift? Twelve? I didn't know what time it was, but I wasn't unsteady or even truly cold. Jog to the coiler while the line winds in. Jump to keep blood in my toes. Laugh obligingly at Steve's crab penis joke. Move an arm back to clear the knot in my shoulder, move the sorting table forward, even as Steve and Mark clean out the pot, rebait it, launch it. We're on the crab. We're on the crab. Swing the tote around, fill it with keepers. Pitch them in the tank. Start over.

Drawn, maybe to the point of obsession, at least to the point of compulsion, to Ted's unconventional, hard-working, dangerous, distant life, I followed resolutely behind him. I convinced him and the others through my quickness at finding a rhythm on deck, through never hesitating, through proceeding quietly, my Grundens snapped and belted, out the wheelhouse door behind the boys and out across stacked pots or an open deck shining in ice, seawater, or sodium lights. I scrambled to gear up for work when we were nearing a string. Bob and I traded off on the cooking chore, and I jogged into the galley to scramble eggs as shifts neared their end. I staggered from my bunk to the wheelhouse for my driving duty after the man closing out his watch before me woke me up. I radioed the cannery when our tanks were full and we were heading for land. And when we turned back out to sea after delivering, heading into the towering mountain ranges of the gray Bering Sea, Ted, at the helm, would sometimes say, "I like this image, the bow of the boat iced up, moving forward in the night." I began to know what he was saying. I fell into a partnership of work with him that felt remote from my first rubbery journey across the pots, distant from my other lives, from the calendar, from the movements of other people I'd known.

One night on deck I was bent over, clearing keepers into the live tank, when a wave the size of a SeaLand container cleared the railing and hit me full against my backside with the force of a frozen concrete wall. I went down on one knee. My other foot lost the surface, went plunging forward into the tank hole. Suddenly I was flat on my stomach on deck, up to my hip in the tank. Water was filling my boot. I could feel the rubble of crab shells through rubber. I didn't say *Shit*. I didn't say *Fuck-ing shit*. I coughed for air. Another wave caught on the rigging, shattering across the forepeak, the deck, me, my back, left the deck awash, its own small sea. Thirty feet above us, even the windows of the wheelhouse were dripping and shining.

I didn't know what had happened, but I did know a flash of terror, peril that could finish me—something I hadn't felt in weeks, even years. I'd just lost my balance. One hit of sea. One submerged limb in a tank full of king crab. I pulled my leg out, my sock dense with freezing seawater, my bones and brain vibrating. I ran back to the shelter deck, hoping the boys hadn't noticed how long I'd been down. All the data I could take was legible in that hit. Buried in all the wool and rubber gear, I shook with a fear that carried into my eyes. The skin on my hip was raw against my sweats. No one said anything. They barely looked to my eyes. A few minutes later, Ted got on the hailer and said, "I can't see shit out here and I'm lost. Let's finish up in the morning."

Once inside the wheelhouse, the boys went down below to mow through hot dogs, pizza, and Mountain Dew. I sat up in the dark pilot room, looking out at the replays of that wave. They rose, rose some more, overbalanced, and smashed across the deck boards. Another trough, another rise. A shower on deck. Categorical. From up here, silent, a movie screen on mute. I pulled salt and herring scraps out of my hair, rubbed my swollen hands. Ted methodically reset the electric plotter and changed our course. At the top of the loran screen, the numbers read 55.23.21 N, 167.10.27 W. The radar screen lit up snow squalls as blue blurs. He saw that wave, I thought. He pulled the weather map off the fax machine. When he spoke, it was gently, as if to himself. "You don't have to stay out here. You know, working this fishing job."

I looked at his face, oddly aglow by the neon of the dials. The fax machine continued to tick and print. All our weather came to us from Japan, so I'd somehow started imagining that the weather maps did too. Or sometimes that we were actually near Japan. When I looked up from work some afternoons on deck I saw the red sun breaking the shaley clouds and then slipping silently below the horizon, right into Asia. I didn't say anything to Ted, even if, for a second or two, I thought I had a response. "There are a lot better jobs out there than this one," he said. "I know that." I had the funny sensation of both: Ted's detachment from me, and his investment in me. Reliable in will; unfamiliar in form: I was both. Closely attached to my fear, a kind of pride from bumping back up on deck, for the endorsement the boys' silence granted me. I said nothing, and Ted and I never broached the subject that directly again. After that, events made decisions for us.

Two weeks later, tired and very hungry after an afternoon of work that ran until midnight, I balanced an overflowing plate of spare ribs and potatoes and a glass of milk to the galley table, but I couldn't put my plate down, because the table was covered in *Playboy* magazines. "Can't we please just get the *Playboy*s off the galley table so we can just eat?" I half-mumbled it, pushing a few back with my glass. Steve immediately hit the roof, stacked up three dog-eared magazines and slapped them down on the Formica table right in front of my plate. Unwisely, I persisted, by, doubly unwisely, baiting his expertise: "Those are all just silicone breasts in those pictures anyway," I said, trying for a ring of authority. Deconstruction did not suit the boys. Was I sorely mistaken? I was sorely mistaken, because Steve himself knew exactly what a silicone breast felt like, he had felt plenty. But so had Mark and Bob and Bill, and what ensued, as I peeled a gummy paste from the ribs and stared passively at the breasts on the cover blonde, was a long and heated discussion about, yes, which of the men had felt more silicone breasts.

Lies, lies, lies. I'd told my mother enough to comprise an entire parallel life, a fiction as intricate as a ton of webbed crab legs. The fact of lies, in fact, seemed part of the fabric of our knowing one another. Somehow, sometimes, I guessed that enactments of dramatic physical freedom were the best ways to pull against her. Mother wrote me long letters, front and back sides of the page, which I picked up at the cannery in Dutch when we made it into town. Her long reports, her insistence on close presence, wore me down with a kind of dim exasperation. I was free. I was free. I could hear myself, see myself. But when I got her letters, spoke to her, it felt like a surrogate truth.

If I could have explained crab fishing to myself, I'd have explained it to her. But how could I justify something that seemed, at bottom, really about extending a question? I thought my attachment to Ted was the tie I needed, but, looking back on it, it wasn't really—couldn't really be—the thing keeping me there. The costs, potential and actual, of the freedom of crabbing are too high for many people. For me though, at that time, the ultimate freedom of the enterprise appeared to be the drawing card, the real lure, but it was actually the cost that compelled me. How far would I go to realize a self that no one had articulated, that I had found merely by guts? I didn't and couldn't know how much the cost was, how far I was willing to go, how much I could cash out in pursuit of this most private force. That overwhelming unknown was more compelling to me than the freedom, the love affair, the stories, the money in my half-share pocket. Selfishly, I sent Mom postcards. Selfishly, I told her the crabbing was excellent, that we never worked at night, that Ted and I were good working friends. *The men on the crew are protective and kind. The weather's been unseasonably mild.* I'd almost made enough money to justify the worry. I'd be home in the summer to look for real work in a real place.

The more weeks and months passed, the faster they seemed to fly. Time had a cryptic way of simplifying, of depicting the advantages of fishing. The work, while tough, was made easy by its attainability. There was one job to do, one objective. The day could be met in a day. I could often awaken to these actions— actions that had formerly appeared insignificant, even crass— and see them as clear, the propulsion of the matter and importance. Chopping herring, mending webbing, painting 54374, the Fish and Game number, on buoys. Dangers and securities became weirdly blurred. The more necessary I felt and became, the more old fears slipped swiftly behind.

When on the crab, we baited the pots and threw them right

back over. A string like any other: I left Bob to finish sorting at the table, turned, raced to grab a bait setup, and came back to the launch. We were in forty-foot swells, but it wasn't difficult anymore. Mark hauled the shots out of the coiler and tossed a couple of them on top of the pot that sat hip-high on the launch. With the door of the pot open, I sat backward into it, as if I were leaning, my head low, back into my bunk. Once inside the pot, with one hand grasping the top iron bar of the doorframe, I leaned even farther back, the other arm reaching with the dangling bait setup that would fasten to the middle of the pot. It was like lying almost flat on my back and, with an arm extended overhead, lifting a twenty-five pound weight off the floor—all in a flash. My feet stuck out the front of the pot and came up off the deck as my torso, arms, stomach and neck all reached back. No pausing here. For a second, I was deep in the pot. I saw all the sky and sea between the diamonds of webbing. Mark and Steve were coiling lines. Bob was stuffing bait jars. Ted was up in the wheelhouse, driving. I was sitting, even momentarily, in the most dangerous spot onboard, inside a crab pot that was moments from tipping seaward.

The dangers were these: One, if Bill hit the launch switch, the bars that the pot sat on would lift my legs farther from the deck and I'd fall to the waves, a ballerina in a music box. Two, if I thought about this, I wouldn't be able to keep up, or even to keep working. The muscles of my stomach ringing from the reach, I snapped the bait string in place in the matter of a second and swung forward, my head low to clear the upper bar of the pot, and then out. One step to the side, and Bob and I pulled the door over and down with a yank, stretched and fastened the rubber door ties, and stepped back. Steve hit the switch.

Of all the distinctive sounds from the crab fishing world—the whine of the coiler, the hiss of the hydraulic block, crab refuse cracking between rubber boot soles and deck boards—there is no more impressive sound than that of a crab pot falling into the sea. A crash and a seethe all at once, a mass of foam, a percolation, it falls. The water gathers in it. The water gathers it in. Mark bent to gather a shot of line and tossed it, then another, then a third, in after the pot. Then he stepped out of the way and I moved to his spot by the railing, a buoy in each hand. They went, just as suddenly, first awkwardly skyward. Then they slapped down and bumped behind us—resolute beacons on this passing segment of sea.

A run into Dutch, in the middle of my second season, and I dashed to the cannery to check for the *Obsession*'s mail messages. In the pile was a pink note for me, telling me to call home as soon as I could. When I did, I was impatient, more possessively sealed into the world of the boat than ever. I was competent, accepted; more of Ted's equal, less of his project. I'd passed muster with the boys, understanding their odd camaraderie. Tired, intrepid, important, I'd adopted their gaits, their cadences, the safe and predictable way we behaved as a unit of orphans, righteously, faithfully severed from the world outside.

Mom answered the phone in Virginia, and quickly, excitedly, got down to business. Someone from an office in Denver had called her, looking for me. They wanted me to fill in on a crew that was leaving to work in Antarctica in a month. I was shocked, and had to work to remember that I had excitedly applied for that job, ostensibly driving forklifts as part of a cargo crew at the South Pole station, over two years ago.

"You'll consider it, won't you?" Mom was trying to be diplomatic here, trying not to plead, but I could hear the pull in her voice. Through the window of the cannery office I saw the mountains of Dutch smudged and muddy, the *Obsession* motoring wearily across the harbor toward the fuel dock, snow ripping sideways between it and me. One tether bound me tautly to Ted, the *Obsession*, and the crew. One tether, however buried, bound me to her. When would one of them snap from the strain? When would both snap? When did Antarctica become a better option for a daughter?

"Yes. Okay, Ma." I suddenly wanted to move, to get going. "I'll call the guy. I promise." I had to run to meet the boys, but as I did, I saw them ahead of me already different, as if my perception of them were out of my control, and had shifted even as I resisted its shift. Were they dirtier? Less united? Less hopeful? I'd tried to commit my every cell to them, and now the events were rendering me a traitor, someone they'd suspected me of being all along, someone with a few too many options.

We pulled out of town by midnight, late. On that trip, I learned about momentum on an afternoon when we were stacking empty pots on deck. What had once appeared impossible came to be, with a few tricks, manageable, energizing. A small series of moves could create a staggering geometry, a geometry in motion: Wait for the right rolling wave under the boat. Use it for the gravity it lends. Grab the crossbar, chest-high, of an empty pot and push it, high on its end, away from the launch and across the slick deck to the corner below the wheelhouse. Keep a wad of pot-ties in the belt of your gear and use them to tie it off, the bars of the pot to the bars of the railing. Get another pot, do it again, securing the second pot to the first. Build an entire layer. Build another as the crane raises, dangles, and sets pots before you. Stack them cleanly, as if they were books on a shelf. Build a third, climbing and balancing stories above the sea. That afternoon that became that night, the five of us were working in a speed and rhythm of baiting, sorting, and stacking that was a pure addiction. I didn't tell the boys I was leaving or even thinking of leaving.

Toward the end of that trip we worked almost incessantly against the closing date of the crab season, and almost always in the vicinity of the 168th parallel. Some nights, in a half-sleep, finishing a watch, or starting one, I could, without arranging it, think of Ted, and the thought would inadvertently begin, "Years from now . . ." as if I could already look back and hear its imminent silence. Something authentic had come of something fabricated, but my hold on its matter, my hold on comprehension of it, seemed to slide away as certainly as the season, with a will, a sense of timing, and a pace that matched even my own.

In the end, at the end, many stretches of work seemed to meld into one tale that I repeated and repeated, long after I'd left for Antarctica, returned, fished again, quit, taken up life with other people, in other places, sometimes with Ted, ultimately without him. In the tale, it's night when we start working, or else we've been working and night fell and I didn't see it fall. A night like any other, our orange raingear blurred against the crab and equipment, an ice-railed stage. Snowflakes fling stupidly down across the deck, the pots, the rim of the bait box. I look up. I can't see anywhere, anywhere outside the sodium lights, can't make out a single feature of night. It's like I'm in space. It must be like space. It's the only thing I can think of. I see the wheelhouse, its windows black, knowing Ted is inside, driving, setting the plotter, watching us. A roller, high as that wheelhouse, shines at a crease of foam on the peak. It's much bigger than the wheelhouse, but nothing is crashing. We're just rolling, up to take the crest, and back down. I'm on a tiny deck, so minute. I don't feel a fear like I'm going to die here, but I feel I could so easily die—I could so easily be extinguished and there would be nothing to account for it at all. We pause at the base of the mountain, iridescent as always, foolishly new. Infinite smallness is what I separate out, only a piece of this unscrupulous voyage.

THE LONG
ROAD HOME

JOE UPTON, *gillnetting in southeast
Alaska, is reluctant to end his summer
salmon season. Against better
judgment, he stays, pushing his season
too far into fall.*

W E'RE TAKING A CHANCE, you know." Harley's nervous twitch was worse than usual. Losing his boat and being in that cold water, even for just a few minutes, had aged him. Now he was squeezed in with his nephew's family on their thirty-four-footer. "If we were smart we'd get out of here while we still could. . . ."

I looked down the beach where my wife, Susanna, was walking with our dog. Beyond her the hanging glaciers loomed over the waters of bleak-looking Chilkat Inlet. I could tell just from her posture that she was ready to call it a season.

"I know," I said, "we were here last year—stuck for a week, blowing every day, but just one more good opening and we'll have our winter money in my ass pocket."

Susanna came up just then, as if she knew exactly what we were talking about.

"You know," she said, "the really smart ones left ten days ago, when we got that first dusting of snow. They're probably home by now."

"When you boys see fresh snow on the hills," an old-timer had told us, "better start smokin' 'er south." But he was probably thinking about the old days when salmon weren't worth so much. At ten bucks a fish, we could double our season in just a few lucky days. Dusting of snow or not, I wanted to stay up in that remote fjord north of Glacier Bay as long as we were allowed to fish, even if it was just a one- or two-day fishing period a week.

The early fall dusk closed in around us and we crowded close to the beach fire. The smoke rose straight into the still air, and our boats lay mirrored in the still water, but across from us was an awesome wall of rock and ice, a reminder of the true nature of the place. As we sat there eating and drinking around the fire, a good end to a mediocre season seemed within our grasp—just one more period of good fishing and we'd have our winter made.

Lynn Canal, where we lay, was a treacherous wind tunnel, sort of a storm corridor running from the Yukon Territories in the north to the North Pacific Ocean in the south. Sometimes, especially in the fall, the battles between the Pacific lows and the Arctic highs would go on for weeks. A norther had hit at night during the fishing period the week before, sending half a dozen boats ashore or to the bottom, fortunately without any casualties.

"I knew we were drifting fast," a friend of ours had told us. "but we had a hell of a set and I couldn't stop picking. Besides, I figured as long as I could see lights to leeward of us, we were okay, so I didn't go in and check the radar. Then POW! We hit the beach, and we were right over on our side, driven up by the waves in no time. Then I realized that the lights I had seen were other boats that had been blown ashore, too. All I could do was grab my sleeping bag and wade through the surf, try to get out of the rain and stay dry until the chopper came. When they picked me up, there were four other guys in there, all soaking wet and half in shock. What a night. . . ."

Another friend had just finished picking up a big set when the wind came. But he set out again anyway. When you're pulling five thousand dollars out of the water in just a couple of hours' work, it's hard to stop. That set was even bigger than the first one. By the time he was halfway through the net, the hold and the fish boxes were all full, and the husky thirty-six-footer was riding low in the water.

"Don't you think this is enough?" his worried girlfriend asked, as they threw a deckload forward and began filling the stern with fish as well.

"Naw, babes," the skipper said, "this is just like one of those Errol Flynn movies. . . . everything comes out okay!"

They got the last of the fish and the net aboard at last, and, wallowing deep in the water, headed for the tenders, or fish-buying vessels, two miles away. They made the point and were almost in the lee when they took a sea broadside. The boat slowly rolled to port and began to settle in the dark water. Luckily another boat was running in right behind them and plucked the two of them quickly out of the water, but their boat and all the fish were lost.

Later that night, after we had returned to our boats, I stumbled out on deck to take a leak. There was a moon dog, a great circle around the hunter's moon, and I heard in the hollow stillness a faraway booming that made the very water tremble. It was a million tons of ice, one of the glaciers on the mountains around us, inching forward, tumbling pieces of ice the size of small houses or trucks down into the trees far below. In the morning, there was fresh snow on the hills, extending almost down to the waterline.

"We could go," Susanna said, "We could be home in three days. We could enjoy what's left of the fall before the weather turns." But even as she spoke, boats started to move out of the anchorage around us, to look for fish, to be ready for the noon opening of the twenty-four-hour fishing period, and I couldn't turn my back at a crack at another four or five thousand bucks.

We started out in Chilkat Inlet, a few square miles of water surrounded by high mountain walls with a couple of hundred other boats. Sometimes, even in the middle of a big fleet, you can do well. The fish that are milling around below our shallow gillnets can suddenly rise in mass toward the surface and we all load up, big boats and small.

But that day there were no big hits, just steady fair fishing as we slowly worked north toward the mouth of the Chilkat River, where hundreds of bald eagles had begun to congregate to feed on the spawning salmon. High clouds moved in from the south at dark, and the raw northerly increased to twenty-five knots. I knew we were in for a lousy night, but we hit a little bunch of fish and had almost four hundred aboard by midnight—good fishing for us. Each time Susanna and I would come in from picking and resetting the net, we'd hang up our foul-weather gear and just huddle, shivering, as close to the diesel stove as we could get, until we could get warm again.

"If we'd left three days ago, we'd be home now." Susanna said, her face pinched with cold.

I waited until my teeth stopped chattering before answering. "I know. When it's like this, I wish we had, too. But, hey, four grand looks pretty good in February, too."

"Sure, but then there's the grand after that and the one after that. We've made our boat payment, we've got enough money to get south for a while this winter. . . . I mean, how much is enough?"

There it was—the "how much is enough" thing. I envied the guys who had been able to turn their back on this and head south when there was traveling weather. We probably had "enough," whatever that was. We'd always been able to make do with whatever we had at the end of our season. I just wasn't ready to quit yet, though.

The thirtieth of September came, black, windy, and cold. When it was time to pick the net, Susanna and our dog Sam were sleeping cozily together and I didn't have the heart to wake them. The weather was so rotten by then, a steady thirty-five with blowing snow and sleet, that I was tempted to go in and anchor up after I'd picked. But still, there were over forty fish in the net at ten bucks a whack. I ran up close to the shore and looked for a spot in the lee to set the net out again. Finally I got it out, and lay down to rest with the boat pounding heavily, and the wind howling through the rigging.

Dawn, when it came, was grim, with snow and sleet falling from a leaden sky. I had gotten a chill the night before, and couldn't seem to shake it, not even by standing right beside the almost red-hot stove. Our net had been "end-o" for hours by then, pulled straight downwind by the boat. A less cold and more aggressive fisherman might have jogged clear rather than have the boat pull it out of shape, but with the snow and all, the risk of losing sight of the net was too great for me.

At 9:00 A.M., the wind was 35-plus, blowing the snow horizontally. I put on nearly all the clothes I had and went out to pick. The corkline was like a steel rod; I had to put the boat in reverse to take some of the strain off before the hydraulics could wind it in. There were another thirty some fish in the net, but I just threw them into the hold and went inside to start steaming for the tenders. We could have set out again, but with the weather obviously still deteriorating, it seemed prudent to go in early, and I was totally chilled.

Susanna came up then and steered while I stood as close to the stove as I could get without igniting myself. She didn't even ask me how many fish we'd caught that night; she wasn't interested.

For almost four hours, we bucked into a five-to-six-foot chop in driving snow and zero visibility. The spray was freezing on the antenna. I had a real hard time keeping a picture on the radar screen.

"Where you guys at, Joe?" the radio asked. The usually calm voice of our friend Bob Dolan was noticeably tense.

"Ah," I said, glad to have a voice to talk to. "We're out in the middle somewhere, bucking up toward Twin Coves. It's rotten here. Can't see a thing and the radar's about useless, what with the snow. How 'bout you?"

"We're up inside the inlet now, just jogging, waiting for it to let up a bit. Windows are all iced up. We'll be some glad when we get in." His wife and two young daughters were aboard, as well as his uncle Harley, whose boat had sunk in the blow the week before.

I kept fiddling around with the radar and occasionally got enough of a picture to keep us going. Just before 2:00 P.M., the anchored Icicle Seafoods' tender *Emily Jane* appeared out of the snow ahead and we slid alongside to unload. The hills above us must have funneled the wind, for as the skipper, Gene Sheldon, and I worked to unload, williwaws gusted around us at a good fifty knots plus, and the boats worked noisily against the fenders.

Over the noise of the engine driving the refrigeration system, I could hear the anchor wire complaining in the hawse pipe. Afterward, Susanna and I sat down in their galley to have a cup of coffee and catch up on the news while waiting for our fish ticket.

A call came over the radio, and Gene went forward into the pilothouse to answer. It sounded as if some more boats were waiting to be unloaded thirty miles farther down the canal. It hadn't occurred to me that anyone would leave shelter in such a storm.

"You're not going out there, are you?" I asked Marilyn, Gene's wife.

She shook her head. "We've still got the *Belle K* and four others to get in Bridgit Cove." She didn't seem real happy about the idea. I heard the engine room door open and close and a moment later, the sound of the hydraulic system going on for the anchor winch. Outside, though it was not yet 3 o'clock, the light was going fast. The sun was already over the ice mountains and the snow was coming on thicker.

"You heard about the *Babs*, didn't you?" Marilyn asked. The *Babs* was a well-found thirty-six-foot gillnetter.

"No, what happened?"

"Frank was fishing on the outside of Sullivan and I guess a big sea caught him and filled the hatch. She went quick."

"How 'bout Frank?"

"There was another boat a little ways away. They came right over and picked him up, but Frank got real cold."

Gene came in then. He had his oilskins on again and the weather report was plastered all over them. It was time to go.

The lines came off and the *Emily Jane* was lost to our sight, blotted out by the thick snow, the wind, and the early dark. It was getting to be a wild, wild night out there and I wasn't sure I'd ever see them again.

As we jogged slowly over toward the head of the anchorage, I called Bob, the friend who had been trying to get into Cannery Cove, a few miles to the north.

"Bob, what's it like up there?"

"It's better than nothing . . . but it's pretty wild. The outer floats are breaking up and blowing ashore. We're on the inside with about eight lines on the float, but I'm afraid the whole ball of wax'll go if it gets any worse. Where'd you guys end up?"

"We just pitched off. We're jogging up into the head of the anchorage now. Chuck and Alan and the rest of the guys are in here—we'll just lay alongside them."

"Well, just be ready to move if this northerly ever quits. Sometimes it switches right around to a hard southerly after one of these."

A raft of boats appeared out of the snow and gloom ahead: the *Firkin, Arctic Tern,* and *Kay II,* all small gillnetters and friends from our Sumner Strait/Point Baker summer fishing grounds.

I ran up ahead of them and laid out both anchors in a big V while Susanna maneuvered the boat. Then I payed out line and wire until we could lay alongside the other three. In a momentary break in the driving snow, I counted fifteen other boats crowded into the little anchorage, which was little more than a bight in the shore.

It was full dark by then, and though we all lay as close to the steep shore as we dared, the wind was gusting down through the trees with force, heeling us all over and working our fenders and lines. It was a good night for friends, a cozy foc's'le, dry clothes at last, and a bottle to pass all around, and we had all of those things. But I went to bed listening to the hiss of the snow on the hull just a few inches away and the moan of the wind through the rigging, and I wished we were back at Point Baker, our season done.

The first of October came off cold and windy. At 2:30 A.M., I was up to check the anchors. On both sides of us, other boats were re-anchoring, their spotlights casting shafts of swirling snow. But our little bunch of tired people and boats seemed okay. I went back to an uneasy sleep with the wind shaking the boat.

The gray dawn came, with low skies and everything blasted white—hills, trees, beach, and boats. Clusters of boats were anchored together, their anchors almost on the beach, seeking every available foot of lee. As we ate breakfast, we listened to the radio. All the packers had anchored up last night and this morning's tales were of dragging anchors and parted lines. All up and down the coast, hundreds of boats were tucked into all the coves and anchorages, talking about the storm.

At three, the wind suddenly dropped, and our little group was quickly under way for the small town of Haines, ten miles away, keenly aware that if a southerly hit, this would all be lee shore. Near Seduction Point, we saw something sticking up out of the water and stopped to investigate. It was the bow of a sunken gillnetter, iced up and half hidden by the snow and early gloom. We circled it but there was little that we could do.

Night came early, and we led with our radar, each boat in

line, following the masthead light of the boat ahead. When at last we made the breakwater and the harbor at Haines, all of our windows were opaque with snow and frozen spray. I slid back a side window and gingerly idled in toward the snowy darkness until, finally, the lights of a float deep in snow materialized out of the gloom. We snuggled in as close to the head of the harbor as we dared and tied up, third boat out.

The southerly came in at midnight and for the next three days the wind never dropped below thirty and the temperature never went above it. We played cards in the Harbor Bar and someone built a snowman at the head of the ramp down to the boat harbor, but it was only a bitter reminder of the prison that Lynn Canal had become for us.

On the seventh we hitchhiked across the peninsula to Cannery Cove. It was a bleak and wintry sight. A few boats still lay there with tripled-up lines, but the ramp and outer floats had broken to pieces and been blown up on the beach. Where the floats had been lay another sunken gillnetter, with only its rigging above water.

The eighth came clear, but with a nor'west at 40 as four days of accumulated southerly winds blew their way back out of the Yukon country. The next day dawned fair, with little wind—our first good day for traveling in a week. But fishing opened at noon for twenty-four hours.

"We're heading to Point Baker, right?" Susanna asked cautiously.

"Well, let's just see what's out there. If it's dead, we'll blast out of here."

In my heart I knew Susanna was right, and by midafternoon, with very skinny fishing, and another southerly gale making up, I knew I'd made the wrong choice. But by then it was too late to run, and we could only keep fishing and hope for a lucky set. Some time after midnight, when it took two hours to pick jellyfish and juvenile codfish out of the net for nine dog salmon, we called it quits.

So, on a black and mean night, with sleet slashing down from the ice mountains above, I rolled the net on for the last time. We snuggled in close to the mainland shore, opposite the southern end of Sullivan Island, to drop the hook, and our season was done. The moment we had talked about and looked forward to came with no emotion save exhaustion.

At first light, we got under way to sell our fish and get out of that lonely and windy canyon. After rubbing the "N" off the compass, we were ready to do the same with the "S."

The next morning, when at last we headed out and around the point and began beating our way south, the weather was marginal: southeast wind at twenty-five knots and an ugly chop. But one hundred other boats had the same idea—ahead and behind as far as I could see were the white smudges of spray flying as the fleet pounded south—we couldn't get out of that bleak canyon fast enough! All were soon lost in the gray and the sleet. It was one tough ride, but Susanna and I had decided that comfort be damned; if we could travel without breaking a window out we were going to keep going. Eldred Rock Lighthouse rose stark and bleak from the water to the east and we were glad to finally put it and Lynn Canal behind us.

The wind let go at noon, when we were at Vanderbilt Reef, where the big Canadian steamer *Princess Sophia* had stranded on a bitter night in October of 1918. A rescue fleet had shown up the next morning, ready to take off passengers, but decided to wait until better conditions. They never got them: a wild northerly howled down the canal at dusk, driving the rescuers to shelter. Late at night came a single desperate call: "For God's sake, come, we are sinking!" In the morning only her masts were sticking up—she had been driven off the reef and sank with all 343 aboard.

The tide was up as we passed Lena Point, and all of the boats traveling down the canal with us took the shallow shortcut across Mendenhall Flats to the bright lights and fuel dock at Juneau. But the draw of our cozy Point Baker cabin just 150 miles south kept us going, around the back side of Douglas Island, where the wind found us again, just at dusk, for a long, dirty hour before we finally made Taku Harbor and tied to an empty float, the only boat there.

Maybe the Juneau crowd were the smart ones: our bowline parted in a violent gust around 2:00 A.M., the boat swung around sideways, and a moment later the stern line parted too and away we went. Three-quarter-inch lines and barely a month old. I started her up quick and spotlighted our way up to the very head of the harbor to anchor, then sat up for a bit afterward to make sure we weren't dragging anchor. I flipped on the radio to hear a big eighty-foot packer just a few miles away say he was giving it up and heading for shelter before the seas blew a window out.

The morning came calm, with only light airs and a leftover swell. We were up and away at first light, down Stephens Passage, with the hills rising dark and steep on either side and here and there small icebergs from the Tracy Arm glaciers. Once we saw a tender, hull down way ahead of us, bound for Petersburg, and heard a few faraway voices on the radio, but other than that we were totally alone in that vast and humbling landscape.

In the early afternoon a front came through just as we were passing Point League, for as nasty an hour as we'd had all season. We finally made the cove at Entrance Island at very last light, dropped the anchor, found the rum bottle, and baked up the last coho of the season. By then it was truly roaring out there.

We could hear the wind working the woods outside even over the music on the tape deck. But we were in the lee and our anchor deep in the mud, so let 'er rip. Deep in the night something big in the woods fell nearby, and I lay there for a long time listening to it all again and giving thanks for a secure harbor on a wild and mean night, and asking for just one day between storms so we could get home.

Someone must have heard our prayers, for the wind let go in the hours before dawn. We slid out of the empty anchorage again at first light for the last, last miles with the gray skies pressing down on the land and water, the shores lost in the overcast, and not another boat in sight. In the late afternoon's failing light we passed the Tlingit village of Kake, a line of houses and an old cannery along the shore with wood smoke smudged against the dark hills behind. We entered Rocky Pass, a constricted and twisting passage between Kuiu and Kupreanof Islands, so narrow that at times the tree branches seemed to almost graze our trolling poles and raft after raft of ducks traded back and forth in the shallows. Our little Cummins diesel seemed to speed up, as if it knew that the barn was close. On another trip, we might have stopped, dropped the hook, spent a peaceful night, and taken the morning to get in some good duck hunting with the dog. But we'd come too far to stop so close.

On we went, the early darkness finding us in Sumner Strait, with a long swell driving up from the unseen ocean to the south. Finally at ten, in a cold drizzle, we spotlighted our way into the black and empty cove on Prince of Wales Island where our cabin waited and tied up to our float.

After a six-week season, the longest we'd ever fished, everything was as we had left it, except the skiff had sunk. Our dog went off to sniff around his old haunts, and we lit the kerosene lamps, built a fire in the wood stove, and got out the old rum bottle again.

We'd traveled three long days to get home, laid overnight both times in deserted and empty harbors. Beyond our kerosene lamp–lit windows Sumner Strait and the whole back side of Kuiu Island was totally black—all that land, all those bays, without a cabin or any sign of man at all.

Outside the wind began, working at a loose shingle like a dog at a bone, and our lights shone out on another wild and unfriendly night.

"Was it worth it?" Susanna said, her only reference to what we'd just come through.

I shook my head. "You were right. We should have left sooner."

But we'd made our winter money and coming back to our cabin and our cove after that fall season, our lives seemed filled up in a way they never did in the south.

NIGHTS OF ICE

SPIKE WALKER *relates the tale of the* Tidings, *returning to home port* Kodiak *after crabbing in one of the coldest winters on record. When their vessel suddenly rolls, the skipper is trapped inside and the three crewmen, without survival suits in frigid waters, face impossible odds.*

F OR JOE HARLAN, captain of the fifty-three-foot crab boat *Tidings*, and his crew, the 1989 Kodiak Island tanner crab season had been an exceptionally tough one.

From the opening gun, they'd ignored the weather, fishing hard through the merciless cold of an arctic storm. They were working the waters down in the Sitkalidak Island area on the southeast side of Kodiak Island, some eighty nautical miles from the fishing port of Kodiak. But Harlan and his men had been pleased at their luck.

They'd been pulling gear in the biting cold of the short winter hours of light, grinding through a total of some one hundred crab pots. Harlan had agreed to pay his men a 10 percent per-man crew share that season. In just two weeks they'd boated more than forty thousand pounds of tanner crab. Crew shares had already topped ten thousand dollars—per man.

But they had been pounded night and day by wild northwest winds packing chill-factor temperatures of minus fifty degrees and williwaw gusts that made fishing that 1989 season one of the most perilous ever. One crab boat had gone down not far from Harlan and his men, near Chirikof Island. All four of the crewmen had died. So far, only one body had been recovered.

On another crab boat, one deckhand had lost three toes to frostbite when he ignored the water sloshing about in his boots while working on deck. As a fellow crewmate recalls it, "Before he knew it was happening, it had already happened."

On the very first day of the season, Joe Harlan had lost one of his own men to frostbite. He had rushed the man into the ancient Aleut village of Old Harbor on the south end of Kodiak Island and hired a bush plane to fly the man to the hospital in Kodiak for treatment. The man had broken no hard-and-fast rules of the sea; he had merely tried to sort crab wearing only cotton glove liners. And he had developed large blisters on the fingertips of both hands, which would keep him out of commission for the rest of the month-long season.

Less than two weeks later, the tanner crab catch fell off dramatically. And skipper Joe Harlan turned to his crew, hoping to cut his losses and call it a season. "Well, you know what you've made so far," he began. "And the way the crabbing has been going these last few days, you know what you can expect to make. The way I see it, we have two choices. We can stay out here and scratch away on a five-or-ten-crab-per-pot average until the Alaska Fish and Wildlife Department tells us to quit. Or we can quit burning up our fuel, store our gear away back in Kodiak, and get out of this cold son-of-a-bitchin' weather."

After weeks spent working in the single-worst extended cold spell ever recorded in the Kodiak weather books, the crew of the *Tidings* did not hesitate. They'd been "successful enough" for one season.

Built in 1964 in the shipyards of Seattle, the fishing vessel *Tidings* had a wheelhouse that was mounted forward on the bow. She was considered one of the nicest boats around at the time because she had a toilet, something that was considered rather extravagant in those earlier, "hang it over the side" days.

Packing the recommended load of some thirteen crab pots on her back deck, the *Tidings* was closing fast on Chiniak Bay of the port of Kodiak, cruising through moderate seas, paralleling the coast of Kodiak Island about one and a half miles offshore, when, late on that frigid night, "all hell broke loose." Joe Harlan had been looking forward to slipping into the close and comfortable shelter of the Kodiak port, and with the exception of ice forming on the wheelhouse and railings of the *Tidings*, their journey north along the full length of the island had gone as planned.

But at Narrow Cape, they ran into some bad tide rips. Spray began exploding over the length of the ship, and they began making ice heavily.

Joe Harlan soon rousted his crew from their bunks.

"Guys, we've got to get this ice off of us," he said as he woke the men. With his crew gathered in the wheelhouse, Harlan pointed at the windows surrounding them. They were encased in ice. Only a clear space the size of a quarter in one window remained.

"Knock the windows clear, and then be sure and get the ice that's stuck to our railings," directed the skipper. "But don't let yourself get frostbitten. As soon as you get cold, come on in!" he insisted.

In an amazingly short time, a thick layer of ice had formed on the *Tidings*. Ice covered the boat—except, that is, for the crab pots themselves. Harlan and his crew had wrapped the commonly ice-drawing forms of steel and webbing in a layer of slick plastic, one that drained quickly before the spray from the ocean had time to harden.

The crew of the *Tidings* made good work of the ice-breaking task. But they longed to get back inside, out of the murderous cold. There they would flop down on the floor and warm themselves in front of the heater in the galley.

Back inside, skipper Joe Harlan was making a routine check of his engine room when he spotted seawater rising fast in the ship's bilge. Seconds later, the *Tidings* began to list to the port side.

Either the crab tank's circulation-pump pipe had ruptured inside the engine room or the steel bulkhead separating the engine room from the crab tank had split a seam. Nobody would ever know for sure. But it "put a lot of water in that engine room right now!" The moment Harlan spotted the water, he rushed to the back door and yelled to deck boss Bruce Hinman, "Grab your survival suits! And then start kicking the pots over the side!"

Joe Harlan was standing in the wheelhouse when he felt the *Tidings* roll. Instinctively, he was certain the ship would not be able to right herself. Yet he "couldn't believe it." He found he was unable to accept what was happening to the *Tidings*, a vessel he had come to trust and even admire. Then a ridiculous thought shot momentarily through his mind: He had an unspoken impulse to order his crew to "run back there, hop overboard, and push the thirty-ton vessel back upright."

With the *Tidings* sinking fast, Joe Harlan knew she would finish her roll and sink completely in about the time it would take him to utter a single sentence. Turning to his VHF and CB radios, he made a snap decision.

In the past, he'd listened to many Mayday calls to the U.S. Coast Guard in Kodiak. As glad as he was to have them standing by for his fellow fishermen, Harlan also knew that the Coast Guard usually wanted to know "who your mother's sister was, the color of your boat," your date of birth, your last checkup, proper spelling, and the like. So rather than shoot off a Mayday to the Coast Guard, Harlan decided to take a gamble.

For much of the night, he'd been listening on VHF channel 6 to the friendly chatter of the boats traveling ahead of him up the line. He grabbed the CB mike then and yelled, "Mayday! Mayday! Mayday! This is the *Tidings!* We're off Cape Chiniak and we're going down!"

As he spoke, the *Tidings* fell completely over on her starboard side. Below him, Harlan could see batteries breaking loose and flying across the engine room. He felt his heart freefall into his belly. Before he could unkey his mike, he "lost all power. Everything went dead."

Harlan heard a tremendous crash, and it seemed that all at once everything inside the boat—pots, pans, toasters, even rifles—came flying loose. Then the large hulk of the refrigerator came tumbling from its mounts. Harlan was thrown across the width of the wheelhouse. He struggled to regain his footing, but instead he tumbled backward down into the fo'c'sle.

Then, like a whale sounding, in one continuous motion the stern kicked high, and the *Tidings* sank bow-first, straight for the bottom. She slid toward the ocean floor in one steady motion, burying herself full length in the night sea. And there she paused, floating with only a few feet of her stern showing above the surface, with Joe Harlan still trapped inside.

As Bruce Hinman recalls it, shortly before the *Tidings* foundered and rolled over, his skipper had slowed the vessel to allow all six-foot-three and 290 pounds of Hinman's huge frame, as well as his fellow crewmates Chris Rosenthal and George Timpke, time to get dressed and make their way outside. A ten-inch-thick layer of sea ice had already formed on the *Tidings'* superstructure, and was growing fast. Clad only in their work clothes, they hurried outside to do battle.

Hinman, Rosenthal, and Timpke attacked the ice with baseball bats. They broke ice and tossed the chunks overboard as fast as they could move. And as they did, they squinted against the sharp, eye-watering gusts of arctic wind, and winced at the biting cold. They worked in drenching conditions in a chill-factor reading of some −55°F., the coldest ever recorded in the area. And they swung at the growing layers of ice now encasing the bow railings and bulwarks surrounding the wheelhouse, certain in the knowledge that their very lives hung in the balance.

Suddenly, the crab boat began to list sharply. The growing list soon tilted past forty-five degrees. Seawater rose over the portside railing. Hinman was removing his survival suit from its bag when a tall wave broke over the twisting slope of the deck. And just as suddenly, he and the others found themselves dodging a deadly shuffle of fifteen thousand pounds of crab pots sliding forward toward them down the steep slope of the deck. As the bow of the *Tidings* nosed farther forward into the icy sea, the seven-ton stack of crab pots accelerated its slide, further distorting the already-untenable balance of the sinking ship.

Accelerating as it came, the tall and deadly stack of sliding crab pots closed on the terrified crewmen like a moving mountain. The square-fronted stack of steel and webbing plowed into the back door of the ship's wheelhouse like a runaway freight car. It slammed against the rear of the wheelhouse with the effect of a door closing on a bank vault, leaving their skipper trapped inside.

With the shifting weight accelerating the angle of the plunging bow, the *Tidings* rolled with an astonishing velocity, pitching the four crewmen scrambling across her back deck bodily through the air and overboard.

The suddenness of the portside motion caught everyone off guard. It was as if an all-powerful force had suddenly gripped the *Tidings* and flipped her—as if her fifty-three feet and forty tons were no more substantial than a bathtub toy in a child's hands.

Bruce Hinman felt the sudden shift, and he found himself hurtling through space; several of the crab pots followed. His right arm became entangled in the webbing of one of the pots—and just as suddenly, the six-hundred-pound crab pot began to "sink like a rock" toward the bottom, dragging Hinman, kicking and struggling, along with it.

It all happened so quickly. Hinman had been knocked senseless by the sudden shock of the Kodiak waters, ensnared by one of his own crab pots, and was now being dragged along on an unforeseen journey into deepest darkness toward an ocean floor more than a thousand feet below.

He knew instinctively that if he allowed panic to rule him, he would be lost. And he fought to choke back the rising tide of unreasoning fear within himself.

As he descended through the darkness, Hinman gained a measure of composure. He would fight against the building fear by taking action. He was perhaps seventy feet beneath the ocean surface when he managed to jerk his ensnared right arm free. Then he placed both of his stockinged feet against the webbing of the crab pot and pushed away violently. The fast-sinking crab pot disappeared quickly, tumbling off into the black body of sea below him.

When Hinman looked up, he was awestruck by what he saw, for a blinding orb of radiant light hovered above him. There was something beautiful, even angelic about the vision before him. Brilliant in splendor, it bathed him in spirit-lifting columns of golden light that seemed to beckon him home.

He ascended feverishly then, stroking overhead toward the comforting swath of inexplicable light like a man with a building hope, a hope tempered by the fear that at any moment another toppling crab pot might very well descend upon him and carry him back down again.

And at that moment, Bruce Hinman's past life flashed before his very eyes. Launched instantaneously through time, he watched the events of his life play out before him with "the speed of thought." The prevailing feeling was of being cast adrift on a wondrous journey, unhindered by earthly impediments of time, matter, or communication.

Hinman felt "lost in time without an anchor." And the look and feel of special moments long past came back to him now with complete clarity. They flashed and froze there in his consciousness, in a kind of nostalgic collage of all that had once mattered in his life.

He saw his two little boys; his former wife, Carol; his two

adopted foster daughters; and both of his parents, as well. Then Hinman was back under fire in Vietnam, just as it had all happened, with soldier buddies dropping all around him. A millisecond later, he was a boy again, scrambling along the banks of Lake Shasta in northern California. And he was swept back into the very moment when he had come so close, as a child, to drowning. It all scrolled past him now, and each memory carried with it the exact same heart-tugging emotion he had felt at that time.

Bruce Hinman exploded through the surface, leaving the visions behind. He rose bodily into the bitter night, then wrenched hard and began inhaling deep lungfuls of the precious air.

When he regained himself, he spotted the stern of the *Tidings* drifting nearby. She was hanging straight down in the water.

Adrift now, without a survival suit, lost in a whiteout of silvery gray ice fog, Hinman knew the odds of outliving his predicament were slim. He dog-paddled and fought to catch his breath.

When he could, he yelled for his crewmates, "Hey, Chris! Where is everybody?"

A voice sounded out of the darkness perhaps fifty feet away. "Hinman!" He recognized the voice of his good friend and crewmate Chris Rosenthal.

"Harlan's in the boat! He's down inside the boat!" Chris shouted.

George Timpke, their third crewmate, soon acknowledged him, as well. He was clinging to a piece of flotsam off in the darkness approximately one hundred feet away.

Short of diving equipment, Hinman knew he had no way of reaching his trapped skipper. Swearing aloud, he soberly acknowledged to himself that his good friend Joe Harlan was a goner. And a single thought shot across his mind. What am I going to say to his wife, Mary Ellen?

Now Hinman felt the almost caustic effects of the bitter wind and numbing ocean against the flesh of his face. He also knew there would be no way to climb back aboard the sinking vessel, no way for him or his other shipmates to climb clear of the life-sucking cold of the Gulf of Alaska water, and he felt at once helpless and angry.

"Now what?" he shouted into the arctic night.

Harlan had been roughed up considerably when the *Tidings* had rolled over. In fact, he had come close to breaking his right arm. He scrambled to gather himself and climb out. Ordinarily, the ladder leading from the engine room to the sleeping quarters stood upright and led down into the engine room. But now the vertical leg of the ladder posed a serious obstacle. With the *Tidings* tilted straight down as she was, the ladder now lay unevenly across the inverted space before him, sloping as it stretched between cabins. Scaling it would be a little like trying to climb the underside of a stairway. With his battered right arm, it would be a difficult gymnastic feat.

Now the startled skipper found himself "all the way forward" in the darkest inner reaches of the ship's bow, some fifty feet below the surface of the sea. As the boat continued to leap and roll, he could hear the ongoing crash and clutter of stored parts falling and scattering overhead.

Suddenly, in the gray-black light, a roaring blast of seawater broke through the door to the engine room. The tumultuous white water broke heavily over Harlan, lifting him bodily and washing him out of the fo'c'sle. He gasped for air as the icy flood cascaded over him. As he was carried along through the inverted space of the ship's galley, Harlan reached out and snagged the handle to the wheelhouse door. He tugged frantically, but with the water pressure sealing it shut, he found it immovable.

As the small galley continued to flood, Harlan found himself struggling to remain afloat in the narrowing confines. The galley sink and faucet were now suspended on end below him while beside him, in the claustrophobic space, floated the gyrating hulk of their refrigerator.

Harlan gulped air and dived. He knew he had to think of a way out. He swam down through the watery cubicle of the galley to the sink, grabbed the faucet with both hands, and kicked viciously at the starboard side window behind it. But the leaden cold of the water seemed to drain the power from his blows. This is hopeless! he thought, as he swam humbly back toward the pocket of air above.

The moment his head emerged, he was greeted by a terrifying roar. The flood of gushing seawater into the room seemed to be accelerating. The sound of it echoing in the small sliver of space was deafening. The water sloshed back and forth between walls that rolled and dipped in a dizzying motion around him. Again, the refrigerator drifted into him. And he fought against a building sense of horror.

Treading water, Harlan tilted his head back in the narrow space next to the ceiling and tried to inhale the precious air. But the shocking cold of the seawater continued to make breathing difficult, and his breath came in shallow huffs.

Well, this is it, he thought. This must have been how Jim Miller died on the *George W.*

Harlan considered praying, but it occurred to him that doing so would be an admission that he was going to die. He also made up his mind "not to snivel." He would not pray, and he would not blubber. He would face the outcome, whatever that might be.

Joe Harlan weighed the chances of escaping through the galley door and out onto the back deck. But with the *Tidings* standing directly on end as she was, he knew the entire fifteen-thousand-pound stack of crab pots would be pressing down against the door at that very moment. And, with the refrigerator floating in front of it, he conceded the escape route had been lost.

Yet even at the time, in the midst of all the terror and commotion, Joe Harlan realized that there was something strange about his ongoing ordeal. For he could see virtually everything. With his adrenaline flowing, his senses had somehow become heightened—and now a whole new world seemed to open up before him. When he dived again, he saw, through the blue-green tint of the water, the forms of the faucet and the window behind it, while the blocky brown figure of the refrigerator bobbed above him, suspended in the water overhead.

There was something strange about it all. Harlan knew there were no lights burning on the boat. Everything had gone dead. There was "zero power." Perhaps it was moon-bright up top. But then he recalled that there had been no sign of the moon on such an inclement night. Yet, submerged as he was, Harlan could see clearly through the seawater inside the boat, as well as out into the light green sea space on the other side of the window.

Adrift in the ocean current, the hull of the *Tidings* bounced now in the lumpy winter seas like a floating berg of ice, with barely 10 percent of her whole self still showing above the surface.

Entombed inside the sinking hull of the *Tidings*, Joe Harlan was also feeling the weight of his impossible predicament close in on him, and his emotions built toward a breaking point.

He thought of his lovely young wife, Mary Ellen. She had soft brown hair and beautiful blue eyes. They had met four years before in Kodiak; Harlan had hired her to do the cooking for the boat during a herring season. They had married soon after that, and now they were the proud parents of a beautiful one-year-old daughter, Chelsea.

In the hardworking and yet contented years since then, Joe Harlan and his wife had built a fine house together outside of Kodiak in the Bells Flats area along Sergeant Creek. Harlan could see the ocean from the balcony of his home. And he had one of the best silver-salmon fishing holes on Kodiak Island right in his own backyard. During the salmon-spawning season in the lush and beautiful summer months on the island, he often had to put up with Kodiak bears who wandered onto his backyard property and competed for those same spawning salmon.

Joe Harlan loved his family. Besides, he had mortgage payments to make, and a lot of living to do. The whole damned thing just wasn't fair. He couldn't bear to accept it! He couldn't "just give up!"

The injustice of the moment sent Harlan into an emotional spiral that carried him over the edge. And he erupted into a blind rage. Wild with anger and determination, he sucked in another brief pull of air and dived again for the sink. He would make another attempt to break out the window. But this time, he would try another method. He swam to the sink, then grabbed the faucet tightly again with both hands and began repeatedly ramming his head into the glass.

Suddenly, the window exploded from its mounts. Harland watched as it tumbled out into the pale green void and fell into the watery oblivion below.

All of a sudden, Harlan felt outside of himself. Imagining himself to be a sea otter, he swam nimbly ahead through the small opening as if it were the most natural thing, arched his back, and headed directly for the surface.

In the strange and unexplained illumination that still remained, Harlan was able to see the hull of the *Tidings* as he swam upward. Man, I can't be *that* far from the surface, he thought as he stroked "up and up and up." The moment he broke through the surface, he felt himself return to his old

334

self. It was like breaking into a "completely different world again!"

Harlan gasped wildly for air.

Bruce Hinman was drifting next to the bobbing stern of the *Tidings* when a man's head exploded through the surface, popping up right alongside him.

Choking, thrashing against the water, the man coughed heavily and spun in his direction.

"Hinman! You ugly son of a bitch!" he yelled.

It was none other than his skipper, Joe Harlan.

"Joe! Damn, I thought you were dead!" shot back Hinman, elated to see him.

Hinman's levity at seeing Harlan was quickly tempered, however, by the hopeless realization that there was no way to survive the present predicament. The canister containing the life raft had apparently failed to release when the *Tidings* rolled over, or perhaps it had released, only to get tangled up in the rigging or the crab pots. It didn't matter. Without that life raft, they knew they were all "as good as dead."

"What are we going to do?" shouted Hinman to Joe Harlan. "Did we get off a Mayday call?"

Harlan had tried, but he couldn't be positive that anyone had heard it.

There was nothing the men could do now but tread water and wait. With the wind blowing offshore, there would be no way to try to swim to shore. The deadly effects of hypothermia commonly paralyzed and drowned most men adrift in such seas in a few short minutes, at least those wearing only work clothes. Some began to sink the moment they hit the water. Even if Harlan and Hinman and the others could remain afloat, the wind and waves would eventually carry their bodies out to sea, where they would be lost forever.

When one crewman realized how grim things looked, he announced that he might just as well swim back down into the wheelhouse of the *Tidings*, get his pistol, and shoot himself.

Suddenly, an object "as large as a dinosaur" exploded out of the water between Hinman and his skipper. It was the fiberglass canister that housed the *Tidings'* life raft. The canister was about the size and shape of a fifty-five-gallon oil drum.

"Grab that SOB!" yelled Hinman.

The four crewmen converged on it. "Pull the cord!" yelled Joe Harlan.

While his crewmates treaded water nearby, Hinman began to peel off the line as fast as his numbed arms could move. He pulled and pulled, and after what seemed like several hundred feet of line later, he aired what everyone was thinking.

"God Almighty! This must be some kind of joke! We've got nothing but a coil of line here!"

"Pull! Pull faster!" yelled one terrified crewman.

"Damn, man! I'm pulling as fast as I can," shot back Hinman.

Moments later, Hinman was forced to stop. The frightening cold was beginning to press in on him, and he'd run out of breath.

Joe Harlan soon rejoined Hinman in the effort. He pulled what seemed to be literally hundreds of feet of line from what they had supposed to be the life raft canister. It was beginning to look like a fisherman's prank—an unbelievably cruel prank—had been played on them. What if the white fiberglass canister floating in front of them, the canister designed to house the ship's life raft, was filled with nothing but a large, unending, useless coil of line?

Minutes dragged by as Hinman continued to extract the line. As hundreds of feet of useless and entangling line played out in the water all around the floundering crew, their worst fears began to take on the feel of reality. When they came to the end of the line, a winded Bruce Hinman wrapped the line around his numb, pain-racked hands and gave a final tug.

Nothing happened.

The crew treading water around him let out groans filled with disbelief and a mounting panic.

Harlan's mind raced. I just can't believe this is happening! he thought. After all we've been through, to come up short like this.

Joe Harlan moved in to help. He leaned back in the water, placed both feet on either side of the end of the canister, and wrapped the rope around both of his clumsy, cold-ravaged hands. He reached down all the way then and pulled with everything he had.

The stubborn knot on the other end of the line gave way suddenly. Then came the pop and hiss of the CO_2 cartridges discharging within. In the next instant, the bright orange canister exploded open and the raft began to inflate. But it inflated upside down.

As longtime fishermen, 290-pound Bruce Hinman and 200-pound Joe Harlan continued to work together. They quickly assessed the situation and, without comment, approached the task at hand as if driven by the logic of a single working mind.

Inflated and upright, these rafts are fluorescent orange in color and round in form, with a diameter of eight feet. Floating, they look like giant inner tubes, or perhaps like those inflatable backyard pools that small children use, but with a dome tent mounted on top.

Swimming to one side of the raft, they crawled atop it. Then, planting their feet (and combined weight of five hundred pounds) on the downwind side of the overturned raft, they reached across, grabbed its upwind edge, and lifted it in unison. When the twenty-five-knot wind caught the exposed upwind edge of the raft, it flipped it upright, scooping more than a foot of icy seawater along with it as it did.

"All right!" yelled one shivering crewman as he breaststroked nearby.

Drifting in the murderous cold of the ocean currents, the entire crew was thoroughly chilled, their movements sluggish with the steadily advancing effects of hypothermia. Hinman and Harlan decided to drift alongside the raft in the painfully cold seawater and help their crewmates crawl aboard through the narrow doorway of the raft.

Being by far the huskiest of any man in the *Tidings* crew (or in the entire Kodiak crab boat fleet, for that matter), Hinman insisted on going last. It was a wise decision, for when all had been helped aboard, so numbed was he, and so completely had his strength been sucked from his body, that it took not only all of his own failing strength but also the body-wrenching efforts of the entire crew to haul him aboard.

Never in more than a century of brutal Alaskan winters had a storm front this cold struck the Kodiak Island area. A −25°F. reading in Alaska's dry interior country near Anchorage or Fairbanks was considered cold, even dangerous, although not unusual. But it was unheard of in the moist marine waters of the Gulf of Alaska.

The storm winds howled incessantly. The unrelenting gusts turned the raft's doorway into a virtual wind tunnel. Caught without a single survival suit among the four of them, and constantly awash with more than a foot of icy Gulf of Alaska seawater crashing about inside their raft (and with more seawater washing inside all the time), the crew of the *Tidings* knew their lives were still in serious jeopardy.

In truth, the record cold front threatened to freeze them where they sat. Packed tightly inside the cramped and drenching confines of the dome-covered raft, the cold-ravaged crew of the fishing vessel *Tidings* huddled together, shivering violently as panting columns of steamy breath jetted from their mouths.

Bruce Hinman rubbed his hands together furiously. He crossed his forearms, folded his hands under his armpits, and turned numbly to his skipper.

As if the record cold and unconfirmed Mayday hadn't been enough to worry the crew of the *Tidings*, they now discovered another unsettling fact: Their painter, leading out from the life raft, was still tethered to the sinking hull of the *Tidings*. In theory, the raft was attached this way to keep the crew members in the close vicinity of the boat as long as possible. But the status of the inverted *Tidings* was tenuous at best, and they knew she could be heading for the bottom at any moment. If she did, the life raft and all its occupants would likely be pulled down along with her.

The bridle cord attaching the raft to the painter was designed so that it was tethered directly in front of the raft's entrance hole. In any windy conditions, this meant that as long as the raft remained tied to her mother ship, the gaping hole of the doorway would always end up facing directly into the prevailing wind. That wind now drove close-cropped ocean waves against the stationary side of the raft. And icy walls of sea spray began exploding in through the front door and over those inside. Short of cutting the cord and casting themselves off into the mercy of the night, there was nothing to be done.

In only minutes, the blunt force of the record cold, the knifing edge of the arctic wind, and the drenching blasts of icy sea spray had rendered the men almost unconscious. They prayed then, and waited. And as the murderous cold bore down on them, a heavy silence fell on the crew.

Like the rest of the men, skipper Joe Harlan could no longer feel his fingers. But when he sensed the growing sense of hopelessness in the raft, he turned to his men.

"Look, guys, we're going to make it. Try not to worry about it. We're in the raft. That's the important thing." He paused.

"We've just got to keep fighting it," he added. And he set about to keep the men busy. "Now is the time to get things done. And the first thing we need to do is to get that door flap tied shut!"

Those nearest the door opening soon discovered that the flap ties were frozen fast to the walls of the domelike ceiling of the raft. The going was slow and painful. No one in the entire crew seemed able to carry out the simple task; their numbed fingers had lost all dexterity. Yet if the crew was going to survive, it was imperative that someone tie the thin strips of nylon fabric to the bonnet of the raft itself and shut out the deadly chill of wind and sea. Harlan encouraged them to keep trying.

With the rest of the crew now on task, Hinman and Harlan worked frantically to open the survival kit. Perhaps there was a knife inside that would allow them to cut themselves free of their mother ship. They soon came upon the small package containing the essential lifesaving equipment such as flares, water, and food. But whoever had packed the raft had wrapped the package in layer upon layer of silver duct tape. Joe Harlan discovered that his fingers were no longer taking messages from his brain. His fingers had given out, and so Harlan began attacking the wide silver-gray tape, ripping at it with his teeth.

One crewman started praying again. "Dear God, help us! Dear God, help us!" Over and over he repeated it.

At first, Harlan appreciated the prayer; then it began to wear on him. With the icy weight of the Alaskan cold front bearing down heavily upon them, the freezing crewmen were "starting to fade." Finally, Harlan spoke to the crewman. "You know, you need to shut up now," he said steadily. "This is not good for our morale." The young crewman fell silent.

"Guys, we're going to make it. We're going to make it. So let's just keep thinking that way," Harlan added.

Joe Harlan was proud to see how his crew worked together.

In a situation where fatalism might not have been out of line, they were doing all they could to save themselves. There isn't a coward in the bunch, he thought.

When they finally got the survival package open, Hinman and Harlan found no knife; they did manage to locate a small flashlight, yet its batteries had lost most of their charge. And they were forced to squint hard in the dim and intermittent flashes of light to read the flare instructions and figure out how to work them.

Harlan held out one of the flares and turned to Hinman. "Bruce, how do you work one of these damned things?"

Hinman looked at the oddly constructed flare. It had foreign instructions printed on it. He handed it back to Harlan.

"The goddamned instructions are in French!" shouted Hinman. And he cursed a streak.

Unable to read the instructions, and fearing they might accidentally launch the flare into the face of someone inside the raft, Joe Harlan decided that for the time being he would not attempt to launch one at all. Joe Harlan now felt himself slowing down dramatically. And each time the cord line leading from the raft to the *Tidings* pulled tight, the life raft would once again contort wildly beneath them, and the severely hypothermic men inside would be drenched in yet another icy blast of seawater. It soon grew so cold inside the raft that the men agreed that they'd felt warmer while immersed in the sea itself.

Finally, after herculean efforts, they managed to get the flap tied shut. But even then, it only partially blocked the painful, drenching blasts of exploding sea.

Adrift in the cold and utter darkness, they remained tethered to the bouncing, drifting hull of the *Tidings*, blown back and forth across the rugged face of the sea by a knifing twenty-five-knot wind and battered by an unforgiving sea. With nearly a thousand pounds of men sprawled on the floor inside, Harlan felt certain that the constant jerking of the waves would soon tear the raft in two.

Harlan knew what he had to do. He searched for his own knife. He felt a lump inside one of his pockets, reached in one pocket, and pulled out a stray shotgun shell. Finally, he managed to locate his knife. But when he ordered his hands to open, they refused. Then, holding the knife in the palms of his stiff hands, he bent forward, took the edge of the steel blade in his teeth, and pried it open. Leaning outside through the doorway of the raft, he slowly and deliberately sawed on the line.

The line parted, and suddenly they were adrift. The violent, neck-snapping action of the raft vanished abruptly. Now as they rode up and over the rolling seas, they could hear the roar of the wind and the breaking of unseen waves off in the darkness all around.

Then a thought came to Harlan: Hypothermia isn't a bad way to die. After the initial cold goes away and you go numb, you just start slowing down. Pretty soon, you get lethargic, and you just feel like going to sleep.

He fought against the seductive nature of such thoughts by admonishing himself. "Don't you give up! Don't you go to sleep, now!"

Bruce Hinman furiously rubbed his hands together. He crossed his forearms and folded his hands under his armpits. Then he pulled the door flap a few inches to one side and scanned the late-night seascape all around.

The sinking of the fishing vessel *Tidings* brought with it an especially insistent message. This was the second ship to sink out from under Hinman in the last month. Both had sunk off that very same point of Kodiak Island coastline—Cape Chiniak.

The U.S. Coast Guard squad, flying out of the Kodiak Island

base, had been kept hopping all season long. The rescue of Hinman from the sinking *Cape Clear* several weeks before had been performed in huge seas in yet another blinding snowstorm.

The Coast Guard helicopter pilot had descended bravely out of the night and hovered down over the sinking vessel. But the helicopter's rotor blades had struck the ship's mast, very nearly killing Hinman as well as the eight men on board the chopper.

Adrift then in the tall seas, Hinman had fought hard to keep from drowning as the torn and flooded suit he wore threatened to sink him. He was completely played out by the time they finally managed to hoist him aboard the Coast Guard chopper.

And now he and his crewmates were waiting to be rescued from yet another crab boat. Hinman was staring out through a silver moonlit haze of ice fog swirling across the lonely black face of the sea when he spotted a set of approaching mast lights.

"Hey!" he yelled aloud. "Here comes a boat!"

The fifty-eight-foot fishing vessel *Polar Star* had been under way several miles off Cape Chiniak when the *Tidings* first called for help. The skipper and owner of the *Polar Star*, Pat Pikus, was wrestling with poor visibility himself at the time. He had been standing alone at the helm, moving ahead through a steamy, boiling cloud of ice fog, when the call for help suddenly leapt from his CB radio: "Mayday! Mayday! This is the *Tidings*! We're off Cape Chiniak and we're going down!" Then, just as suddenly, the frantic voice fell silent.

Pikus quickly awakened his crew. "Everyone get up right away!" he yelled. "We've got a problem!"

He paused while his crew scrambled to life. Knifing, thirty-knot winds, with a bladelike edge, of $-26°F.$, were driving across the face of the sea. More important, Pikus knew there were no charts that could adequately describe the chill factor—nor the utter aloneness a drenched and drifting crew would know on such a night. When crewmen Shannon McCorkle, George Pikus, Gene LeDoux, and William De Hill, Jr., had gathered in the wheelhouse, he turned to them. "Boys," he said, "we've got a boat in real trouble nearby us here. And cold as it is outside, I'm still going to need one of you men to go climb up on the flying bridge and keep a watch out from there."

The wind was blowing offshore at the time, and Pikus began his search by making passes back and forth across the brackish water between the shoreline of Kodiak Island and an imaginary point several miles offshore. He had no sooner begun his effort when another skipper's voice jumped from the radio.

The skipper claimed that the last time he'd seen the *Tidings*, she'd been cruising several miles offshore. Still another skipper added that he believed he'd seen a tiny blip on his radar screen in the very area where the *Polar Star* was now cruising. But his radar had only fastened upon it once; then it had disappeared, and had never shown again.

After completing several grid-line sweeps, Pikus was about to head back into shore for yet another pass when, squinting through the boiling fog, he thought he saw something dead ahead. It turned out to be the silver flash of a small piece of reflector tape and it was stuck to the side of the dome of a life raft.

Slowing his approach, Pikus and his crew soon spotted the stunning figure of the *Tidings*' stern bouncing slowly and rhythmically through the choppy black seas. The *Tidings* had somehow managed to remain afloat, standing on end, with almost her full length buried beneath the sea. Only the last few feet of her stern and rudder now showed above the surface.

As he watched, the exposed stern of the wave-slickened hull performed an eerie ballet. What remained to be seen of her rose and fell through a jet-black world of swirling fog and howling wind, a void as cold and oppressive as a journey into the unlit bowels of a walk-in freezer.

Pikus was afraid that, in the strong winds, his vessel would drift right over the top of the life raft. So he swung in downwind of it, then maneuvered in close.

"Hello! Hello! Is anyone there?" Pat Pikus yelled out his side wheelhouse door.

A muffled cry came back. Then the door flap on the side of the raft's dome flipped out and someone yelled, "Yah, we're here!"

The raft was caught in the bleak glare of his sodium lights. When he pulled alongside, Pikus "looked right down into the raft." He had never seen a more pathetic sight. "No one wore survival suits," he recalls. "A couple of them were without shoes. There was a lot of water slopping around in the raft." The entire crew looked as weak and hypothermic as humans can get and still remain alive. "They wouldn't have made it another ten or fifteen minutes," he recalls.

By the time the *Polar Star* came abreast of their raft, Bruce Hinman was barely conscious and completely unable to stand. The crew of the *Polar Star* climbed overboard and literally dragged him from the raft, up and over the side, and aboard their ship. Hinman remembers landing on his back and the icy crackle of his sopping-wet clothing freezing instantly to the deck.

Joe Harlan reached up and tried as best he could to grab hold of the railing. When they saw that he, too, was unable to be of much help to himself, the rugged young crewmen aboard the *Polar Star* reached down and, in one motion, hoisted him up and over the side. They tossed him onto the deck and out of the way in order to make room for the rest of the survivors.

Lying on the deck where he landed, Harlan spotted the door

leading into the heated space of the *Polar Star*'s galley. Unable to walk and unwilling to wait, he rolled over onto his stomach and began crawling toward the door. Pausing en route, Harlan gathered himself, and, raising up on one elbow, took one last glimpse at what remained of the *Tidings*. Waves were exploding off the few final feet of her stern.

"Good-bye, girl," he said aloud. Then he collapsed back down onto the deck and began crawling again toward the warmth of the ship's heated interior.

So intent were they on rescuing the other survivors that no one among the ship's crew noticed Harlan go. He managed to crawl in through the galley, down the hallway, and into one of the staterooms, where he pulled himself "up into somebody's bunk" and lay there "shivering violently."

"Don't let them go to sleep! Keep them awake," ordered the Coast Guard repeatedly over the radio set.

When the crew of the *Polar Star* found him, Harlan peered up at them with dark, sunken eyes from the soft, warm bunk in which he lay.

"Look," he said, "I want you to know that I'm married. And I've got a kid. And I don't want you to think I'm a homosexual or anything. But I need someone to take off all his clothes and climb in bed with me here. Because if you don't, I think I'm going to die."

It was *Polar Star* deckhand Shannon McCorkle, son of well-known Kodiak harbormaster Corkie McCorkle, who did the honors.

"He was the one who brought me back to life," recalls Harlan gratefully. "The real heroes of this thing were the crewmen of the fishing vessel *Polar Star*," claims Joe Harlan. "There's no doubt in my mind. If we'd been out there even another fifteen minutes, we would have died. We were that close to buying it."

By the time the *Polar Star* men managed to lift aboard the

nearly frozen crew of the *Tidings*, nearly a foot of ice had accumulated on the decks and superstructure of the *Polar Star*. The instant the last man arrived on board, they left the raft to drift, and immediately struck out for Kodiak.

When the *Polar Star* arrived back in town, there was an ambulance waiting for the *Tidings* crew, but Harlan wanted nothing to do with the hospital. "Look," he told the EMTs, "I want you guys to take my crew to the hospital. Have them checked out and make sure they're okay. But I'm going home to see my wife and my daughter."

Throughout the entire ordeal, Harlan knew that it was the love of his wife and daughter and home that had kept him going.

Now barefoot, his wet hair still matted against his head, Joe Harlan was clad in nothing more than a wool blanket when a friend drove him home. His wife came out to greet him. It was a tearful reunion.

That winter, during the bitter cold of the crab season, Joe Harlan had grown a beard. Now even his one-year-old daughter did not recognize him. When he approached and picked her up, she asked him, "Are you Santa Claus?"

Once inside, Harlan took a long, hot bath, devoured hot platefuls of food, and spent time relaxing with his wife and daughter. At 8:00 A.M. the very next morning, Joe Harlan called a ship broker in Seattle. It was time to start shopping for a new crab boat to buy.

CONTRIBUTORS

Marie Beaver has worked as a wilderness guide in the Alaska Brooks Range for more than eight years. She commercial fished for salmon for two seasons. Currently she lives in Fairbanks with her husband, Tony, their new son, Cassiar, and their sled dog, Whoozit. She has an M.F.A in Creative Nonfiction from the University of Montana.

John Cole lives in Maine and has written about commercial and sportfishing for several decades with such books as *Striper, Stripers: An Angler's Anthology, Fishing Came First,* and, most recently, *Tarpon Quest.*

Michael Crowley has fished six years in the Bering Sea and Alaska on halibut schooners out of Seattle. He lives in Maine and makes his living now as a writer, addressing fishery issues as an editor at *National Fisherman,* and as contributing editor for *Seafood Business* and *Workboat.*

Wendy Erd lives in Hanoi, Vietnam, where she has taught English to government officials through Harvard's International Development Institute. She and her husband, Peter, summer in Alaska, where they have commercial-fished for twelve seasons in Bristol Bay. She has received local and statewide awards for both her poetry and nonfiction. Her most recent work has appeared in *Alaska Quarterly Review* and *An Inn Near Kyoto: Writing by American Women Abroad.*

Leslie Leyland Fields lives in Kodiak during the winters, where she is Assistant Professor of English at the University of Alaska, Kodiak. Summers she commercial-fishes with her husband and five children off a three-hundred-acre island. This season was her twenty-third. She is the author of *The Water Under Fish, The Entangling Net: Alaska's Commercial Fishing Women Tell Their Lives,* and numerous essays and poems, which have appeared in *The Atlantic Monthly, Creative Nonfiction, Orion, The Christian Science Monitor,* and others. "Hurled to the Shark" is excerpted from her recent book *Climbing Water Mountain.*

Robert Fritchey fell in with Louisiana's coastal finfishermen at age thirty, deciding after graduate school that he would earn his living "only from renewable resources" and that "he would never work for another man." Since his entrance into the fisheries in the early 1980s, he has witnessed and recorded in his book, *Wetland Riders*, the ongoing loss of the redfish and other marshland resources to corporate and sport interests. When not writing for *National Fisherman*, he still fishes shrimp and oysters in the bayous.

Joel Gay lives in Homer, Alaska, where he is currently managing editor of *The Homer News*. He is an aspiring musician and a prolific writer with essays in *Alaska Geographic, Alaska Airlines Magazine, National Fisherman, We Alaskans*, and *Pacific Fishing*, where he is a field editor. He has fished herring and salmon, but has given up the seafaring life for an office.

Linda Greenlaw has been a commercial fisher for more than twenty years, the last eight of which she skippered the seventy-six-foot *Hannah Boden*. She is still recovering from the publicity, cover photos, and tour surrounding the release of her book, *The Hungry Ocean: A Swordfish Captain's Journey*. She is now quietly fishing for lobster off the coast of Maine.

Seth Harkness lives on an island in Maine, where he worked as a sea urchin diver for seven years. He now works as a fisheries consultant. Most recently he worked on biota counts in Labrador for the University of New Brunswick. He writes fiction and covers fishing issues for *The Fisherman's Voice*.

Nancy Lord lives in Homer, Alaska, where she is a writer and a commercial fisher of salmon each summer. She is the author of three short story collections, the most recent *The Man Who Swam with Beavers*. Her two books of creative nonfiction are *Fishcamp: Life on an Alaskan Shore* and *Green Alaska: Dreams from the Far Coast*. She also teaches creative writing as a Visiting Professor at the University of Alaska.

Peter Matthiessen is the author of *Snow Leopard, Blue Meridian, Cloud Forest, Men's Lives*, and other best-selling works of fiction and nonfiction. For three years he worked as a charterboat fishermen off Long Island. He lives in Sagaponack, New York.

Gavin Maxwell lives on the coast of Scotland, where he writes and conducts marine research. He has written a number of books, among them *Ring of Bright Water, A Reed Shaken by the Wind,* and *Lords of the Atlas. Harpoon Venture,* excerpted here, has been recently reprinted in paperback by Viking.

William McCloskey was a senior staff member at the Johns Hopkins University Applied Physics Laboratory, and at the age of forty-five became a commercial fisherman. Since then he has fished all over the world and written several books, among them *Highliners, Fish Decks,* and most recently, *Their Father's Work: Casting Nets with the World's Fishermen.* William Warner has said of him, "No one writing today can match William McCloskey's knowledge of fishing or the breadth of his experience at sea. He is the writer of record on world fishing."

Paul Molyneaux lives in Maine and has worked for twenty-three years in the fishing industry, trawling for groundfish, lobstering, scalloping, shrimping, and longlining for cod. For three years he harpooned swordfish aboard the *Irene & Alton,* Maine's last boat to go out strictly for that fishery before it was outlawed. After earning his B.A. in 1997, he has written on fishery issues for *The New York Times, National Fisherman,* and *Wildlife Conservation Magazine.*

Debra Nielsen lived in the Alaskan bush for ten years, earning a living by salvaging sunken boats and commercial fishing. She began as a cook and deckhand and worked her way up to skipper, running her own boat for five seasons, until the tragic sinking of *The Wayward Wind* that killed her husband and three others. Since then she has run an import shop in Kodiak, traveling extensively throughout Asia, and now spends her time with her husband, Mark, and her daughter, Danica.

Toby Sullivan has fished commercially year-round for twenty-five years in Alaskan waters, working king crab, pollock, cod, and salmon. Injuries from deckwork have sent him back to college, where he is earning a degree in computer science. His creative writing has earned him state and local awards and made him a favorite at the annual Fisher Poet's gathering in Astoria each year.

Martha Sutro fished tanner crab in the Bering Sea for three seasons while on sabbatical as a high school English teacher. She worked recently in Antarctica, and has just returned from Asia, where she was on assignment for *Outside Magazine,* writing about Mongolia's newest tourist draw—mountain biking.

Joe Upton divides his time between Seattle and Maine and has seined for salmon in southeast Alaska for more than twenty years. His *Alaska Blues: a Season of Fishing the Inside Passage* has just been reprinted. His other books include *The Coastal Companion, Journeys Through the Inside Passage: Seafaring Adventures Along the Coast of British Columbia and Alaska,* and *Amaretto.*

Spike Walker fished the Bering Sea during the king crab boom years of the 1970s and '80s, then turned author with his best-selling *Working on the Edge: Working in Alaska's Most Dangerous Profession.* Since then he has written *Nights of Ice* and *Coming Back Alive,* and is currently at work on his next book of at-sea rescues. He lives in Seattle and still halibut fishes every spring.